# FATHER'S LOVE JOURNEY:

## A Devotional Commentary on the Gospel of John

—ɯ—

**By**
**Fount Shults**

**Forward by**
**Bob Sorge**

*FATHER'S LOVE JOURNEY:*
*A Devotional Commentary on the Gospel of John*
by Fount Shults

Printed in the United States of America

ISBN 978-1-60266-263-6

www.xulonpress.com

# Readers' Responses

—ɤɤ—

This book will teach you what it means to really follow Jesus, not just give you ideas of who He is. Fount's intimate use of John the beloved's insight into the character and work of Christ will transform your belief system. This in-depth study into the heart of John's Gospel will also bring you to a place of abiding rest in Father's bosom. Enjoy!

Bob Mumford
International Bible Teacher
Lifechangers

I highly recommend this book to anyone who is serious about the truth. This is a one-of-a-kind book. I found *Father's Love Journey* inspiring and instructive. In it Dr. Shults brings out hidden truths that make all the difference in the world to understanding the message.

As I read it, I thought of one of my favorite authors, G. Campbell Morgan. There is no question that this book is not for a "quick fix." It is for the serious student or a person who is reading it for its devotional content.

This will certainly be one of those books that, wherever you open it, will have a message for you. In fact, if it had been divided up, it would have made daily devotional study for one year.

May the God who has given enlightenment also give others the commitment to see it through.

Paul Johansson
President Emeritus
Elim Bible Institute

To take a walk with Dr. Shults through John's Gospel is to experience a feast of the love and the Father's heart of God like few others experiences you'll ever have. He has spent countless years wading through and teaching from these rich chapters, making him one of the best men I know fully qualified to take on this tour into a fresh experience of revelation of Father and His relationship with you in His only begotten Son.

Jeff Clark
President
Elim Bible Institute

Dr. Fount Shults has found something in John we all need to hear; it is the embrace of the Father and it is delivered to us with a father's passion and caring. This is a word for the serious disciple as well as for the leadership of the Church to grasp. I can feel and hear the Father compelling us into a fresh understanding of how we fit into His eternal heart. Well done, my brother!

AJ Baisch
Sr. Pastor, New Harvest Church
Myrtle Beach, SC

When my good friend, Dr. Fount Shults, asked me to read this book, based on his meditations from the book of John, I was delighted. Because of his deep insight into the scriptures and especially John's gospel, I couldn't wait to get started. After completing the read, I declare that my friend has written a classic. The message and impact of *Father's Love Journey* is timeless for every believer, those who are curious, those who are confused, and those who are seeking more.

I found my spirit being delighted as revelation after revelation secured me in the love the Father has for me. As I read I was drawn to a place of meditation, reflecting on my relationship with the Father and His desired relationship with me. This is a book not to be read only once, but to be picked up over and over by those who desire to venture into the Father's embrace, through His son. *Father's Love Journey* will remain, over the years, a source of revelation, inspiration, and meditation in our understanding the Heart of our Father.

> Don Richter, Director
> Harvest Preparation International Ministries
> Sarasota, FL

Dr. Shults has done it again. Using his expertise, experience, and the amazing gift of God in his life, he has mined the golden truths of the Gospel of John and is sharing the wealth of revelation with us in this book. This treasure will be a blessing to every reader.

> Stephen Schlabach
> Pastor, Shining Light Bible Church
> Sarasota, FL
> Regional Director
> Rhema Ministerial Association International

Fount Shults has given us a treasure in this commentary on John's Gospel. There is much scholarly meat, seasoned with practical insight and experience. Individuals and small groups alike will find *Father's Love Journey* inspiring, challenging and helpful.

Fount's training, ability, and long experience as a Bible teacher are clearly seen in the depth and insight of his writing. Foremost, Fount is a disciple loved by Jesus, just like the evangelist whose Gospel is the subject of this book. Like the Apostle John, Fount's purpose is to help his readers know the one of whom he writes, and have life in that knowledge. He has achieved his goal.

Mark Burlinson
Director of Pastoral Ministries
Shiloh Place Ministries
Conway, SC


For many years Dr. Fount Shults has been holding serious students of the Bible in the palm of his hand, while imparting great truth to those who desire both a thorough knowledge of the Word and practical insight into the testimony of God as found in the Scriptures. With a bold approach and keen insight into the literature of the Apostle John, Fount has captured the essence and validity of one of the most beloved books of the New Testament, inspired by God and communicated through the beloved disciple.

In this book Dr. Shults has brought the compassionate life of Jesus, as articulated through John, into unparalleled focus.Through interpretive wisdom and the author's powerful communicative style, the reader will not only know this Gospel, but sense that they are right with John as he was penning this most remarkable account of the life of

Christ our Lord. Without reservation I endorse this book and encourage you to "...get on the path and follow it..."

> Dale Haight
> Senior Pastor and Author
> *Radical Vessels* (Xulon Press)

I once heard a theologian described as a person who is able to take the simple things of God's Word and make them complicated. My friend Fount is not like the theologian mentioned above, because he has the ability to capture the wonderful realms of God's Word and makes them come alive. I highly recommend this book.

> Dr. Leon van Rooyen
> President
> Global Ministries and Relief.

If I want to learn about abiding in Christ from the Bible, the first book I go to is the Gospel of John. If I want to learn about abiding in Christ from a teacher, I'll go to Fount Shults. Dr. Shults is humble and wise, transparent and tested, and able to dig treasure from the Word that others miss. He invites us to come along on this exploration of the testimony of John, the beloved disciple. You may find yourself abdicating some preconceived notions about the Christ you thought you knew.

> Dr. Ron Burgio
> President
> Elim Fellowship

This is an inspiring and insightful read! I was drawn in to the person and encounters of Jesus. Tracing the various emphases of John makes for a rewarding study for the leader or serious student of Scripture. I recommend this for a small group study. The insights are so compelling that you'll want to read it together…sharing back and forth with one another.

Randy Stewart
Care Pastor, Zion Fellowship
Canandaigua, NY

# Table of Contents

—⚊⚊—

# PREFACE

—⁂—

As I was putting the finishing touches on this manuscript, Jack Frost's new book arrived in the bookstores. In *Spiritual Slavery to Spiritual Sonship*, Jack exposes the root of many of the difficulties facing individuals, families, and churches. Even though we have accepted Jesus, many of us have not yet experienced the depths of the Father's love. We know God loves us, but we live as though we are unloved—as though we're orphans.

Many frantically strive to become acceptable and get discouraged or backslide because they don't really believe they have a place in Father's house. Jesus prepared a place for each of us in the Father's heart of love and invited us to follow him into the Father's bosom. Those who follow become sons and daughters of Love because God is Love. They have a home in Father's heart. But some act and feel as though they're unloved and homeless.

We all desire to be fruitful in our Christian walk, but we often live defeated unfruitful lives. Jack identifies the problem when he writes, "Intimacy precedes fruitfulness." We have tried to be conformed to the image of Jesus. We aren't able to become like Jesus because we focus on Jesus' teaching or his morality rather than focusing on what was the center of Jesus' life—intimacy with his Father. Jack put his finger on it when he wrote, "Jesus wasn't sinless because He was God; it wasn't His divinity that made him the man He was. Jesus was the man He was because of the Father He had."

## *The Essence of John's Gospel*

The essence of John's Gospel is the Father's love. His love is on a journey to the world he created. The Son comes to the world with the Father's love, and the Father's love draws men and women to Jesus. Jesus leads those who follow him into the bosom of the Father where they find love. We are invited to join him in his journey of love.

Jesus is continually on a journey which makes a full circle—from his Father to the world and back to his Father. God is Love. The life of Jesus is a movement out from Love (the Father's bosom) into the world which God created for love. He returns to Love (his Father) with as many as will believe in his Father's love and join him in his return journey to his Father's bosom. First the Son was in Love—he was in the Father. Then Father sent the Son into the world with Love in himself—the Father (Love) was in him.

Our origin is also the bosom of the Father. The Word—the Son of God in the bosom of the Father—created all things. When God spoke, this Word came forth from the heart of the Father in creation. That's the Son's journey. But our journey is different. We were created by love and for love. But we, like the prodigal son in Luke 15, went out from the Father's house *without* love. Or, like the elder brother, we spend our lives in the field trying to earn love. This puts us on a journey downward into the pit of alienation from ourselves, from our fellow pilgrims, and from the Father of love.

The Son of God had to come from the Father into our foreign country to woo us back into the Father's house by making us aware of and hungry for our true inheritance. Our journey back to the Father's love begins when we hear a word of testimony, like the two disciples of John the Baptist who first followed Jesus. When we hear the testimony, we recognize our need for love and are no longer content with the counterfeit love we found in the foreign country. If we don't make this journey we will remain in the pit of loneliness even if we think we're fine.

The call to become a disciple is a call to follow Jesus. The pattern in Jesus' life which we are called to follow is simply this—*he lives his life as a Son of the Father*. He lives with the knowledge and confidence that his Father loves him. The Father loves the Son. The Father also loves the world and gives his Son for the world. The Son loves what his Father loves. He gives himself over to death so that we can return to the Father. This is the essence of John's Gospel. It's about the journey of the Father's love into the world to draw men and women into his bosom of love.

Jesus is the Way to the Father. When a true disciple comes to Jesus, he comes into Love (the Father) and is filled with the love of the Father for the world. A true disciple, following Jesus' journey, will live his life as a son of this Father of love and will invite others to come see and receive this Love.

## *My Personal Journey through John*

This devotional commentary has been in my spirit for many years. I was fascinated with John's style very early in my career as a Bible student and teacher. The Gospel of John was part of my undergraduate studies program and I began to teach it in 1964. Every academic dean I have worked under has allowed me to teach John and his writings. After over forty years of ever increasing insights into the nature and message of the Gospel, I still feel there is much more there than I have found. John wrote in very simple language but the content is so profound that it takes decades of study and meditation to scratch the surface.

The teachings in this volume have been tested in churches, conferences, and retreats as well as the college campus. Deep ministry has come to many who have attended meetings where these meditations were presented. The Gospel of John is all about coming to know the Father through Jesus and entering into intimacy with him. Having scratched around on the surface for over forty years I've uncovered a few things that are valuable for those who desire to experience a deeper relationship with our Father.

The basic teaching is this: Jesus is the way to the Father. There are no steps of action. There is only a call to follow him and an indication of the direction he is going. The challenge will be for the readers to look away from their preconceived notions long enough to find him where he really is. He may not be where we expect him to be. When he was in the flesh he did not hang out with religious folks too often. He was a friend of sinners while at the same time abiding in the bosom of the Father. This book is for those who desire to join him there.

## How to Use this Book

There are twelve chapters. It can be used for a quarterly study in churches and small groups. A thirteen week survey of this book will not satisfy those who are seriously seeking intimacy with our Father. It will only create a hunger for more and deeper intimacy. It may even create frustration because there is so much. But you have the rest of your life to pursue more of God's manifest presence in your daily life.

The book may also be used for personal quiet time, perhaps taking one chapter a month for twelve months. Even a year is not enough time to digest all that's in the Gospel of John. You can expect to increase your hunger even more as you spend more time with John.

There are challenging questions in each chapter. Leaders of study groups can prepare ahead of time by reading the chapter and asking themselves where they personally are on the path toward the Father's bosom. Honesty and vulnerability on the part of leaders will release others to share. Participants should also read ahead and be prepared for lively discussions.

Those who follow the lines indicated in these chapters will learn the process of coming into a deeper relationship with our Father. The value of this book will not come to those who are merely looking for more academic understanding. All of us must enter the path and follow along to the place Jesus leads: into the Father's embrace.

## Acknowledgments

I am indebted to many for the insights in these meditations. I am grateful to all the administrators and deans who allowed me to teach. Teaching requires a greater concentration than mere reading or sitting under teaching. My grasp of the Gospel increased each time I taught it, and it continues to increase as I write about it.

Many students have played a significant role in the developing insights. Their questions and comments challenged me to look more intently for the Father, Son, and Holy Spirit who live behind the text. Watching as students receive the Father's love during the course of study increased my commitment to do more than impart information during class. It's always something very special when a teacher sees his or her students receiving the reality indicated in the teaching.

Eric Taylor and Scot Magann, former students of mine, have contributed greatly to the process of making the language readable to the men and women in the daily walk of life in the 'real' world. My tendency is to try to sound academic, as though I were in a class full of students. Thanks guys.

Without the support of my wife Lynda, I would not have advanced very far on my personal journey into the

Father's bosom. She and our six children and ten grandchildren continue to give me an arena to work out the details of allowing this welcoming love of the Father to come through me into their world. Lynda was also a vital part of preparing the manuscript for this book. She is an expert proof-reader. Thanks, Sweetheart.

The Scripture quotations are from the RSV. The quotations from John and from I John are in boldface type when it is the phrase I am commenting on.

Fount Shults, Myrtle Beach, South Carolina,
February, 2007
fount@valiantlee.com http://www.onword.org

# FORWARD

—◊—

If I told you I knew the Master Key to the Christian life, would I pique your interest? Would you like to know what it is? The truth is, there is one single key that, when engaged, opens to us the panoramic vistas of Kingdom possibilities. And I know what it is.

What's more, I'll tell you what it is—if you'll just hang with me for a few moments. The answer is so important that it deserves a little bit of build-up. Allow me to set it up with a hypothetical situation.

They banish you to live by yourself on a remote Pacific island, and they tell you that you can take only one book of the Bible with you. Question: Which book would you take?

If it were me, I'd be in a whole lot of pain. You're telling me I've got to toss 65 of the 66 Bible books and narrow it down to just one? Ugh, this is awful! I can't think of one book I could possibly do without. Psalms? I live in that book every day, don't take Psalms away from me! And Hebrews, I couldn't survive without Hebrews. Nor Romans. Isaiah! Don't touch Isaiah! Revelation—just try and take Revelation away from me. Job? Job is my buddy. Deuteronomy? I'm in love with that book! Acts? How could anybody live without the book of Acts? And then there's Ephesians—ah, Ephesians!

You're serious? I have to choose only one Bible book to keep for the rest of my life? Whew, this is tough! But if you're really gonna force me—I mean, if I really had to choose just one book of the Bible—I think I'd have to... uh...mmm...uh...I'd have to go with...John. Final answer. The Gospel of John.

Wow, what a book! It's just gotta be one of your favorite books in the whole Bible. It's an unparalleled beholding of Jesus that sets your heart to burning for a relationship with the Father. It sets your spirit to soaring with Jesus on the way to the bosom of the Father. O the wonder of the Man, Christ Jesus! And O the wonder of His Father's embrace.

Then, if they said, "Narrow it down to one chapter," I'd *really* be in trouble! What? Throw away 20 chapters and keep only *one* of John's 21 chapters? Don't take chapter 14 away from me! Nor chapter 3. Nor 17. Don't remove the crucifixion and resurrection in chapters 19-20! I've got 20 reasons why I can't cut any of the chapters. I'm in pain over here. I've got to choose just one chapter in the Gospel of John?? Well, if you absolutely *made* me choose just one chapter, I think I'd choose...uh...mmm...uh...I'd have to go with...chapter 15. You forced me into it. Give me John 15.

Why chapter 15?

Because it's got the key. The Master Key. When I say it, you're going to go, "That's so simple!" And you're right. The Master Key to the Christian life is a very simple invitation from Jesus' lips: "'Abide in My love'" (John 15:9). There, that's it.

"Abide in My love." So simple—and yet the greatest challenge you'll ever face. It's what the human heart longs for—an intimate, knowing, reciprocating, fiery love relationship with He who is "The Desire Of All Nations" (Hag. 2:7). It's here that we find our reason for being. Herein is true success. Nothing else exhilarates the human spirit like the wonder of beholding the extravagant beauty of the One who died for us.

"Abide in my love." You can explore that goldmine for the rest of your days and at the end of your life realize that you hardly scratched the surface of the glorious depths of the love of Christ.

Why am I talking like this? Because the book you hold in your hands has been crafted specifically to guide your steps into an abiding love relationship with Jesus Christ as he abides in the Father and the Father abides in Him. A book could hold no nobler purpose. Fount Shults lays the Gospel of John plainly before us as a roadmap to intimacy with the Father in Jesus Christ.

Fount has the expertise to write a book that would have impressed us with its footnotes and quotations from erudite sources. Instead, he chose to write from the heart in order to engage our heart. Simply because he wants us to see Jesus and, in seeing Him, to see the Father.

If you come away saying, "Now I know the Book of John," you will have missed Fount's message. If you hear from the heart you'll come away saying, "I'm seeing Jesus and His Father like never before."

Fount was my classroom teacher 27 years ago when I was a Bible School student. Even back then his teachings on the Gospel of John impacted my life. My point is that this book is like a flask of well-aged wine. Drink deeply of every chapter. May the intoxicating love of Christ capture your soul!

> Bob Sorge
> Author, Conference Speaker

# CHAPTER 1

# John's Basic Themes

—⚡—

Picture a young woman gazing at a young man. A cartoonist's imaginative balloon floats over her head. In that bubble stands a knight in shining armor. She doesn't see the young man actually standing in front of her; she sees her hero—a man who exists only in her imagination. Her image eclipses the real man. If you try to convince her that the real young man she's looking at is nothing like the one in her mind's eye, you'll recognize how powerfully preconceived notions influence what we see.

### Preconceived Notions

A preconceived notion is an idea or expectation we bring into a situation. It's the mental picture of a thing before we see the thing itself. It's like a dream, but more dangerous, because it changes the way we see the real thing when it shows up. When we dream we eventually wake up and realize it was only a dream; but with a preconceived notion we don't know it's only a dream.

When we're under the influence of preconceived notions we have a form of spiritual blindness. It's the most serious kind of blindness because we think we're seeing clearly. *There are none as blind as those who refuse to see.* If our young woman protects her preconceived notion too carefully, she'll end up married to a man she doesn't know and doesn't even like.

In Jesus' day the Jewish people had preconceived notions about the coming Messiah—ideas and expectations they brought to the situation from their study of Scripture and their national history. They had orthodox reasons for expecting the Messiah of their balloon, but their image was nothing like the real Messiah who was coming. They knew what they were looking for, but they were looking for the wrong Messiah. When the true Messiah refused to conform to their preconceived notions, they walked away from him looking for another Messiah. The only other Messiah is a false Messiah.

## A Human Problem

The Jews of Jesus' day had this problem with preconceived notions, *not because they were Jews but because they were human.* We Christians also have concepts of Christ based on our study of the Bible and our denominational history. We fill our theological imagination with orthodox ideas and convincing arguments. Like the Pharisees, we prove our devotion by a life of piety and good deeds. We may even invoke his mystical presence among us when we're together.

Some of us even try to expose as heretics those who disagree with us. We want to destroy their reputation because we want others to reject them as we do. In all this the question rises: If Jesus himself were to appear in our midst, would I recognize him? Would you recognize him? Would we recognize him? *Pharisees are always certain.* How certain are you? Can we be certain?

## A Form of Idolatry

Idolatry in our culture takes the form of preconceived notions. We don't mold metal, clay, and wood to reflect our image of God, but we try to pressure the real God to conform to the balloon-images we've made of him. It matters little that these images are not in stone; they are still in that mythical and demonic world where gods are merely extensions of our rebellious imagination.

Our claim to the name of Christ is void to the extent that we have false images of him. "Claiming to be wise, they became fools, and exchanged the glory of the immortal God for images resembling mortal man…" (Rom. 1:22–23). We're in danger of exchanging the glory of Christ for our human image of him if we stubbornly cling to the image in our mind's eye.

## *Effect on Church Life*

People often enter churches expecting great things and walk away when they realize God isn't doing things their way. Thinking they've seen clearly, they've not seen at all. In their private religious enterprise, they become 'church hoppers' in search of the church of their bubble. Too many Don-Quixote-Christians are only chasing figments of their imagination. One can only hope and pray they never find what they're looking for. If they become disillusioned, they may open up to an encounter with the Christ who is Jesus. In Miguel de Cervantes' novel, Don Quixote does not become disillusioned until his death when he experiences a conversion of sorts.

My prayer is that more and more Christians, me included, will forsake their illusions and have a fresh encounter with the true Christ daily so we, the Church, can give an effective witness to the world.

It's also possible to go to church looking for the real Christ and find a group of people preoccupied with a distorted image of him. None of us have images of God that perfectly reflect the reality of who he is.

Our problem isn't images in our bubble; we all have them. God created us with an imaging faculty because he desires to fill it with himself through dreams, visions, and insights. All of us have ideas in our bubble that are based on what we have been taught or what we have imagined to be true. We also have many pictures in our imagination that are true because we have experienced God personally.

Our problem comes when we fiercely refuse to consider the possibility that some of our mental pictures of Christ may be wrong or misleading.

## *John Speaks to the Problem*

John's Gospel is unique among the Gospels. Understanding this uniqueness unlocks the meaning of the stories and teachings presented in his Gospel. Why did John record the life of Jesus so differently from the other Gospels? It isn't enough to notice the differences; we must discern the *significance* of these differences.

John has a twofold purpose. He calls the church of our day to recognize Jesus as the Christ, the Son of God. And he calls the church to follow Jesus into the Father's presence. Jesus is the way to the Father. In the meditations which follow, I will *not* try to draw a better picture of Jesus for you to carry in your mental backpack. I will challenge you to follow the Jesus who *"is in the bosom* [embrace] *of the Father"* (Jn. 1:18).

He made our journey into Father's bosom possible when he disarmed 'the principalities and powers'—those 'gods' who reign in the domain of our rebellious imaginations. These powers try to control the 'space' between ourselves and the true God (see Col. 2:15). Jesus made a way for us to walk through enemy territory into our Father's presence. We can follow this way only as we each let Jesus reveal himself by the Spirit and replace our favorite images with a true image of him.

## *Our Goal: Following Jesus*

Our goal is to pursue the basic question of discipleship: What does it mean to follow Jesus the Way? We can ask this in two ways:

We can ask, "What does it mean to *follow* Jesus?

Or we can ask, "What does it mean to follow *Jesus*?"

This distinction is more than one of emphasis, for a real problem emerges with this shift. With the emphasis on *our following*, we can follow the imaginary Jesus in our bubble rather than Jesus himself. This can look like true discipleship while it's really an exercise in unbelief. It's a work of man apart from God's presence. It's an exercise in *unbelief* (or it's belief in the wrong Jesus) because the object of this faith is the Jesus of our imagination. Paul warned us about those who preach "another Jesus" and a "different gospel" (see II Cor. 11:4).

If there's another Jesus, a valid question arises: Which Jesus am I following? True faith and true discipleship can only follow the *authentic Jesus as he really is—yesterday, today and forever.*

Yet true disciples will *follow* Jesus. How could it be discipleship otherwise? The danger of false following doesn't relieve us of the responsibility to follow.

### *Jesus is the Way*

To follow implies a way. Here again we come face to face with Jesus. He said, "*I am the way, and the truth, and the life; no one comes to the Father, but by me*" (Jn. 14:6). The way isn't a path we can follow apart from the presence of Jesus because he is himself the way. *Jesus in you is his way for you.*

A way also has a goal—a destination. In this case both the way and the destination are in Jesus Christ who is in the bosom of the Father (see John 1:18). The ultimate goal is to be in the Father. Jesus is in the Father. To be in Jesus is to be in the Father's embrace. To be in the Father's bosom is to be on the way.

"On the way to what?" you may ask. For that answer we must wait.

As we develop the themes of John's Gospel, we'll keep before us three basic truths. First is the absolute uniqueness of *this man Jesus.* Second is the uniqueness of the *way he walked.* And third, we will also remain alert to the truth that he is walking among us today as well.

## Words and Images

In approaching this, I'm aware of the dilemma we face with words and images. *Words create images.* If I say "dog," you automatically picture a dog in your mind. But the dog in your mind might be quite different from the dog I'm talking about. To be certain we have the same dog in mind, the dog I am referring to must be there so I can point and say, "This dog."

The only way any of us can be sure others see Jesus when we are speaking of him is if Jesus Christ shows up for the one we are talking to. Another complication is, if I talk about Jesus who is present to me, the audience can still be thinking of the Jesus of their childhood Sunday school lesson. If they've not matured in their personal relationship with Jesus, true words can still miss the mark.

Here's our problem. On the one hand, we use words. I know the concepts and images in your mind might be different from those in mine. On the other hand, we must use words to present Jesus Christ because there's no other way to present him. Well, that's not quite true. There's no other way to present him in a book. We present him all the time with our lives. We're like little incarnate words to the degree that we portray him with our grace, hope, and peace. Whether by words or by actions, we can't make him present to you the way he was to the disciples in his day. We can only use words and actions to point the way and pray that you turn to see the one we speak of.

## *Our Method: Watching His Walk*

In the meditations of the following chapters we won't deal with all the themes of John, but only those that relate to the question of discipleship and its goal: "What does it mean to follow this man Jesus and to walk in the same way he walked? How can we experience the Father's embrace and make his love known to the world?"

In unfolding the key words and phrases, we'll refer to virtually every story and dialogue in the Gospel, but not in the order they appear. I'm taking this approach because of John's style. He introduces a theme in one place and develops it in different ways through other stories and dialogues throughout the Gospel.

### *John as Our Guide*

John 21:30, 31 will be our guide. John is *"the disciple who is bearing witness to these things, and who has written these things; and we know that his testimony is true"* (Jn. 21:24). He identifies himself as *"the disciple whom Jesus loved"* (Jn. 21:20). He gives testimony as an eye witness. He was on the scene when the events took place. He saw with his own eyes and heard with his own ears.

This disciple whom Jesus loved obviously knows he has the same name as the Baptist. Like the Baptist, he did not come to bear witness to himself. That may be why he doesn't even mention his own name. Like the Baptist, he is not the Light. Nor does he want to be in the limelight. His purpose is to point to the One he met. As he writes, he points in the hope that we'll follow his pointing quill.

Our methodology is to trace the various themes through the Gospel in an attempt to discover what John witnessed—

what he wants us to see. These basic themes are outlined in John's explanation of why he wrote the Gospel.

## Believing

Let's begin with John 20:31; we'll look at verse 30 later. John writes, *"...but these are written that you may believe that Jesus is the Christ, the Son of God, and that believing you may have life in his name."* These phrases contain the purpose behind the writing of the Gospel.

*"These are written that you may believe."* We can understand the whole of John's Gospel in terms of his purpose. He doesn't leave us to guess. He stated it clearly. *'You'* includes all who read his account, even you and me today. Everything he recorded in his Gospel was to bring us to the place of believing.

John weaves a number of themes through the fabric of his Gospel. Studying them is interesting and valuable, but they aren't there for their own sake or to draw attention to themselves. The themes are also not the light but bear witness to the light.

It's easy to get caught up in themes and miss the light. John develops his themes with an explicit purpose: he wants us to become believing disciples and receive life.

## A Personal Relationship

Believing isn't doctrinal or biographical; it is *personal*. John's purpose isn't just to portray the major details of Jesus' life accurately so we can give mental ascent to their historical accuracy. He does give additional information about the life of Jesus which isn't in the other Gospels, but we've not heard what John is saying if we simply come away with more information. His concern is much deeper. The facts are there and we can derive true doctrine from them (if we leave our bubble behind). But the facts are not the light, they're there to call us to believe, to connect with the Father through Jesus the Son.

The root of the Greek word translated 'believe' in John's Gospel implies binding yourself to another. It involves a personal commitment of yourself and your resources to the one in whom you believe. In biblical faith we bind ourselves in a relationship by a covenant. That's why we call a man *faithful* when he honors the marriage covenant. When we believe in the biblical sense, we *bond* to the one we believe in. God intended bonding to be a normal part of human life because he created us for intimacy.

Believing, then, has everything to do with intimate relationships. To "believe in his name" means to bond with him as a follower, as a disciple of the one who bears the name. To "believe in him who sent me" means to enter an intimate relationship with the Father who sent him as well. To commit to the Son is to commit to the Father.

Believing in John's Gospel is more than a commitment of your mind to a doctrine; it's a commitment of your whole life to a person and to his way of living.

The faithful God gives his life in love to his creation. He then calls for faithful followers willing to lovingly give their lives to him as channels of his love to the world.

## *The Content of Belief*

"*...That Jesus is the Christ.*" John seeks to impart a very definite content to believing: "The Christ of God whom you've been expecting," John says, "is Jesus and I want you to believe." Believing that Jesus is the Christ means giving your self to him for the sake of *his Father's mission* in the earth. It's all about bonding to a unique person with a unique mission—to reconcile the world to his Father's love.

John isn't asking us to ascribe to some doctrinal system built around a concept of Christ which man conceives in his bubble. He isn't interested in the ideas and concepts of the leading theologians of his day or of our day. His concern is that we see Christ in Jesus and recognize him as the Son of the Father. He wants us to bind ourselves to this person. That's why he writes and that's why he calls his writing a testimony. He testifies to things he's seen and heard to bring others to commit and bind their lives to Jesus, the Christ.

He isn't writing a biography, at least not in the sense that we have biographies today. We can understand his Gospel better if we think of it as a sermon, because preaching is designed to call people forth to a commitment to the person of Jesus Christ.

## A Person with a History

The content of John's theology is a person, not an idea or a concept. This person has a history. His history didn't begin at his birth. He was God's Word in the beginning with God and he was God (see Jn. 1:1). He is eternally in the bosom of the Father (see Jn. 1:18). He had already been involved in this world before he came in the flesh. *"All things were made through him"* (Jn. 1:2). Nor did his coming begin at his birth. *"He was* [always] *coming into the world"* (Jn. 1:9).

This Word came out from the bosom of the Father into our world of flesh (see Jn. 1:14). We must see the details of this man's life in light of where he came from and where he was going—back to the bosom of the Father.

Just as Jesus' coming didn't begin with his birth, so also it didn't end with his death. He's still with us today. He's still coming to us daily. He doesn't leave us desolate; he walks with us as we follow him. Any reading of John that fails to keep these things in view falls short of John's purpose. The interpretations in this book are not exempt. They also fall short because I haven't yet fully seen what John saw. We can only bear witness to what *we've* seen.

## *The Person Defines the Name*

Jesus is the one John presents for us to observe. He's the one John wants us to believe in. John's message is: "The Christ for whom you wait is *this man* Jesus." We aren't at liberty to supply the meaning of the title 'Christ' from our own understanding or to project onto Jesus our ideas of what the Christ 'ought' to be. We simply look to *this man* Jesus and acknowledge him to be the Christ. The title 'Christ' derives its meaning from the person and work of *this man* Jesus; it's never the other way around. Jesus doesn't derive his meaning from any preconceived notion about his title.

No matter how lofty our concepts may be, the reality of who he is overrules our ideas. He is Lord over our bubble.

## *His Identity*

"*...The Son of God.*" Many ideas also orbited around the title 'Son of God'. Kings and emperors often presented themselves as sons of the gods. People of those days also thought of Angels as sons of God in some sense. However, we can't define Jesus in terms of some philosophical or theological notion of the Son of God. John gives details of the life of *this man* Jesus to define the title. Again, this can never be reversed by using some humanistic concept to define Jesus' identity as the Son of God.

We learn what Son means by reading what is written. If we try to project the image from our bubble onto Jesus, we'll never see him for who he really is. We might say that John has written these things to pop our balloons. It will be unfortunate if our balloons don't pop until we face him in the final Day.

In the chapters that follow we'll look at the events of Jesus' life, seeking to be open to what's beyond the external details. Our goal will be to discover the Jesus John wrote about and to pursue the way he walked, recognizing that there's "another Jesus" and a "different gospel" that some preach (see II Cor. 11:4). We aren't looking for one who conforms to our mental images, nor are we simply seeking more information about the one we think we know. We want to see Jesus himself.

In this attempt, we may deflate some balloons. Many of my own false images decomposed during my personal study of this Gospel over a period of many years—some even as I was writing these meditations. I've been on this journey long enough to expect that others will come under the spotlight, but I've learned to welcome with gratitude each challenge as it comes.

## The Goal of Believing

Our approach in these reflections comes, in part, from what Jesus said when Philip asked to see the Father. Jesus said, *"He who has seen me, has seen the Father"* (Jn. 14:9). If we don't see the Father, we haven't yet seen Jesus as he desires for us to see him. It won't satisfy us merely to see historical details about his life. In seeing Jesus, we want to see the Father. In looking *at* Jesus, we're looking *for* the Father.

*"And that believing you may have life in his name...."* Some surprises are in store for those who've never looked carefully at this theme of believing as John develops it. Remember though, the theme isn't there for itself. We're looking for the one in whom we are to believe, the one with whom we are to bond. And we want to understand how to enter into the kind of believing that brings us into an intimate relationship with the Father who was and is present to the world in Jesus Christ. In relating to him we receive life. With that life we receive the commission and the ability to love as he loves.

## Levels of Believing

We'll discover different levels of believing in John's Gospel. There's a believing that brings life: *"He who believes in the Son has eternal life*" (Jn. 3:36). He who enters into this kind of believing won't be condemned (see Jn. 3:18) and will be raised up in the last day (see Jn. 6:40). However, there's also a believing that Jesus won't commit himself to. *"Many believed in his name when they saw the signs which he did; but Jesus did not trust himself to them*" (Jn. 2:23–24). There's a critical distinction here. Those who desire all that God has made available in Christ Jesus must make sure their believing is of the first category and not the second.

If Jesus won't trust himself to us—if there's no mutual bonding—there's no value in pursuing a relationship with him through this kind of believing. He won't adjust himself to our belief system; we must adjust our belief system to him. Our focus must shift from our 'trusting Jesus' to the more radical question, "Does he trust himself to us?"

We can detect a transition from one level of believing to another in several of the stories. In the healing of the nobleman's son, for example, the man *"believed the word that Jesus spoke*," but later it's said of him that "*he himself believed*" (see Jn. 4:46-54). The difference between the first and the second believing is not clear in that text; but something extra is obviously implied in the second. Something happened as a result of the second believing that hadn't yet happened in the first.

There are also negative examples. To the Jews who had believed in him, Jesus said, *"If you continue in my word, you are truly my disciples, and you will know the truth, and the truth will make you free*" (Jn. 8:31, 32). They weren't willing to admit their bondage: *"We are descendants of Abraham, and have never been in bondage to any one*" (Jn 8:33). In their minds they were free; they needed no liberation. Believing you are already free isn't the believing Jesus will commit himself to.

In the text that follows these statements, John makes it clear that they weren't on the path to life, even though they had believed in him. They had apparently believed in the Christ of their preconceived notions rather than the Christ who was offering them freedom. They were on the wrong track from the beginning. To continue on that track is to miss him completely.

## The Father is the Ultimate Goal

As we pursue this theme through the various texts we'll receive direction from the words Jesus cried out after his triumphal entry: *"He who believes in me, believes not in me but in him who sent me"* (Jn. 12:24). The goal of believing is to bond to the Father through the Son. If we've believed in Jesus without coming into an abiding relationship with his Father, we've not yet effectively believed in Jesus.

*Jesus is the way; the Father is the destination.*

## The Significance of Signs

The rest of this chapter will focus on John 20:30. We saw in verse 31 *why* John wrote. Here we find *what* he wrote. *"Now Jesus did many other signs in the presence of the disciples which are not written in this book."* He wrote signs. He didn't write *about* signs; he wrote signs. Keep this in mind as we continue.

*"Now Jesus did many other signs...."* The key word here is *signs*. Understanding how John uses this term opens the way to understanding what John is saying. The Gospels refer to the supernatural deeds of Jesus in three ways: miracles, wonders, and signs.

*Miracle* refers to the power necessary to accomplish the deed.

*Wonder* draws attention to the response of amazement on the part of those who witness the deed.

*Sign* draws attention to the fact that the deed points beyond itself. In other words, the deed does not merely accomplish something, it *means* something. The only proper response to a sign is to find out what it's pointing to and to follow until you find the thing itself.

If I were on a long trip and got hungry, it would be foolish to stop and try to eat a sign advertising a restaurant. I need the sign to find what I'm looking for, but the sign isn't what I'm after. My goal is to find the restaurant and eat.

## *The Pointing Finger*

One of my sons helped me see this when he was in middle school. I asked him to carry out the trash as I pointed toward the door. "Dad," he exclaimed with excitement as he took my pointing finger in his hand, "I just learned that the number of hairs between the knuckles of the finger are inherited. Look, Dad. You're almost bald between the second and third knuckle; and so am I." An accurate observation, but the trash hadn't moved. He'd noticed details about the pointing finger; he neglected what it pointed to.

We all do the same thing with the Scriptures sometimes. Many Bible teachers and interpreters spend years analyzing the text without ever following the sign to discover the person the Scripture speaks of. Many believers are impressed with teachers who analyze the texts, identify all the Greek words, and explain all the cultural and historical background. Yet their lives remain unaffected by the most obvious command: "Love one another." They argue and fight over doctrines that amount to nothing more than splitting the hairs between the knuckles of the pointing finger. I have personally participated in many of these kinds of arguments only to wake up and realize how insignificant it all is.

As John the Baptist points and says, "Behold, the Lamb of God," we don't want to begin counting the number of hairs between the knuckles of his finger. We want to follow the direction of the finger and find where he's pointing. In order to find our way we sometimes need to consider the Greek words and cultural background. But those things are not the point. They are only indications of the direction to face as we seek.

## More than Miracles

We usually think of *signs* only in reference to Jesus' miracles and wonders. These were definitely signs, but John is thinking of all the acts and sayings of Jesus when he speaks of the many signs Jesus did. The cleansing of the temple was as much a sign to John as the changing of the water to wine. When Jesus stoops to the ground and forgives the woman caught in adultery, this is a sign to John. All the acts and statements in the Gospel are signs pointing beyond themselves to a reality found in Jesus and his relationship with his Father and to the world.

John records these signs so we readers might find a pointer leading us to a reality beyond our bubble, to the reality John himself had seen with his eyes and touched with his hands (see I Jn. 1:1).

John chose the signs he recorded for a reason. From the many signs, John chose these particular signs because they bring readers to have life in his name. As we begin to look for life in his name we're already on the way to what the sign points to. But if we're merely looking for more historical information, we're in danger of missing the point and foundering in our attempts to know the Father.

Approaching the stories as signs doesn't deny their historical truth, but it's infinitely more valuable because the reward is life in his name. The goal of seeking is to find life, real life in the bosom of the Father.

## Events and Stories

It will help if we make another distinction before we develop this thought. The way the signs were available to John is quite different from the way they're available to us. Jesus was there in the flesh for John. For us he's there in the stories. I don't say that he's there *only* in the stories. He is really there in the stories for those who have eyes to see. He's *there* because he's *here*. He went away, but he comes to us again in a form the world can't see (see Jn. 14:19). Today he comes to those who have received him, who have believed in his name. He really is here and he can manifest himself to us as we read the text with openness for him to dissolve our false images.

When I first started studying the gospel stories, I thought it would've been more exciting to be alive in those days. "It would've been easier to get to know him then," I mused. As we continue our study, we'll see that it wasn't any easier for those who saw him in the flesh than for us who see him in and through the stories.

The Father was available to them in the presence of Jesus Christ in the flesh, but many missed him. God is available to us in the presence of Jesus Christ in the stories. We sometimes miss him as well. In either case, whether in the actual events or in the text that witnesses to those events, only the Spirit can reveal the real presence of the Father in the person of Jesus.

They needed to follow the arrow of the *events*. We must follow the arrow of the *stories*. The Pharisees got hung up in the external details of the events because Jesus didn't fit the image in their minds. They saw Jesus working miracles but still failed to recognize him for who he was. Even the disciples had trouble following the line of the signs until after the resurrection and outpouring of the Holy Spirit.

We don't want to get hung up in the external details of the stories and miss the person the signs point to. The arrow can be followed in either case only by the Spirit. But it can be followed. We must follow it if we desire to be in the fellowship of the Father and the Son by the Spirit.

## *Application to Bible Study*

Let's develop this. If John, the disciple whom Jesus loved, was writing these stories as signs, then it behooves us to follow the line indicated by the stories as one would follow the arrow on a sign advertising a restaurant.

John would be disappointed that some of us today are satisfied with learning new details about the earthly life of Jesus. Our human tendency is to prefer concepts that we can control and facts we can interpret as we see fit. Are we avoiding a personal relationship with the Father because we can't control it? Do we prefer a relationship with a text over a relationship with a living God?

It's much easier to *talk* about having a relationship than to *actually be in* one. Like some men who can talk about relationships but are afraid of facing a real woman in the flesh, we're more comfortable with external details of the stories because those details require nothing of us. In this way we can maintain the illusion that we're actually in a relationship. Preferring a fantasy world where we can control all the characters, we have the feelings of a relationship without having to face the real Christ. It's easy to get bogged down in details for their own sake when we focus on the text. That's the tendency of much of the scholarship of the nineteenth and twentieth centuries.

For example, scholars have spent much time and effort trying to determine which tomb in Jerusalem is the actual place where Jesus was buried. There's historical value in such studies. But even if we could prove which place was the actual burial site, we'd only be able to notice that the grave is empty. We already know that. Nor is it enough to stand in wonder and amazement at the fact that he is risen. We would do better to join Mary as she lingers around until the risen Lord appears.

The stories haven't had their intended effect until we experience his presence and worship him as our Lord and our God.

We can spend our lives studying the original languages and the historical and cultural background and still be totally unprepared to approach the text with eyes to see him. I know because I've done that. Having learned to use the various tools for Bible study, I was able to analyze the text and produce an exegetical masterpiece that's accurate in terms of linguistic and cultural background. But in all that effort, for many years I missed the point.

We must learn from the rabbis of Jesus' day. They knew the Scriptures better than any scholar of our day, yet they missed the one the Scriptures point to. They were looking at the external trappings of the life of Jesus and interpreting them based on their preconceived notions. They didn't see the signs as signs. They didn't follow the arrow to find rest in the bosom of the Father. If it was possible for them to miss the point, it's also possible for us.

## *Theology and Biography*

The word 'sign' indicates that John was not focused on biography but on the theological implications of this man's life, death, and resurrection. In this Gospel, John is trying to orient us to the Father in this or that event in the life of Jesus and to show how we can *join him in the bosom of the Father.*

John isn't so much interested in the fact that Jesus actually fed the multitude with only five loaves and two fish. It was a miracle and a wonder, but the miracle isn't his point. He wants us to ask, "What does this mean?" He wants us to discover and partake of the "Bread of Life"—not just to articulate an accurate doctrine of Jesus as the Bread of Life.

Once I was presenting this concept and a student challenged the notion that John is more interested in theology than biography. He'd been exposed to a theology that stripped Jesus' life of all miracles and supernatural overtones. Like so many in our day, he equated 'theology' with academic intellectualizing of the gospel. There is a theology that presents the gospel in philosophical terms, speaking as though it were nothing more than a series of doctrinal propositions or biographical details to be affirmed or denied. This isn't true biblical theology. It's only human philosophy in theological clothing.

This humanizing of the gospel is similar to what prompted John to write his first letter. Some Greek intellectuals of his day tried to explain the life of Jesus Christ in terms of their philosophy, a philosophy that came to be known as Gnosticism. They used the stories of Jesus' life as signs, but they were pointing to the Christ of their preconceived notions. They even made up a few stories themselves. The stories that came down through the disciples who knew him personally couldn't easily point in the direction of their false Christ. John almost certainly had these philosophers in mind when he said, "...*many antichrists have come*" (I Jn. 2:18).

Paul addressed a similar situation when he warned about those who preach "another Jesus" and offer "a different spirit" (see II Cor. 11:4). The true Christ never fits into the bubble of humanistic intellectuals. On the other hand, the spirit of antichrist will gladly enter your bubble and draw you away from the pointing finger of the signs in John's Gospel.

## *Failure to Follow the Signs*

My response to the student's challenge was to draw attention to the real problem. The failure to see the Gospels from a theological perspective is the very thing that leads to such philosophical nonsense. Theology is words that point in the direction of God, words about God. Whether it is good theology or bad theology depends on the direction the arrow is pointing. Wrong words point in the wrong direction. False theological constructs produce false concepts.

One can even use all the proper terminology and still point in the wrong direction. Even speaking the right words and pointing in the right direction doesn't guarantee the hearers will get the point. Jesus used all the right words and pointed in the right direction but many didn't see because they were listening through the grid of their mental images.

## Which Disciples?

This brings us to the critical point that we began with. When we approach the life of Jesus with preconceived notions based on our own human understanding apart from revelation, we can only see what our bubbles have programmed us to see. The believing that comes from such seeing is a believing produced by blindness. Jesus didn't entrust himself to this kind of believing. Jesus didn't show himself to the Pharisees who thought they could see, but he did show himself to the blind man who admitted his blindness and received his sight.

"...*In the presence of the disciples.*" We'll look at the implications of the word disciple before we turn to the question of presence. '*Disciple*' represents another major theme in John's Gospel. There are some surprises here also for those who haven't yet followed John's way of presenting different kinds of disciples.

A disciple is one who follows a teacher, but there were many disciples who drew back and no longer followed Jesus when he didn't do what they expected. These obviously weren't true disciples. Then there were the few who followed him until he was arrested. How could they be called disciples since they forsook him? Yet John calls both groups disciples. And there were the two who followed him to his trial. One of those, Peter, denied him there. Was he still a disciple? Somehow! But how? Only one, the disciple whom

Jesus loved, followed him all the way to the cross. Was he more of a disciple than the others?

## Disciples and their Dreams

If a disciple is one who follows, and that's the biblical definition of the term, then the multitude could be called *"un-disciples"* since they only followed as long as he was going the way they thought the Messiah should go. They were the 'believing unbelievers' to whom Jesus would not commit himself. He wouldn't trust himself to them because they weren't really following *him.*

These 'un-disciples' were merely excited because they thought they'd found in him the fulfillment of their messianic dreams. As Jesus continued to go the way the Father had set before him, they saw that their messianic ideals were in opposition to the way he was walking. They chose to follow their dreams and leave Jesus behind. Really Jesus left them behind. He would've left the others behind as well. *"Will you also go away?"* he asked (Jn. 6:67). Love doesn't control; it freely offers.

A serious question rises at this point. What is a true disciple? How far and in what sense does one have to follow before he's really a disciple? How much failure is allowed before one becomes an *un-disciple*? Judas followed all the way to the last night but was then exposed as the betrayer. As it turned out, the disciples who ran away in the night were still disciples in the end, somehow or other. Peter became the chief of the apostles even though he denied him.

## True Disciples

We'll discover that a true disciple is one who follows until he sees the Father in the Son and the Son in the Father and joins in this peaceful life of God on his way into the hearts of the present generation. Discipleship consists of following Jesus as the Way to this destination. There are degrees of entering into this peaceful life on its way into the world. If we've not entered the Way into fellowship in the bosom of the Father we've not yet begun to experience what's available to every true disciple. But as long as we're advancing in that relationship, we're disciples.

## The Problem of Presence

"*In the presence*...." Jesus did these signs *in the presence* of the disciples. Another question surfaces here. In the presence of which disciples? Only the ones who followed him all the way? What about the ones who followed him until he made a 'wrong' turn? The curious thing about this is that Jesus did the signs in the presence of the unbelievers as well as the disciples. He worked his miracles in public.

These *deeds*, done in the presence of many, were *signs* only to true disciples. The deeds became signs only to those who followed the arrow until they found the Father.

## There, but not There

One key to understanding this distinction between deeds and signs is to notice the implications of the word 'presence' as John uses it here. Every teacher knows that students can be in class without being *there*. Many, like Calvin and Hobbs in the old comic strips, are off on some journey into space while the teacher is presenting the material. These students are simply not present to the teaching. They're there, but not really *there*.

During the ministry of Jesus, many were on the scene but were not present. They saw the *deeds* but missed the *signs* because they were living in their bubble. The only thing really *present* to them was the image in their imagination.

Everyone recognized the feeding of the multitude as a supernatural deed. They even recognized it as a sign indicating that Jesus was "*the prophet who is coming into the world*" (Jn. 6:14). When they tried to make him King, Jesus withdrew himself from them. He didn't withdraw the natural bread; he withdrew *himself*. He wouldn't commit himself to the fulfillment of their human expectation. He performed the *deed* in their presence, but the *sign* was hidden from them because of their false notions of the coming prophet.

The fact that they thought the deed was pointing to the fulfillment of *their* expectation shows that they hadn't seen the reality of what (or who) was before them.

## Bread of Life or Bread of Death

When the crowd came for more bread, Jesus tried to draw their attention away from the deed to the sign. *"Do not labor for the food which perishes,"* he said, *"but for the food which endures to eternal life, which the Son of Man will give you"* (Jn. 6:27). The arrow of that sign pointed to Jesus himself as the Bread of Life coming down from the Father to take us back with him to the Father. Jesus came down to give us eternal life and to raise us up at the last day (see Jn. 6:38-39).

To eat of the bread of the *deed*, without following the *sign* to the True Bread, is to partake of what can only sustain a life on its way to death. *"As the living Father sent me, and I live because of the Father,"* Jesus said, *"so he who eats me will live because of me."* He spoke very clearly to those present to the sign. *"This is the bread which came down from heaven, not such as the fathers ate and died; he who eats this bread will live forever"* (Jn. 6:57, 58).

The choice is clear. Partake of the bread of the *traditions of the fathers* or partake of the Bread provided by *the Father*. Eat the first and die like the fathers died; eat the second and live with the Father eternally—even here in this life. Be satisfied with the external blessing of the deed and seek more of that external blessing, or follow the sign and find the Father from whom all true blessings flow freely and eternally. This looks like a no-brainer.

Their choice was determined by their presence or absence to the signs performed before them. *"After this many of his disciples drew back and no longer went about with him"* (Jn. 6:66). The Father was there for them, abiding in the person of Jesus, but their bubble blinded their minds.

Our choice today is determined by our presence or absence to the signs which are written and by our presence or absence to the signs he is still performing. Are you there?

## *Seeing without Seeing*

Like the men of Jeremiah's day, they were "foolish and senseless people, who have eyes, but see not, who have ears, but hear not" (Jer. 5:21). The crowd had seen Jesus in an external way, but they had not seen the Son of the Father because they were satisfied with their human insight. Having eyes, they saw not. They didn't see because they didn't look for anything deeper than their own human perception.

The Pharisees had heard the voice of Jesus, but they missed the voice of the Father (see Jn. 5:25). They only listened for statements they could use against him or statements which seemed to confirm their dream-messiah. Having ears, they didn't hear. They didn't come out of death into life (see Jn. 5:24) because they were content with the life they had. Even though they had a doctrine of resurrection they didn't realize that the life they had was a life with no future, a life with no promise beyond death. This life with no future is the death that comes by seeing the deed (in an event or in the written code) apart from the Spirit who draws us to the one the sign points to.

Paul states this same truth. He speaks of "him who has made us competent to be ministers of a new covenant, not in a written code but in the Spirit." He draws attention to the fact that we can read the "written code" apart from the Spirit, and identifies the results of reading the text apart from the Spirit: "For the written code kills, but the Spirit gives life"

(II Cor. 3:6). The "written code" refers to the biblical text seen by one who doesn't follow the arrow of the sign to find the one who gives life. And the only ones who can follow that arrow are those who are in tune with the Spirit.

Those imprisoned by their balloon find fulfillment in their interpretation of the text. They feel no need to look for anything beyond that.

## Reading Scripture without Listening

Jesus addresses this same problem when he says to the religious leaders, "*You search the scriptures, because you think that in them you have eternal life; and it is they that bear witness to me*" (Jn. 5:39). The scriptures bear witness to Jesus Christ from Genesis to Revelation.

I still 'wake up' sometimes to realize I've been off in my bubble trying to force the text to agree with me. When I do that I only receive better ideas, not revelation. The Spirit gives revelation and life as we follow the line of the pointing finger of the text and receive the miracle of the opened eyes. The power of the bubble is broken and we are free. Are you there? Or are you still in your bubble?

Let's return to the feeding of the multitude. When Jesus turned to the twelve and asked if they would also go away, Peter answered, "*Lord, to whom shall we go? You have the words of eternal life; and we have believed, and have come to know, that you are the Holy One of God*" (Jn. 6:68, 69).

This is an amazing response considering what Jesus had just said, "*Eat my flesh. Drink my blood.*" The disciples didn't yet understand the Lord's Supper as we know it today. This must have sounded much like a call to cannibalism. Furthermore, the Law forbids the drinking of blood (see Lev. 17). How much more repulsive the drinking of human blood must have sounded. Jesus didn't try to make their decision easier by explaining what he meant. Nor did he insist they continue to follow. Love doesn't control.

He left each to make his own decision based on what he'd already seen. Had they seen the signs or only the deeds? Whether they stay or leave will indicate what they've seen and the level of their believing.

## *Peter's Example*

We can capture the significance of Peter's answer by reading between the lines. Peter was saying, "Lord, we don't understand what you mean about eating your flesh. But if that's what it takes to be your disciple, then give me a bite. 'Drink my blood' sounds repulsive, and it's against everything we've been taught from the Law. But if the choice is between drinking or going away from you, then fill my cup." The decision to continue following Jesus is always a radical one.

All the popular ideas and concepts of the Christ were being challenged at the very core. But the twelve (or at least eleven of them) were willing to leave their concepts behind. If you've really seen him as the "Holy One of God," you have no choice but to accept his challenge and leave your preconceived notions behind. You'll continue to follow him even if it means turning your back on all you thought you knew. "I am here, and I am staying," Peter says.

## *Present in the Secret Place*

Matthew 6:6 will help us understand this concept of being there but not there. Jesus instructs us to go into our room and close the door when we pray. Then he speaks of the Father being "in secret" and rewarding "in secret."

The secret place is a place where the disciples are present to the Lord and the Lord is present to the disciples. Others may be in the neighborhood but they aren't in this secret place. The closed door to the room is not referring to a literal door. It simply indicates that those who have no relationship to Father have no access to the reality we're experiencing with him while we're in the secret place.

Jesus did the deeds in public but the signs remained in the secret place where disciples meet with their Father to pray. Jesus spoke many words to the multitude; but his voice reached only the ears of those willing to forsake their bubble to follow him into the Father's bosom, into the secret place. The disciples saw and heard because they weren't merely in the vicinity of Jesus of Nazareth. They were in the presence of the Father who abides 'in secret'—in Jesus.

They didn't fully understand why they were so drawn to Jesus, but they were really there because the Father was drawing them (see Jn. 6:44). They were in that secret place because of their willingness to continue following Jesus even when his way surprised them and challenged their preconceived notions.

Even though Peter didn't follow Jesus all the way to the place of his crucifixion, he did follow Jesus. He stumbled as he followed, but he followed. Like the other disciples, his understanding of the way Jesus was going was clouded. But when Jesus made a turn Peter hadn't anticipated, Peter continued to follow at a distance. He did have preconceived notions but he forsook them to follow Jesus the way Jesus was going. He did deny the Lord in a moment of confusion but he was the first to enter the empty tomb. He was still following in spite of his failure to understand.

Are you in that place where Peter was? Are you ready to be surprised by Jesus? Are you ready to follow him, whatever that means?

Let's continue to the next chapter with openness for the images in our bubbles to be challenged.

# CHAPTER 2

# The Day of Transition

—⟋ⁿⁿⁿ⟍—

In our first chapter we saw the danger of coming to the Scriptures with preconceived notions. We also noticed that the mental pictures in our imagination influence what we are able to see. These embedded notions may keep us from seeing what's right in front of us. John wrote his Gospel using the stories as signs to challenge the images in our bubble. He wants us to see the relationship between the Father and the Son as we follow the story lines. He wants us to see the Father's love and become believing disciples. In believing we receive life.

Our next project will be to look at the four consecutive days in John's introductory chapter. As we unpack these verses we'll be looking for signs of the transition from the Old Testament to Jesus Christ and the Church. We'll begin by looking briefly at the poetic structure of the first chapter of John.

## *The Structure of John's First Chapter*

The prologue (Jn. 1:1-18) presents the basic structure of the relation between God, his Word, and his world. The center of the poetic structure of the text speaks of God giving "**power to become children of God**" to those who believe and receive the Word (vs.12-13). The ability to become children of God is the central theme of the prologue. Before and after the center John develops three other themes. Before the center (vs. 1-11) the focus is on God's relationship to the world in general as he moves toward the sending of his Son in the flesh. After the center (vs. 14-18) the focus is on the coming of the Son and his ministry to those who receive the Word.

On either side of that center there is mention of this Word which is the light of man coming into the world. Immediately before the center (vs. 9-11) the Word comes as light to those who are his own, but they reject him. Immediately after the center the Word comes in the flesh and the disciples (the "we" of verse 14) behold his glory. That's the first theme — the coming of the Word into the world he created.

As we move another step away from the center we find John the Baptist and his testimony. It's a negative testimony before the center. *"He was not the light, but came to bear witness to the light"* (vs. 6-8). It's a positive testimony after the center. *"He who comes after me is before me"* (vs. 15). That's the second theme — the testimony of John.

One more step away from the center the prologue begins with the relation of God to the Word, *"...the Word was with God, and the Word was God"* (vs.1-5). This Word was active in creating and giving life and light to man. The prologue ends with the disciples receiving grace and truth from his fullness. Then the Word of God is identified as the *"only Son, who is in the bosom of the Father"* (vs. 16-18). It's this Son that makes the Father known to the world he created. That's the third theme — the relationship of the Father and the Son and the Son's ministry to the world he created.

The *sign* of this structure points to God's dealing with the world. The world first rejected his dealings but he overcame that rejection by becoming a part of the world through the incarnation. In this way he made it possible for men to become members of his family. We shouldn't necessarily think the 'before and after' is referring to historical time before and after Christ. It can also refer to the condition of individuals in the world before and after they 'see the light' and receive Christ. The 'old man' becomes 'new' when he sees the light of the glory of God in the face of Christ (see II Cor. 4:6). In John that experience is called being "born anew" (see Jn. 3:7)

As we present the following meditations, be alert to John's answer to the question of how the incarnate Word makes the Father's love known in the world. The four days of transition follow a pattern similar to what we noticed above in the prologue to the Gospel. The rejection of the Baptist's testimony (first day) is followed by the appearance o Jesus (second day). The transition begins as disciples hear John's testimony and begin to follow Jesus (third day). Jesus then begins the process of calling disciples to himself and the Baptist is left behind (fourth day).

## *Four Days of Transition*

After the prologue John presents the *transition from John the Baptist to Jesus* over four consecutive days (see Jn. 1:19-51). In this chapter we'll focus on the third day when two disciples heard John's testimony and followed Jesus. These two disciples become a sign pointing to the kind of following that leaves the old behind and turns to follow the new. They show the way to enter into the reality of what the Father offers in Jesus Christ. These two disciples will hold our attention all the way through chapter six because they really heard and really followed Jesus to the place prepared for them—the abiding place in Father's bosom.

## *Overview: First Day*

On the *first* day Jewish leaders sent priests and Levites from Jerusalem to check out John the Baptist. They're trying to find out if he's claiming to be Messiah (see Jn. 1:19-28).

53

*"I am not the Christ,"* John confesses. His answer is short. God didn't send him to testify about himself. So he says no more until they press him.

*"Are you Elijah?"* the inquisitors ask.

*"I am not."* His answer is briefer still.

*"Are you the prophet?"* They need an answer for those who'd sent them.

*"No,"* he replied.

Why is John so short with these men? He was sent to bear witness to Jesus the coming Messiah, so why is he avoiding the issue? He knew that those who sent these men were not truly seeking Messiah. They came to judge him. This happened near Bethany, which means 'House of Sorrow'. John often uses places and times to clue the reader in to the spiritual realities the sign is pointing to. How sad it is when we live in that place where heaven's messenger withholds his witness.

Here's the message of the first day: "Heaven withholds its testimony from those who set themselves up as judges of religious orthodoxy."

## Overview: Second Day

On the *second* day (see Jn 1:29-34), John gives a definite testimony. Pointing to Jesus, he says, *"Behold, the Lamb of God, who takes away the sin of the world."* Seeing the Holy Spirit descend on Jesus as a dove, he proclaims: *"This is the Son of God."* He delivers this testimony as Jesus walks toward him on this second day. John couldn't have spoken more clearly, "God sent me to point out this man Jesus. He's the one God promised would come; he's more than you expected. He isn't just another man; he's the Lamb of God and the Spirit of God is upon him. He's the Son of God."

There's no record of anyone turning to follow on the second day. John may have left out that detail to draw attention to the sign. Many may have chased after him on that second day thinking he was the fulfillment of their expectations. Chasing after God is not the same chasing the image in your mind. Chasing after God is turning to follow when you've really heard the testimony. That may be why many chase God and never find him. They're only chasing their dream. By God's grace the blessings and promises are still available to those who don't yet get it.

Here's the message of the second day: "God fulfills all his promises in this man. We receive forgiveness of sin and power for living life by the Spirit through him."

## Overview: Fourth Day

We'll save the third day for later since it's the main topic of this chapter.

On the *fourth* day (see Jn. 1:43-51) Jesus begins to call his own disciples and his disciples begin to call others. The Baptist is no longer active. Philip finds Nathaniel and invites him to come and see.

The transition is now complete. At the end of this fourth day Jesus recognizes Nathaniel and affirms him as "*an Israelite with no guile.*" The phrase *without guile* points to one whose 'bubble' is clean and ready to receive revelation. Nathaniel immediately confesses, "*Rabbi, you are the Son of God! You are the king of Israel!*" Jesus promises Nathaniel, "*You will see heaven opened, and the angels of God ascending and descending upon the Son of Man.*"

The text identifies Jesus as the Son of God on the second day and on the fourth day as well. After Nathaniel's confession, however, Jesus uses the term *Son of Man*. This term carries some baggage from Jewish apocalyptic expectations developed between the close of the Old and the opening of the New Testament. In Ezekiel the term simply means "human being" or son of Adam.

Taking our lead from Ezekiel, we suggest that the angels ascending and descending on the Son of Man may include all those who enter into the Body of Christ—the second Adam. That interpretation is consistent with Hebrews 1:13, which refers to the angels as servants sent in behalf of those who are being saved.

Here's the message of the fourth day: "Those with an open heart will see heaven opened and will be involved in the coming of the Kingdom."

## *The Third Day in Scripture*

In Scripture, the *third* day often marks the transition in a spiritual journey—the beginning of something new. On the *third* day Abraham lifted his eyes and beheld the place where he would offer Isaac as a sacrifice. On this third day Abraham and Isaac became a picture (a type) of the Father offering his Son (see Gen. 22:4). On the *third* day the Lord came down on Mount Sinai to meet with his people (see Ex. 19). "On the *third* day," writes Hosea, God "will raise us up that we may live before him" (see Hos. 6:2). Being raised up is clearly the beginning of a new life in the presence of God.

There are many other examples: Joseph releasing his brothers from prison, Jonah rescued from the belly of the whale, Esther fasting before entering the king's presence to plead for the life of the Jewish people, Jesus resurrected from the grave—all of these were third day events.

In the final chapter of John, Jesus' third appearance (not a third day, but still significant) was after he ascended to his Father and returned to bring the disciples into the place he had gone to prepare for them (see Jn. 14:2). This event also speaks of a new thing in the lives of the disciples.

The Wedding in Cana follows this transition from John to Jesus. That event also takes place on a *third* day (see Jn. 2:1). The point of the wedding feast is that Jesus "*manifested his glory; and his disciples believed in him*" (Jn. 2:11). We will learn that his glory is related to his abiding in the bosom of the Father.

Here's the message of the third day in chapter one—"We may enter into the abiding place with Jesus, that place where God's glory is revealed to us and through us."

## Standing and Walking

Let's look at this *third* day. "*The next day again John was standing with two of his disciples; and he looked at Jesus as he walked, and said, 'Behold the Lamb of God!' The two disciples heard him say this, and they followed Jesus*" (Jn. 1:35-37).

"*John was standing.*" On this third day the Baptist, who had been on the move, is now standing and Jesus is walking. This is a sign. It points to the shift—the transition that's about to occur. Everything up to this point was preparing the way for Jesus' public ministry. From this point forward all the stories and dialogues bring the reader to a revelation of the Father through Jesus, the Word of the Father in flesh.

On the *first day,* John is the central figure and Jesus is not even mentioned by name. Jesus is *standing* in the crowd as "*one whom you do not know.*" On the *second day,* John sees Jesus "*coming toward him.*" Jesus is beginning to move, but John is still the actor of that day. On this third day, John is standing and no longer moving; Jesus is *walking.* John is decreasing; Jesus is increasing (see Jn. 3:30).

## The Big Shift

This sign doesn't just point to a shift in the story; it manifests a shift in all of history. Before this, everything is moving toward Jesus Christ. The Law and the prophets, including the Baptist, bear witness to his *coming.* After this, the apostles and the Church bear witness that *he has come in the flesh.* Through him all things will be reconciled to the Father (see Col. 1:20). The ultimate goal of creation is now in view.

This third day marks the passing of the old and the coming of the new. The coming Kingdom of God will make all things new (see Rev. 21:5). This day is a pivotal point in history. The ministry of John the Baptist, and with him all the Old Testament prophets, finds its true goal on this third day.

This third day marks the end of a very long night and the beginning of a new day. The sign of this day points to the day of resurrection when Jesus makes his Father available to the world in a new way. In other words, the *ministry* of Jesus has its beginning on this third day but the *events* of this day also point to the place Jesus prepared for us to abide in the Father's love.

From that place in Father's bosom Jesus will send the Church into the world to draw others into the peaceful life of the Father, Son, and Holy Spirit. All the events in the Gospel happen as Jesus is making his way to the cross to prepare a place for mankind in Father's loving embrace. All these events point as signs to the way we come into Father's bosom and go out from that abiding place into the world with love.

## John's Disciples

"*...With two of his disciples.*" A group of men have gathered around John the Baptist. He has disciples. An excitement pervades Israel because they expect Messiah to make his appearance soon. They expect a king to appear and re-establish the throne of David in Jerusalem by leading them into victory over the Romans. John isn't the one they're looking for (he's not the light). He came to bear witness to the one who will come after him, who ranks before him.

The transition from John to Jesus isn't obvious at this time — not even to John's disciples. Most of them remain with John. Apparently, even John later struggled with the ministry of Jesus. Luke tells of John sending two of his disciples to ask Jesus, "Are you the one who is to come, or shall we look for another?" (Lk. 7:19). Nevertheless, in the moment of revelation on the second day of our text the Baptist is not struggling. He clearly and boldly identifies Jesus as the Son of God. In fact his testimony is more complete on the second day than on the third.

## The Eye of a Prophet

"*He looked at Jesus.*" John is looking at the external features of the one who's walking toward him. He's looking with the eye of a prophet, an eye always open and ready for God to show something beyond the surface. He's considering the spiritual implications of what his eyes are beholding. He hasn't been sent to bear witness to what he might be able to discover with his natural human abilities and insights. He knows human insight won't help him recognize the one he'd been sent to identify.

"*I myself did not know him,*" he declares, indicating his own inability to see without help from above (Jn. 1:33). As he looks at Jesus on this third day, he's still waiting for God to show him more of the reality of what he's looking at.

Why is he looking so intently on this third day? On the previous day he'd seen Jesus coming toward him. He'd seen the Holy Spirit descend upon him and remain. God had told him earlier that the one on whom he saw the Holy Spirit descend and remain would be the one he should identify to the people. If he'd already seen so clearly, why is he so eager to see again? The answer is simple. He isn't satisfied with having seen yesterday. He wants to see again today. He understands the principle implied in the statement, "His mercies...are new every morning" (Lam. 3:22-23).

We must never be satisfied with having received yesterday. What he has for us today is new. Yesterday's manna breeds worms (see Ex. 16:20), but God gives fresh provision daily. To receive the newness, we must be open for him to show it to us again today. We must strive to see more deeply today than yesterday. We must not take what we saw yesterday and hold it so tightly that we become unable to see something more today. It's easy to form a new image in our bubble based on our interpretation of what he showed us yesterday.

None of us has seen perfectly and none of us has seen it all. He may have something new to add to our understanding today. We are all in process and must remain open to new insights. Life in Christ is a journey with a destination beyond what any of us have understood or received so far.

## Making the Father Known by Walking

"*...As he walked.*" The Baptist gives his testimony on this third day based on the way Jesus walked. John isn't merely telling us that Jesus happened to be on foot that day. By the time he wrote his Gospel he'd been meditating on the events of the life of Jesus for over fifty years. He'd seen much more—and more deeply—in his later years than what he'd seen before the resurrection. He wrote his 'book of signs' to help us see the 'more' he'd seen.

This '*more*' can only be seen through the grid of the death, burial and resurrection of Jesus and the subsequent outpouring of the Holy Spirit. If it took him over fifty years of seeking for insights to be ready to share, we shouldn't be surprised that it takes us more than one reading of his text before we even begin to see what he saw.

Jesus revealed the Father by the *way he walked*. This is one of John's major themes. His walk—the way he lived life—is a sign pointing to the Father. "*No one has ever seen God,*" we're told. We can't know God except by revelation, and Jesus is that revelation: "*The only Son, who is in the bosom of the Father, he has made him known*" (Jn. 1:18). He made the Father known by the way he walked.

Although Jesus had been exalted to the right hand of God for more than fifty years, John uses the present tense to indicate that the bosom of the Father is the *eternal abiding place* of the Son. When this eternal Word became flesh, he didn't cease to be the Son of God nor did he leave his Father's bosom. When Jesus repeatedly says, "*I am in the Father*," he refers to his abiding place in his Father's loving embrace. He came out from his Father's bosom without leaving Father's bosom. He occupied that place even while on the earth. From that place he made the Father known. His purpose in coming was to return to the Father's bosom bringing "many sons" to glory (see Heb. 2:10).

## *The Bosom of the Father*

Look closely at John 1:18 for two insights, "*The only Son, who is in the bosom of the Father, he has made him known.*" First, the word translated, 'bosom', refers to that part of the body that's in front between the arms. According to Thayer's lexicon it can also metaphorically refer to that part of the loose clothing above the girdle that was used to carry valuables and keep them safe—something of a 'fanny pack', but in the front. Jesus lives his life in his Father's 'tummy pack.' Wherever the Father goes, the Son goes with him because he's abiding in the 'tummy pack.'

When you see Jesus, if you really see what's in front of you, you're looking at his Father. If I'm in Christ, I'm in his Father's tummy pack too. If you're in him, you're also going where he's going because "your life is hid with Christ in God" (Col. 3:3). This is what John has in mind when he presents the beloved disciple reclining on Jesus' breast (see Jn. 13:23). The word translated *breast* is the same word translated *bosom* in 1:18. All disciples are welcome in that position of intimacy but none are forced to recline there.

The full implication of this image of the bosom is much deeper than the tummy pack. The tummy pack is still external to the Father. The message of the bosom speaks of being in the Father's heart of love. Everyone desires to have a place in someone's heart. Jesus went to prepare a place in Father's heart for all of us. St. Augustine was right when he said we are all restless until we find this place. When we do find this place, we've found a treasure in a field and will be willing to sell everything in order to have this for ourselves.

When I first received this insight I used the metaphor of the Father's lap. That's a good picture, but for our purpose the 'tummy pack' is better. A person's lap is not available unless he's in a sitting position. The Father is indeed seated on the throne, but he's also very active in the history of the world.

What we're trying to capture is a dynamic image of our *being carried with him in what he's doing* in the earth today. He's moving toward the consummation of all things—toward the uniting of all things in Jesus Christ, things in heaven and things in earth (see Eph. 1:10). As he moves forward, we're in his tummy pack—in his heart—and involved in his will being done in the earth. We actually experience the intimacy of the Father's bosom as we join him in his work of loving the world.

Henri Nouwen, in his book *The Return of the Prodigal Son*, spoke of "the One who awaits me with open arms and wants to hold me in an eternal embrace." While working with mentally handicapped people, he experienced enough of that embrace to make him hungry for more. We're saying that those of us who abide in Christ are already in that eternal embrace, even as we go with longing toward a deeper experience of that embrace. It's from that embrace that we should be reaching out to embrace our neighbor. When we reach out to others we'll experience a deeper sense of his love for us as well.

We need a dynamic image because a static image would be an idol. A lap disappears when one rises from a sitting position to become active. Thus we use the 'tummy pack' to emphasize God's movement into the world with those who abide in his bosom.

*We are in him and we are in what he is doing* if we are abiding in Christ.

## Teaching by Life Narrative

The second insight is related to the word which is translated 'made him known.' That word can refer to a Rabbi presenting a narrative, a story, to unfold a teaching (Thayer). That's what Jesus was doing when he told parables. But the life Jesus lived on earth in the bosom of the Father became *a living narrative* that unfolds and reveals the character of the Father. John wants us to find that abiding place in Father's bosom, so he presents *a written narrative* of Jesus' life.

As we grapple with this 'lived narrative' of Jesus' life, our life can become a narrative that unfolds the character of the Father through us as well. *"He who says he abides in him ought to walk in the same way in which he walked"* (I Jn. 2:6). John's written narratives of Jesus' life and teachings show us how Jesus lived his life out from an abiding relationship with his Father. We are invited to follow him into that abiding relationship and live our life on earth out from that place with him.

## The Walk and the Abiding Place

John wants us to connect Jesus' *walk* with his being in that *abiding place* in the Father's bosom. His abiding in the Father makes his walk a revelation of our Father's love for the world. Later Jesus will tell Philip, *"He who has seen me has seen the Father"* (Jn. 14:9). Everything Jesus says and does is a revelation of Father's love because the works he does are not his works, *"but the Father who dwells in me does his works"* (Jn. 14:10).

This is true because Jesus is not the source of his own life; *"For as the Father has life in himself, so he has granted the Son also to have life in himself"* (Jn. 5:26). Out of the life of the Father comes the life of the Son; *"the son can do nothing of his own accord, but only what he sees the Father doing"* (Jn. 5:19). The Son initiates nothing. He follows his Father in all things. From that place of abiding in the Father, his walk reveals his Father to those who have eyes to see. That's how he walked, and John saw that walk. And we are invited to walk as he walked.

The Baptist couldn't have fully understood the significance of Jesus' walk at this early stage. Even the closest disciples didn't understand until after the resurrection. This fact is evidence of the way John uses stories to point as signs. The use of this literary device is his way of tempting the reader to look at the text more closely.

The more I study John's Gospel, the more I'm convinced that John, the beloved disciple, is planting seeds in passages like these to prepare us for a deeper revelation of the death and resurrection when his unfolding narrative brings us to that point. As we follow the many pointing arrows within this Gospel, we'll always find the glory of God the Father in the life, death, and resurrection of Jesus the Son.

### What did John See?

*"Behold, the Lamb of God."* The testimony of the third day is actually shorter than the second day's testimony. The second day highlights what he'll do for you. "He'll take away your sins. He'll empower you to live in the kingdom of God by baptizing you in the Holy Spirit. You'll be able to heal the sick, cast out demons, and raise the dead. He'll give you a new past. You'll no longer be what you were. You'll be sons and daughters of the living God. And he'll give you a new future in the bosom of his Father. You'll live in him and be able to live your life here and now through him."

If all these blessings are reflected in the testimony of the second day, what makes the third day more significant? The testimony of the third day—*Behold, the Lamb of God*—focuses on *who he is*. There's no mention of what he'll do for you.

The Lord isn't looking for followers who're obsessed with what he'll do for them. He doesn't want disciples who merely desire to work miracles or to receive miracles. He's looking for those who recognize him for who he *is* and follow him even if this following brings trouble. Certainly he promises blessings and he's faithful to bestow blessings, but those who crave blessings can never follow the way true disciples follow.

The multitudes follow for the blessings—bread, healing, hope of political dominance. As long as the blessings flow they follow; but as soon as he offers what he really has for them, they will draw back and no longer go about with him (see Jn. 6:66). Those who seek him for who he *really is* will continue with him even when his way goes contrary to their expectations.

## Passover and Atonement

To understand the significance of the third day, we must pay attention to phrase '***Lamb of God***'? In the testimony of the second day John adds the phrase "*who takes away the sin of the world.*" Although there are many sacrifices involving lambs, we generally understand that Jesus is the true Passover Lamb sacrificed on the cross during that Passover Feast. In the book of Revelation we see the Lion of Judah which turns out to be the Lamb that was slain (see Rev. 5:5-6).

Jesus is the Lamb that was slain and he did take away our sins, but that doesn't necessarily imply only Passover. There's more to John's testimony than Jesus being the Passover Lamb. Understanding what John meant by "Lamb of God" will help us uncover the implications of the third day sign.

## Passover: Deliverance and Covenant Fellowship

The Passover feast commemorated deliverance from Egyptian bondage and the rescue of the first-born of Israel from death, but it was never intended to take away sin. So why does John mention taking sin away in connection with the Lamb (Jesus) who will be slaughtered at this Passover Feast?

The Passover lamb was not burnt on the altar as a sin offering; it was eaten as a sign of being partners in the altar (see I Cor. 10:18). The phrase 'partners in the altar' simply means that the one who eats of the sacrificial animal acknowledges and experiences covenant fellowship with the god the altar is dedicated to. So the Passover sacrifice was to remind worshipers that they were delivered from bondage and that they have a covenant relationship with the true God who rescued them.

## Atonement: Forgiveness and Taking Away Sin

The Passover lamb, offered in the spring festival, didn't symbolize the removal of sin. That was the work of *two other animals* selected for the Day of Atonement in the fall festival. One animal represented *forgiveness* and atonement—the sin offering. The priests burnt its carcass on the altar and the high priest took its blood into the Holy of Holies and sprinkled it on the lid of the Ark of the Covenant.

The second animal represented *taking away* sin. All the sins of the people were symbolically transferred to the scapegoat—the sins of the nation were put on this animal. Then it was taken outside the camp with the national sins on its head and released in the wilderness (see Lev. 6). Sin was thus taken 'outside the camp.'

The transition from the Old Testament types to the reality of fulfillment actually happened in three days—the days of Jesus' death, burial and resurrection. The sign of the third day of our text points to this transition from type to fulfillment, from the picture to the reality of liberation and intimacy with God.

So we see two separate feasts with three distinct animals, all rich with meaning. Was John confused in his terminology? I think not. John intentionally combines the meaning of the

two feasts into one. He had seen Jesus Christ as the fulfillment of both feasts. Jesus is the reality that all the sacrifices
and rituals of the old covenant refer to.

## *Guilt and Tendency*

Our sins are forgiven *and* taken away in and through
Jesus Christ. Forgiveness deals with guilt—and forgiveness is a good thing. But we should never be satisfied with
forgiveness alone. We should desire for him to take the
*tendency* out of our midst—outside the camp. The blood of
bulls and goats was never able to *take away* the tendency
behind the sins (see Heb. 10:4, 11). God forgave sins in
the Old Testament. David knew forgiveness personally and
spoke a blessing over those whose sins are forgiven (see Ps.
32:1). Forgiveness was available because of Father God's
love for the world.

The primary act of God's love for man in a fallen world
is forgiveness and that forgiveness has always been available
to those who repent. However, the *tendency to sin* was not
*taken away*. The fullness of time had not yet come. The real
blood of atonement had not yet been shed. The real 'goat'
had not been abandoned 'outside the gate' in the wilderness
(death and the grave).

Taking away *sin tendencies* adds a new dimension to
forgiveness. We have often missed the significance of this
dimension of the work of Christ on the cross. It seems to
me that our Father desires to bring the Church into a revelation of this dimension and give us the full experience of this
removal of sin in these last days.

Those Old Testament sacrifices were signs, symbols, or
types of a reality available through the shed blood of Jesus.
The Old Testament saints repeated these sacrifices year after
year because they hadn't received the reality of the cleansed
conscience (see Heb. 10:2, 3). The sacrifices of the Day of

Atonement were only a shadow of the reality that took place at the cross. What is that reality?

## A Cleansed Conscience

Our hearts are "sprinkled clean from an evil conscience" (Heb. 10:22) when the blood of this man is applied. Our life activities flow from the heart (see Prov. 4:23). The heart and conscience work together in determining our action. The conscience is more than the good or bad feelings we have when we've done something. Conscience refers to the source of our behavior, not an inner voice trying to make us feel good or bad because of our behavior. An evil conscience actually produces evil activity. A clean conscience produces clean activity.

The cleansing of the conscience *takes away* that evil inclination that we struggle with so desperately.

John makes a radical statement in his first letter. *"You know that he appeared to take away sins, and in him there is no sin. No one who abides in him sins; no one who sins has either seen him or known him"* (I Jn. 3:5, 6). John ties the idea of 'taking away sins' to a life of victory over sin. To the degree that we abide in him—in the way John uses the term—to that degree we will not sin.

Someone may ask, "Why then do we still have the tendency to sin if it has been taken away?" The answer is simple. All God's blessings are received by faith. The sins of the whole world are covered by the work of Jesus on the cross, but that work has its effect in our life as we exercise faith. What would happen if a generation received this cleansed conscience by faith, a generation whose conscience was actually purified from dead works to serve the living God (see Heb. 9:14)? What a Day that would be!

As long as we continue to *believe* we're bound, we'll continue to be in bondage to sin. The transition is complete as far as the work of Jesus Christ is concerned; but the church as a whole is still on the way to the full experience of what is available in Christ.

Each generation is challenged to go farther on this path than the previous generation. We're going toward that time when "the creation itself will be set free from its bondage to decay and obtain the glorious liberty of the children of God" (Rom. 8:21). In fact "the whole creation has been groaning in travail together until now," waiting for the "revealing of the sons of God" (Rom. 8:19, 22). Some day God will show his sons to be what they really are because they will really believe the gospel and be made free.

## Active Waiting in Full Fellowship

We are now waiting for "adoption as sons, the redemption of our bodies" (Rom. 8:23). We should be actively waiting, by striving to enter that rest (see Heb. 4:11) where we no longer struggle with unbelief and deeds of darkness, where our conscience is cleansed. Will you do your part in this generation and prepare the way for the next generation to go a step farther? Will you believe that the Lamb of God has taken away your sin tendency? Will you dare to walk toward real freedom from sin?

## Summary of Passover and Atonement

In summary, Jesus is the true Passover Lamb of God who brings us into relationship with his Father. He is also the Atonement sacrifice. The covenant is established and we may regularly partake of the covenant meal. In the Lord's Supper we are not partaking of a dead lamb. He is alive. As we abide in him we move toward possessing our inheritance in the 'land of promise.' As long as we remain in his 'tummy pack' we will continue to have victory over our enemies.

The Atonement sacrifice is accomplished through two animals—the Lamb of Atonement and the Scapegoat. Father has provided the way if we would only walk in it. Jesus is the way out of the bondage of sin into the Father's bosom where *victory over sin tendencies is the norm.* He provided a way for our evil inclination to be taken away and our evil conscience to be cleansed. Have you received that by faith?

## *Leaving Sin Behind*

If we see Jesus *as he walked,* we find the Father making his grace and truth available to the world. All the animals slaughtered through the centuries were only types and shadows of this Lamb who is, even now in this gospel narrative, being led by his Father to his death on the cross during the Passover Feast. On that wooden altar he will take upon himself the sin of the world, fulfilling the Day of Atonement. He will take that sin with him outside the camp to the grave thus removing the obstacle to reconciliation with the Father.

From that grave his Father will raise him up on the third day, leaving our sin behind. Jesus will then make himself available by the Holy Spirit as we follow him into Father's bosom. Through his resurrection we become partners with him who was dead and is now alive forevermore (see Rev. 1:18). Through his flesh and blood we're brought into the fellowship of the Father's bosom. *We are flesh and blood sons and daughters of God.* That's what it means to eat his flesh and drink his blood.

Jesus accomplished more than a geographical removal; the scapegoat points to a reality that is in Jesus Christ. Sin is really outside the camp for us if and when we live in the Father's loving embrace.

To the degree that we abide in the Father's bosom—his tummy pack—to that degree we overcome sin. We can still hold on to our sin if we choose, but why? Have we attached ourselves to something outside the Father's heart of love? Why would we want to do that? Do you dare believe this freedom is available for you?

Believing is entering the *path* to total freedom. Abiding in his word is continuing on the path as a disciple. It's only as we continue on the path that we come to know the truth and are made free (see Jn. 8:31-32). How far do you want to go on this path? Are you satisfied with being on the path or do you want to go all the way?

## *Making the Father Known*

Jesus walks in a way that reveals the Father's heart of love by doing *"only what he sees the Father doing."* Living his life in this way Jesus reveals an important truth: The Father is for us, he's not against us. Jesus isn't trying to protect us from an angry God. He's not trying to *change* God's heart toward man. He's *revealing* the heart of the Father of Love. The desire of the Father has always been to have intimate fellowship with his creation. *"For God so loved the world that he gave his only Son"* (Jn. 3:16). It's the Father who so loved the world that he sent his son. That's what Jesus came to show us about his Father. His Father loves you and is available to become your Father.

## *God the Father Seeking Man*

The Bible is not a story of man seeking God. It is a story of God seeking man (see Abraham Heschel's book, *God in Search of Man*, for more on this insight). After Adam sinned in the garden, he didn't seek God or try to placate him and make amends. Adam covered himself with fig leaves, hid from God, and blamed Eve.

Like the prodigal son, man has always been running from the Father into a far country. It was God who was seeking fellowship. He has always been and remains the *waiting Father*. Fellowship between God and man was the Father's idea from the beginning. That's the original purpose of creation. It's our destiny, if we dare pursue it.

Old Testament saints didn't know God as Father. That's why it was necessary for Jesus to come and make him known. Mankind, including the Israelite nation, never understood the Fatherhood of God. By coming to the prophets of Israel, God offered an ever increasing insight into his nature. Even Israel didn't come to see God as Father apart from the ministry of the Son. In fact, those who didn't get it are the ones who condemned him for blasphemy because of his message of the Father. We mustn't judge them for not knowing; many Christians today don't know (experience) him as the Father of love.

## Some See without Seeing

So the Baptist recognizes the Lamb by observing his walk. At least that's the sign John puts up for us to read. Nicodemus also saw something about Jesus by watching him. He came to Jesus and said, *"You are a teacher come from God...No one can do these signs that you do, unless God is with him"* (Jn. 3:2). But Nicodemus missed something. Jesus replied, *"That which is born of the flesh is flesh and that which is born of the Spirit is spirit"* (Jn. 3:6).

Nicodemus saw the deeds Jesus did but interpreted them by the flesh, that is, by his human understanding. He failed to follow the arrow by the Spirit. His confession—that God must be with Jesus—was apparently prompted by a logical conclusion rather than by his openness to revelation from the Father. Revelation never comes through flesh and blood, but only from the Father who is in heaven (see Matt. 16:16). Nicodemus had not seen by the Spirit.

It's true that Nicodemus later became a disciple. He was the one who questioned the rulers when they were condemning Jesus without a trial (see Jn. 7:50). He was also present at the burial of Jesus with Joseph of Arimathea (see Jn. 19:39). This means he was on the right path but was not yet ready to move toward the destination. To come to the bosom of the Father we must stay on the path of revelation until we arrive at the destination. Nicodemus stayed on the path; he continued the journey until he found what he was looking for.

When Nicodemus said, "God is with Jesus," he spoke the truth. But Nicodemus had not yet said all that must be said because he'd not yet seen all there is to be seen in the relationship between Jesus and his Father. Others had worked miracles in the Old Testament and God was certainly with them in some sense. And it could truly be said of many teachers and prophets that they had come from God—he sent them.

None of these came from God in the way Jesus came from God. Nor did they walk like this man walked. God was with this man, and this man was with God in a way that's radically new in the world. Jesus is *in* the Father, not merely *with* him, and the Father is in him still today. And if we're in him, we're also in the Father and the Father is in us.

## *The Father in the Son and the Son in the Father*

Nicodemus had noticed the signs but hadn't yet fully followed the pointing finger to find himself in the Father's embrace. What had Nicodemus failed to see? The presence of the Son *IS* the presence of the Father. The daily walk of Jesus issued from his place in the bosom of the Father. More than that, his deeds were the Father's doing: **"...the Father who dwells in me is doing his work"** (Jn. 14:8-10). Nicodemus had failed to see the Father in the Son and the Son in the Father.

When Jesus said to him, **"...unless one is born anew, he cannot see the kingdom of God"** (Jn. 3:3), Nicodemus thought Jesus was speaking of *motherhood*. The word in Greek for 'being born' can refer to motherhood (giving birth) or to fatherhood (begetting). Nicodemus missed the point. Jesus was referring to *fatherhood*. If anyone could actually repeat the motherhood experience, nothing would really change. The seed comes from the father; and *seed reproduces after its own kind*. If you're born of a new seed, you have a new nature.

The word translated 'anew' can be rendered 'from above'. Jesus was speaking of the possibility of coming into a radically new relationship with God. He was speaking of becoming sons and daughters, begotten of God the Father (see Jn. 1:13).

We'll clarify this in a later chapter. For now, we'll just say that God was doing something in the world through the abiding of the Son. The Father was living out his vision through the obedience of the Son. The Son was living his life in total submission to the vision of the Father. If anyone saw the Son walking, he was watching the Father's vision unfold before his very eyes. *That's what Nicodemus missed.*

## Our Commission to Reveal the Father's Love

That's how the revelation came to that generation and that's how it comes to our generation as well. When we think of our abiding in the Father's love as being a snuggle-bug in his lap, we miss the point. *Abiding in his love means living in the presence of our neighbor as a manifestation of the Father's love to them.* As we allow Father to live out his vision through our obedience we become a revelation of Father's love. Our life becomes an unfolding narrative of God's love for the world.

When he said, *"If you keep my commandments, you will abide in my love, just as I have kept my Father's commandments and abide in his love"* (Jn. 15:10), he was inviting us to walk in a way that might get us in trouble. The Father's love will be available to others through our obedience, but some people are threatened by true love because they've been wounded by a false love. They crucified Jesus even though he was Love Incarnate. Are we willing to follow this love?

## *The Way: Faith, Love and Hope*

So our obedience reveals the love of the Father to the degree that it is the same kind of obedience Jesus practiced. It isn't an obedience focused on rules and regulations. Jesus simply did what he saw the Father doing and the Father's will became an actuality in the history of the community. Obedience is tied to faith, hope and love. Jesus believed his Father was with him (faith) and lived his life (loved) in the expectation (hope) that his Father would do what he promised.

*Faith* believes the promise that he will be with you in what you do in response to his prompting. In faith we bind ourselves to him and to his agenda.

*Love* responds to that prompting—it will always be a loving response because God is love.

*Hope* looks forward to the fulfillment of the promise knowing that the Father will do what he said he will do.

The faith, love and hope that reveal the Father is simply walking in obedience toward the fulfillment of the promised presence of the Father and the Son in us, with us, and through us.

**"He who abides in him ought to walk in the same way in which he walked"** (I Jn. 2:6). The word *"way"* indicates a significant concept in the New Testament. The early Church was simply called *the Way* (see Acts 9:2). The Church is the *Way* only as it follows Jesus who is *THE WAY*. A disciple is in the *Way* only as he follows Jesus and walks in the same *way* Jesus walked. The way he walked revealed the Father's love for the world. Our way should also be a way that reveals Father's love to the world.

This Way is revealed on the third day, the day of transition from the old creation to the new creation.

## *The Transition Begins*

*"The two disciples heard him say this."* When John gave his testimony, probably many disciples were with him.

Many certainly must have heard the words of his testimony, but their hearing didn't affect their walk. Only two of John's disciples actually *heard* the testimony on this third day and began their walk along the path.

How could anyone really hear that testimony without turning to follow? If they heard without following, it makes us wonder if they really heard. However, two disciples who were there on the third day really did hear.

*Someone actually heard.* Someone was *present* to the sign. Someone turned and began to follow the pointing finger. This third day is the beginning of the transition from the Old Testament prophets, John being the last. The focus of biblical history is shifting to this man Jesus.

### Two Disciples Followed

*"And they followed Jesus."* The decrease of the Baptist's ministry begins here. John just lost two disciples. Later when a number of John's other disciples leave him to follow Jesus, those who remain with John say, *"Rabbi, he who was with you beyond the Jordan, to whom you bore witness, here he is, baptizing, and all are going to him"* (Jn. 3:26). These loyal disciples of the Baptist are concerned that he might lose his following. But their concern is not John's concern. John had testified, *"...for this I came baptizing with water, that he might be revealed to Israel"* (Jn. 1:31). John knows he isn't the light. He had come to bear witness to the light.

So John isn't surprised or disappointed when his disciples begin to leave him to follow Jesus. For him the transition is natural. This nonpartisan attitude is evident in his response to those loyal disciples: *"No one can receive anything except what is given him from heaven"* (Jn. 3:27). Those who are given to Jesus will turn and follow. Those who are given! John is not like a controlling pastor who is jealous and possessive over those who gather themselves around him. If God gave them to him, God will keep them.

When these two begin to turn from him toward Jesus, the Baptist is pleased to know they're actually hearing his testimony. *"He who has the bride is the bridegroom; the friend of the bridegroom, who stands and hears him, rejoices greatly at the bridegroom's voice; therefore this joy of mine is now full"* (Jn. 3:29).

The real surprise: John doesn't insist that all his disciples follow Jesus. Why does he let anyone continue with him after he identifies the Lord? Because it isn't his job to *send* disciples to Jesus; his only task is to bear witness to what he's seen. No one can come to the Son unless the Father draws him (see Jn. 6:44). He's at ease with those who stay and at ease with those who go. Love doesn't control.

We find the same candor in Jesus when he asks the twelve, *"Do you also wish to go away?"* (Jn. 6:67). Those who are with him aren't forced to remain when others are leaving. There's no pressure from Jesus there, and no pressure from the Baptist here. If you *hear,* you'll follow. If you *really* hear, you'll continue to follow when Jesus goes in a direction you don't expect.

## *The Significance of These Two*

John's remaining disciples haven't yet seen what he saw. They've heard the words of the testimony but those words haven't yet registered in their hearts. They see the man John is pointing to, but they don't see the reality in him. They hear the words from John's mouth but they miss the pointing sign. Since they haven't yet heard or seen what needs to be heard and seen, they're still disciples of John the Baptist.

Two disciples of John do follow. They follow because they've really heard. The words entered their heart and they responded. With them the transition from John to Jesus has its beginning. The events that take place as they follow will help us in our quest to discover what it means to follow Jesus as a true disciple. Our first clue lies in the question Jesus asks them: "What do you seek?"

The exchange between these two disciples and Jesus will be the guiding principle for the next few chapters. We mentioned in chapter one that John introduces topics in one place and expands them in other places in his Gospel. We drew attention to that in a small way above and will demonstrate it more clearly in the following meditations. It's as if the seeds for the whole Gospel are present in the four days of the first chapter. This will become more obvious as we read each story and each exchange as a *sign* pointing beyond itself to the ultimate reality in the relationship between the Father and the Son as they bring salvation to the world.

Does our obedience reveal the love of God to our generation? Can others tell by the way we walk that we have an abiding place with the Father? Can they tell we are in him and he is in us? Can we honestly say concerning our work that he who abides in us is doing his work? Can we say with Paul, "It is no longer I who live but Christ who lives in me?" (Gal. 2:20). That's what it means to follow this man and walk this way. Has this historical transition had its full effect in your way of relating to friends and foes?

In the next chapter we'll explore the question, "*What do you seek?*" In chapter four we will look at the disciples' response: "*Where do you abide?*" Jesus' response to that question: "*Come and see*," will be the theme of chapter five. Chapter six will focus on the disciples' response to the invitation: "*They came and saw*…and stayed with him *that day.*"

Each of these questions and statements are echoed in several places in the Gospel of John. When we bring them together in this way, the arrow of the pointing signs begins to emerge. There is a story or dialogue specifically designed to open up the meaning of each of the elements of this exchange between Jesus and the first two disciples. As we delve into the context of these stories and dialogues, the integrity of the Gospel should become clear.

We should keep in mind, however, that the focus should not be on these two disciples as individuals. These two are signs pointing to every true disciple. We'll be looking at principles that apply to every disciple that turns from what he's involved in and begins to follow Jesus. Many personal applications will come to light.

We're now ready for the question, "What do you seek?" Be ready to take that question personally. What are you looking for in life?

# CHAPTER 3

# What Do You Seek?

—ຕາ—

We've learned that the third day was the transition from the Old to the New. On that day the old was passing away and the new was coming. That transition was marked by two of the Baptist's disciples who heard his testimony and saw what he saw. They saw the way Jesus walked and sensed something that caused them to turn and follow Jesus. They were following because of who he is, not because of what he might give them. They were beginning a journey toward the bosom of the Father although they didn't yet have a clue about what that meant.

## *My Personal Journey*

The desire for intimacy with the Father had no place in my early Christian walk. My earthly father was an abusive alcoholic during my teen years and there was no possibility of intimacy with him. In fact I avoided him as much as possible, especially in my teen years.

I was born again in the summer of 1945, just before my ninth birthday, and I loved Jesus. He was my daily companion and my friend, but the thought of seeking a relationship with the Father was foreign to me. I thought he would be like Dad.

In 1957, in the spring before my twenty-first birthday, God came to me in an Air Force barrack in Japan. I was immersed in his love for over an hour. The only way I can describe the experience is the room filled with liquid love. From that day to this my heart pants for intimacy with him, even though I experience times of complacency. Having this intimacy as both an experience and as a goal has made the journey from isolation to intimacy exciting, rewarding and bearable.

## *Interpreting the Experience*

At first I interpreted that experience in Japan as Jesus coming to me and affirming his love for me—in spite of the life I was living at that time. Having been immersed in liquid love, I was on a spiritual 'high' for several years before I became complacent. Later, when the Charismatic renewal and the Jesus movement broke into history, I interpreted the liquid love experience as the Baptism of the Holy Spirit. I earnestly began to seek a deeper intimacy. He visited me again and again during that time.

Another period of complacency set in. When the teaching of the Father's love began to rise among God's people, I interpreted the experience in Japan as the Father coming to me with the love I never received from Dad. I began to seek even more earnestly. He's visited me several times since. With each visit I become more intense in my hunger and panting after him. Each new experience sparked a revival of seeking for more.

All three interpretations were correct: the liquid love of the Father, Son, and Holy Spirit came to me in the Air Force barrack. It came more profoundly each time I moved forward in my pilgrimage toward the Father's bosom. I know there's more of that love waiting for me in the future and I continue to thirst for greater and greater fulfillment. This upward spiral never ends because there's always more of God than what any of us have seen or received.

## *Seeking and Finding*

We all experience life as a pendulum of seeking and finding. In the natural a journey ends when we find what we're looking for. But if it's God you're seeking, the journey becomes more like a dance with continual movement back and forth, in and out, up and around. We can also compare it to climbing a spiral staircase, going around in circles but attaining a higher level with each cycle. Each time we go around we see life from a more exalted position. Add to this concept of hearing and seeking the concept of abiding in God and a pattern emerges:

1. We hear a word—perhaps a word of testimony from one who has experienced a deeper measure of God's love than we have. Or we have an experience of something new.

2. We recognize a deep hunger that's always been in our hearts, and the word or experience awakens us to the possibility of something much more satisfying than what we've experienced so far in life.

3. We seek more of the love we experienced or heard about with fresh enthusiasm.

4. When we seek, we find. We experience the Father's love on a deeper level and begin to abide in that love.

5. We grow accustomed to this new level of relationship and become complacent. Life loses its vitality and we become bored.

6. We hear another word, recognize that there's more, seek more earnestly, experience and abide more

deeply, and become accustomed to the deeper level only to discover there's even more...and the dance continues.

Two disciples hear John's testimony, *"Behold the Lamb of God."* They recognize a deep hunger in their hearts and begin to follow Jesus. Their exciting journey of seeking and finding has just begun! They'd barely experienced Jesus when he popped the question: *"What do you seek?"* (Jn. 1:38). In this chapter we focus on that question. As we continue to pursue an understanding of what it means to follow Jesus into the Father's embrace, we are all challenged to hear it as a question addressed to each of us personally.

The goal of being in an intimate relationship with Abba ('Daddy God') gives meaning to the journey. That goal also gives courage to face the difficulties we meet on the road as we follow Jesus.

We are all somewhere on the road between alienation and continual intimacy with God. Between here and there we have difficult times and times of glorious experiences with him. But there's always more of God than we've received even in the most glorious experiences. As we move forward, the way is easier if we remember the goal: receiving more of Daddy God's love and passing it on to others.

Ponder this possibility: *what we seek may determine and limit what we find.* Once again the picture in our bubble can prejudice our vision and our hearing. If we seek one who matches our expectation, we'll be exposed as false disciples when Jesus makes a turn that doesn't show up on our road map. When life takes an unexpected turn, it's important to remember who we are following and where he is leading us—into Father's embrace and then out from that embrace into the world with his love for others.

## *Take Heed How You Hear*

*"What do you seek?"* We all must answer this question before we can approach the true Way. When Jesus sees two of John's disciples following him, he asks this question. It has an almost confrontational quality to it: "I don't know whether I want *you* to follow me or not. First I need to know what you're looking for. What are you really after?" Obviously Jesus isn't out to gain a big following. He knows many will follow him through the country in the geographical sense. Many will be chasing their own vision as they try to force him to conform to the images in their mind's eye. Jesus wants his disciples to consider whether they have a preconceived notion they expect him to fulfill for them. What have they actually heard? Their answer to Jesus' question will tell him what they're looking for.

Hearing determines our spiritual journey. If there's noise in the background from our bubble, it filters out the sounds of heaven. If we don't hear the message right, we draw wrong conclusions. What we are able to hear determines what we're seeking when we come to him. Often what we hear is not what is actually said. When we share with others we share what we heard, not necessarily what was said.

There was probably a lot of talk around the community when Jesus showed up in town. Everyone who heard or saw him filtered the experience through their personal desires and generated their own report through their filter. Then other people filtered these reports through their grids and passed their adjusted reports along to others. If we're interested in the thing we heard through our personal filter, we begin to seek for it; but we may be seeking something that has nothing to do with what Jesus is offering.

It becomes a giant game of "whisper down the lane." That's why Jesus says, "Take heed how you hear" (Lk. 8:18), and that's why he asks, *"What do you seek?"*

We see the same type of challenge in Jesus' response to the rich young ruler in Matthew 19:16-22. This young man knows something is missing, and because of what he's heard he thinks Jesus can help him find what he is seeking. He thinks he wants eternal life and he thinks Jesus has the answer, so he asks, "What do I still lack?" Jesus says, "Sell what you possess and give to the poor and you will have treasures in heaven; and come, follow me."

Walking away sad, the young man exposes that letting go of his possessions isn't part of the image of eternal life in his bubble. It isn't a word he's willing to hear. "What's the value of treasures in heaven if I have to leave my earthly treasures behind?" He wants eternal life and earthly treasures but he wants the earthly treasures more!

Jesus doesn't chase him or try to make him change his mind. He isn't willing to adjust his message or agenda to accommodate followers. He'll let us go another way if we aren't willing to leave the images in our bubble behind.

## *We Must all Answer this Question*

Jesus addresses this question to each of us as we follow him. "What do you expect to find by following me?" We must hear this if we're beginning to follow him for the first time. We must hear it again at each new level of commitment. We must hear the question daily: "What are you after? What do you hope to have in your hands at the end of this journey? What expectations do you think I've come to fulfill?" It's crucial for us to hear the questions in a radical way because what we expect at the end of the journey indicates which way we think Jesus is going. We disciples learn on the way that Jesus didn't come to fulfill our human vision. He's out to empty our bubble and fill it with himself.

The Lord makes himself available to us based on what we're seeking. That doesn't mean he'll give us whatever we want. "Seek and you will find" (Lk. 11:9) isn't simply a promise that anyone who seeks God will find him, at least not in the sense in which it's usually understood. This is clear from what Jesus says to the Pharisees, *"You will seek me and you will not find me"* (John 7:34). One kind of seeking finds God, but the other kind doesn't. It all depends on how we hear. How we hear forms our attitudes and motives. The way we hear influences our willingness or unwillingness to move beyond the preconceived notions that govern our expectations.

If our attitude is one of humility we'll be open for the Lord to challenge the images in our minds. If our motive is to establish ourselves in the way we've chosen, we'll continue to insist that reality conform to our preconceived notions. It never will.

## Three Classes of People

The first three days of transition from the Baptist to Jesus represent three classes of people. John's testimony is different on each day because he addresses a different group each day. Each group is seeking something quite different because each group has heard the reports of Jesus' ministry differently. Some hear the reports as a threat to their position in the community, some hear them as a promise of the fulfillment of their own goals and dreams, and some hear the report as a word from above.

Just as John sees Jesus with the seeing eye of a prophet, he discerns the condition of his audience with sensitivity to the Spirit. Though he doesn't formally ask, "What are you seeking?" on the first two days, the question hovers in the atmosphere as a challenge to each audience.

By the Spirit, John perceives the unspoken answer to the unspoken question and testifies to each group appropriately. He speaks to the spiritual condition of those present. He doesn't have a 'canned' testimony; he isn't passing out tracts; and he isn't repeating the same words to everyone.

Each group's answer to the question of the third day is a barometer of their spiritual condition and determines their ability to receive or reject the testimony.

Let's look at each group separately and notice the attitudes and motives behind their responses to the testimony of John.

### The First Group: Self Seekers

The first group (see Jn. 1:19-28) is made up of priests and Levites—a delegation from the Jewish leaders in Jerusalem. They ask John, *"Who are you?"* They've come to investigate him, to measure him and his message by the standards of their human court. Perhaps they're angry or threatened that the crowds consider him a spiritual leader, even a prophet. We gather from the other Gospels that they didn't think God sent him; at least it is clear that they didn't believe him (see Matt. 21:25).

They probably want to discredit him. They have their own ideas about how a man of God ought to dress and what he ought to teach. They have clear notions about what ought to happen when God moves. John isn't doing any of these things right as far as this audience is concerned. He doesn't have credentials that are acceptable to these self-appointed religious leaders. He can never measure up to their expectations so he doesn't even try.

They're looking for *their* Messiah, but they're quite sure he'd come and reveal himself to them first. They are certain that they'd recognize him without help from other men, especially a madman in the desert like John. They'd never ask a man like that to point them in the right direction. Their answer to the question wouldn't impress the one asking behind the scene. John discerns this, so he doesn't cooperate with them. They're seeking the wrong things for the wrong reasons because they haven't heard the word from above.

## Always Right

People who are always right in their own eyes are seldom open to the testimony of others unless it agrees with what they already think they know. They're blind to see what's right before their eyes, unless it compares favorably to their preconceived notions. They don't ask or seek with an openness to hear or see anything that contradicts their understanding of truth. They come only as teachers or judges, never as students or disciples. They come as those who already know, not as those seeking to learn.

They aren't seeking God. They're seeking to establish their superiority over others. They're not willing to go beyond the preconceived notions that govern their expectations. They want security in their bubble. But bubbles pop too easily, so they build strong doctrinal walls to protect their concepts. Many of these people become controllers and try to bind everyone else to their ideas and practices.

## The Negative Testimony

*"I am not the Christ."* It seems he should've continued, "There he is over there! He's the one you're looking for." But he doesn't. He makes no attempt to take them beyond their present understanding. He knows they aren't seeking the one he'd come to bear witness to. He leaves them in the bubble of their blindness just as Jesus will later do with the Pharisees.

He isn't uptight about getting these men to see what he's come to show. He's at ease with the fact that the Father isn't giving these men a positive witness about the Son. When they ask if he's Elijah or the prophet, he's satisfied simply to answer that he's not the one they're looking for.

*"Among you stands one whom you do not know."* As they continued to press for answers, he does give them something like a testimony. He indicates that the one he came to identify was among them even though they didn't recog-

nize him. We can capture the significance of this moment by reading between the lines.

John implies, "The one you ought to be seeking is out there, if you only had eyes to see! He's among you, but as one you don't know. I can't show you who he is because you're looking for the wrong thing. You're only seeking confirmation for your own human vision. I could point in his direction, but you're blinded by your own arrogance so you wouldn't see him for who he is. I can speak all the right words, but you'll never hear my testimony because you're deaf to anything that doesn't agree with what you think you know. So you don't know who he is and I'm not at liberty to point him out to you."

## *Pride is the Problem*

These priests and Levites are coming to John as the Pharisees would later come to Jesus — for the wrong reasons. If Jesus had asked the Pharisees *"What are you seeking?"* they would likely have given some high sounding answer to give the impression they were seeking God. But even though they put on airs of seeking God, they're really seeking their own glory (see Jn. 5:44). Since Jesus knows what's in their bubble *"he did not trust himself to them"* (Jn. 2:24-25). He refuses to play their religious game. That's why they want to kill him.

The Gospel of John refers to this group as 'the Jews'. John positions them throughout the book as a sign of all those, Jews or gentiles, who oppose the ministry of Jesus and challenge his teaching based on their own religious ideas. They keep trying to arrest him and restrict his movement. They never really hear what he's saying. They hear the words, but miss the message. They see the deeds, but not the signs.

These self-appointed self-seeking leaders are out to kill Jesus from the beginning because he won't conform to their preconceived notions of how a man of God ought to behave.

The way he's walking isn't the way they expect the Messiah to walk. John presents these men as signs of all those who insist on their own way.

They don't have this difficulty because they are Jews. Their difficulty comes from being human beings who aren't open to see beyond their preconceived notions. In their pride they think they know God. They don't engage in any serious seeking, because they think they've already found the prize. They think they know so they only engage in 'proof-texting' to defend the "god" they already know. I use the lower case for *god* because the god these religious leaders know isn't the true God. The god they know is not the Father of Jesus Christ the Son. The god in their bubble doesn't have a son.

Jesus later said to these men, *"You know neither me nor my Father; if you knew me, you would know my Father also"* (Jn. 8:19). No wonder they want to kill him. He dares to suggest they don't know God.

## *Two Kinds of Blindness*

This same group cast the blind man out of the synagogue when he testified that Jesus had healed him. They have to cast out the one the true God healed in order to defend the god of their imagination. Their blindness is worse than his blindness. They're blind to their own blindness. This is the nature of self-deception; your deception deceives you. Jesus said of them, *"if you were blind, you would have no guilt; but now that you say, 'We see,' your guilt remains"* (Jn. 9:41). Guilt will always remain on those who aren't willing to see their own sin and only focus on the sins of others. There's none as blind as those who refuse to see.

So the basic problem of the scribes and Pharisees is that they're seeking the wrong god. If you ask them, they'll insist that they're among the few really seeking God. But the god they're seeking is the god of their own religious imagination, one that exists only in their fantasy world. If this religious

91

god of theirs actually had a son, he would obviously agree with them and affirm their right to religious authority and superiority.

They don't have ears to hear anything that disagrees with what they've already determined as truth. These religious leaders carry the same spirit of superiority found in the devil himself. Jesus reveals their critical condition when they claim that God is their Father. *"If God were your Father,"* Jesus responds, *"you would love me, for I proceeded and came forth from God…. You are of your father the devil."* (Jn. 8:42-44)

In choosing a path that promises to bring glory to themselves, they're walking in a way that leads to death with no resurrection. This isn't the Way of Jesus Christ.

The seriousness of this question becomes painfully apparent. If you're seeking the wrong thing you're on the wrong path; and the wrong path leads in the wrong direction. This is a spiral that goes downward, a dance that ends in the pit. If you refuse to let your religious ideas be challenged, God's appointed witness will be mute and you'll never even know you're on the wrong path. "There is a way which seems right to a man, but its end is the way to death" (Prov. 4:12). May God save us from ourselves!

## *Pride is Still with Us Today*

These leaders are still among us today. They exalt themselves among God's people as judges and executioners. They use the 'sword of the Spirit' to deride and defame those who disagree with them. They step into a revival to stamp out the fire that comes to those who receive newness. They try to arrest and restrict the movement of the Spirit within the community of God's people.

They don't literally 'kill' but, with gossip and slander, they come against those who are open to what God is presently doing. Jesus addressed this attitude when he gave commentary on the commandment: "You shall not kill." He said, "...every one who is angry with his brother shall be liable to judgment; whoever insults his brother shall be liable to the council, and whoever says, 'You fool!' is liable to the hell of fire" (Matt. 5:22).

Some leaders reject the possibility that God might move outside the circle of their influence or beyond the borders of their kingdom. Surely God wouldn't even consider doing anything without checking with them first. They never hear the testimony of others except for the sake of a doctrinal debate. They're too focused on themselves and their programs to listen to anyone. There's someone 'standing among them' whom they don't know and don't understand, and this someone must be silenced at any price.

## We are All Faced with this Question

None of us is exempt from the question, *"What do you seek?"* It's easy for those of us who are not in leadership to think our leaders don't hear from God because they don't agree with us. When we discredit a worship leader, are we seeking to establish God's way or our own way? We can debunk the pastor for debunking others. When we do, are we not doing the same things? Does our ability to see what's wrong with the youth leader make us superior?

That desire to appear superior is the same thing that motivates a leader to criticize and expel those who disagree with him or her. The only difference is that they have the position of power and we don't. When it's time to confront our leaders, we should make sure the Father's love is prompting every motive, attitude, word, and action. The inappropriate criticism of leadership is as destructive to the community of believers as dominating leaders are.

I was with a group of church leaders who went on a retreat. We invited several young men to join us to give them the opportunity to learn something about leadership.

During one of the breaks one young man came to me and began to criticize some of the process and the decisions the leaders were making. He was trying to impress me with his deep insight. When he told me what he would've done if he were an elder, I said to him, "That's probably why God didn't make you and elder." He got the point and received the correction. That humble response was his first step to becoming the leader God had called him to be.

We can't cast out pride with pride. When we criticize leadership, it's often because we want to lead but aren't willing to carry the cross of leadership. We just stir up trouble trying to manipulate the leader to do it our way. We're not following Jesus when we do this. He humbled himself so that others could be exalted to the Father's bosom. We should walk as he walked, in humility.

If the Body of Christ calls you a leader, Jesus calls you to follow him as a servant to those you lead. If you aren't called to leadership, Jesus calls you to follow him as a servant to your leader. Each individual is responsible to present his own motives, attitudes, words, and actions to the Lord. If we are judging others, it's because we're seeking our own kingdom. *What do you seek*, my friend?

## The Second Group: Sensation Seekers

John addresses a second group the "next day" (see Jn. 1:29-34). In his witness to this group John presents Jesus as the one who meets the needs of mankind: *"Behold, the Lamb of God who takes away the sin of the world."* This reflects Jesus' ability and willingness to deal with our past failures. John's testimony continues, *"I saw the Spirit descend as a dove from heaven, and it remained on him…. This is he who baptizes with the Holy Spirit."* John affirms Jesus' ability to offer us a new future; with the Holy Spirit we will be able to move forward in victory.

This testimony is addressed to the general public, the multitude, whom Jesus came to save. The judgmental Jews of the previous day may have been in the crowd but they couldn't hear this message. I suggest the Apostle John is posting a sign that reads: "This announcement is for the whole world!" John the Baptist is saying to the uncommitted crowd gathered to see this new thing in the desert, "All of the blessings of God are available to you through *this man* who is even now coming toward me."

## The Crowd of Unbelieving Believers

We can understand the condition of the crowds by looking at John 2:23-24: "*Now when he was in Jerusalem at the Passover feast, many* [that's the crowd] *believed in his name when they saw the signs which he did; but Jesus did not trust himself to them.*" Here's an important observation from the Greek. The word translated "believe" and the word translated "trust" is the same word. These verses could be translated, "many trusted themselves to him, but he didn't trust himself to them," or "many believed in him, but he didn't believe in them." He didn't commit himself to what they were committed to! They had a picture in their imagination that was not true to reality. Jesus didn't respond to their faith the way they expected him to respond. He didn't *bind himself* to their agenda.

## Expecting 'Thatman'

If we understand the context, we can feel the full impact of these statements. The crowd saw the signs Jesus did in Jerusalem. They saw him as a candidate to fulfill their messianic dreams and hopes. He was *"That man"*—the Christ in their bubble who swings down from above to do violence to their enemies! "With *Thatman's* powers on our side," some may have said among themselves, "we can march in, drive the Romans into the sea, and have political freedom again.

What a way of life it would be with *Thatman* as king. He can heal all our diseases and give us daily bread. With *Thatman*, life would be wonderful. We'd have no problems; he would fix everything. And who knows, maybe he'll let me be Robin, the boy wonder!" Jesus sees this movie playing on the screen of their hearts and says to himself, "I am NOT *Thatman!*"

In so many subtle ways they might have come to Jesus and said, "We recognize you as a man who can fulfill our dreams. We will trust ourselves and all our resources to you. You can be our leader. We have informers in significant places that can monitor the moves of the enemy. We have swords and men trained in guerilla warfare. All this we will make available to you so you can lead us the way we want to go. You can accomplish our agenda for us. You take over the program we've put together and take us toward our goals. How could you pass up a deal like this?"

The answer to the critical question, *"What do you seek?"* is formulating before Jesus' eyes. They're seeking their own success, their own way, and their own comfort. They're seeking to establish themselves as the people of God without any change in their hearts. They're self-seeking at the core of their being. Jesus is seeking those who are seeking an active abiding relationship in the bosom of 'Daddy God.' Self-seekers appear to be seeking God only to others who are also self-seekers.

His simple response was formulating too. "You would trust yourselves and your resources to me to accomplish your will; but my will is not your will. I didn't come to drive out the Romans. I came to bring them into the Kingdom of God. I came to establish my Father's Kingdom, not the kingdom of man. I'll trust neither my resources nor myself to you because I'm faithfully bound to my Father and his mission. The military leader you want isn't the leader I came to be. I have a campaign assigned to me by my Father and I only do what pleases him."

## Feeding the Multitude

We see the same crowd in the feeding of the multitude. After Jesus has provided the meal, while the disciples are collecting the fragments, the people begin to reflect on what had happened, saying, *"This is indeed the prophet who is to come into the world"* (Jn. 6:14). They believe in him and are ready to commit themselves to him, but they want him to be their leader because of what he can do for them.

They haven't yet seen him for who he is. All they know is that *Thatman*—the one in their bubble—could make life easy for them. They've seen the feeding of the multitude as a sign, but they think the sign points to the Christ in their mind's eye—the one with unlimited wealth and the ability to violently destroy their enemies.

The phrase *the prophet who is to come into the world* reflects their understanding of an ancient prophecy that God would raise up a prophet like Moses from among the people (see Deut.18:15). The popular interpretation was that a man of God would appear who, like Moses, would provide manna from heaven. People believed that in this utopia all man's needs would be met supernaturally. There would be economic abundance without work. Who wouldn't want a king like that? With the miracle of the feeding of the multitude it's natural for them to conclude that Jesus is *Thatman*.

## Jesus Withdraws Himself

The text continues, *"Perceiving then that they were about to come and take him by force to make him king, Jesus withdrew again to the mountain by himself"* (Jn. 6:15). We see the same response from Jesus as in John 2:23-24. They believe in Jesus, but he doesn't believe in them. He won't bind himself or his resources to them in a way that will give them control of the situation.

The king they want isn't the king he came to be. He doesn't withhold the natural bread from them. He doesn't ask them to pay him for the bread when it becomes clear that they're only seeking the bread of this natural world. He simply removes *himself* from their presence so they won't be able to force their agenda on him. I wonder how often Jesus withdraws himself from churches today for the same reason.

The crowd isn't prepared to receive the reality he wants to give. They withdraw from him when he explains that he's offering *himself* to them as the Bread of Life. Jesus, knowing what's in man, has already withdrawn himself from them. He knows what they're seeking and he refuses to let them get at the resources available to him from his Father. Those resources are only available to accomplish the Father's will. Jesus is not available to fulfill their human dream.

They can have his presence and all those resources as well, if they're willing to have their heart's desire adjusted. If they're willing to come under his agenda and let him change them, all things will be available to them—but only for the purpose of the Kingdom of Father God.

## *The Triumphal Entry*

The theme of Jesus withdrawing from the crowd also emerges in the triumphal entry (see Jn. 12:12ff.). The crowd goes out to meet him because they heard he'd done a sign (raising Lazarus from the dead). A sensational ministry always attracts a crowd of people seeking sensations. This crowd isn't coming out to Jesus because he is the Lamb of God but because of the sensational thing he'd done in their midst. Like the bread-seekers, they're seeking the bread that would feed their hunger for excitement. They don't get on the field to play the game; they're satisfied to watch. Their thrill is to be in the crowd when 'our team' wins the game.

Later, when he speaks of his coming death, the crowd chimes in, **"We have heard from the law that the Christ remains forever. How can you say that the Son of Man must be lifted up?"** (Jn. 12:34). Rather than receiving his word and following to discover what he means, they challenge him. They haven't perceived the real meaning of Lazarus's resurrection. Most in the crowd have a doctrine of resurrection, but apparently it's a doctrine imprisoned within the walls of the synagogue. When you don't really believe in resurrection you have to have a Messiah who never dies.

They aren't willing to follow him unless he's willing to do things according to their preconceived notions. When they challenge his word we might guess they've already withdrawn themselves from him inwardly. We shouldn't be surprised when we read that Jesus "...*departed and hid himself from them*" (Jn. 12:36).

The question continues to confront the multitude: "**What do you seek?**" Here again they're exposed as those seeking a fulfillment of their human vision. They aren't open to have the content of their bubble challenged.

## The Crowd is Still with Us

In every generation this second group appears as the many that follow a sensational ministry with the hope of actually seeing or experiencing a miracle. They're seeking the thrills, the chills, and the goose-bumps. They may get what they want but they have no way to discern between the work of a man with a "goose-bump ministry" and a real move of God.

The saddest thing is that they don't even notice that *Jesus has withdrawn himself* from them. Why should they notice? He's not the one they were seeking anyway. They've found what they were looking for. They have their reward—goose-bumps.

Today's crowd also tries to bind Jesus to their own agenda. They try to force him into the humanized mold of a god who makes life easy and comfortable for them. I call this a 'waterbed mentality.' They act as though the call to discipleship is, "Come, let me give you a waterbed (not a cross), and follow me in comfort and leisure. Let me establish your superiority over other men (and especially over women) so that you will be the all important one."

They conceive of God as some sort of heavenly Santa Claus who exists to serve King Ego. This god is only there to fulfill the Great American Dream of pleasure and prosperity. Like the rich young ruler, those seeking this kind of Christ have trouble hearing the invitation, "Sell all you have, give it to the poor, and come follow me." It's no wonder they get caught up in the rat race of church power struggles, personal pleasure trips, and programs for self-promotion.

Is it any wonder that the great majority (97% according to statistics) of converts from these methods backslide shortly after they make their commitment? The question keeps hovering in the atmosphere: *"What do you seek?"*

Some evangelists have recognized (consciously or unconsciously) this self-serving tendency in our culture and capitalize on it to gain a large following. "Come to Jesus because he will heal you, make you prosperous, and take you to heaven when you die." The promises of God are sure and he is faithful to fulfill his word. But if people only come for the blessings, they will just go somewhere else when Jesus begins to make a demand on their lives.

Pastors sometimes try to attract the crowd by bringing in famous athletes or other celebrities who 'believe like we do.' This makes 'our group' look good to the people who are sensation seekers.

We know that many genuine conversions take place through these promotions, and I would not suggest discontinuing the promotions. There are always a few "God seekers" in the multitude that attends these sensational events. The promotions are not wrong in themselves; but we should not be surprised when a large percentage of those who come belong to this second group—the crowd of self-centered pleasure-seekers.

## *The Third Group: Son Seekers*

The third group is much smaller. The initial group of God seekers consisted of the two disciples who hear the simple testimony, *"Behold the Lamb of God"* (Jn. 1:36). On this third day John the Baptist offers a simple declaration of who Jesus is—not a word about what he offers. The forgiveness of sin and the baptism of the Spirit of the previous day are certainly available to this smaller group as well, but that isn't why they begin to follow him.

Their reason for following is simple. They've heard the testimony, *"Behold the Lamb* of God." They're following him because of who he is, not because of some popular expectation of the Christ prevalent in their day. They have some preconceived notions that need adjusting. However, because they're seeking God and because they're willing to lay these ideas down when Jesus deviates from their agenda, they're true disciples. On this third day, John sets up one more sign that reads, "True disciples follow Jesus because of who he is."

Are you among this smaller group or are you still in the crowd? Every self-promoting Pharisee will automatically answer in the affirmative, "Yes. In fact we *are* the smaller group." They always think they are the chosen among the chosen because they measure everything by the standards they've established. And they set these standards based on what they're able to achieve (or at least appear to achieve) in their own power.

We're all in danger of answering this question too quickly. We may be trying to shield ourselves from the discovery that our bubble is still full of nonsense. We all want to think we're the ones who have arrived. That's why we must all hear the question again and ask ourselves, "What am I trying to find? In all my religious activity, what am I really looking for?"

## Being Separated from the Crowd

It's here that we begin to see true disciples separated from the crowd. Here we observe the real transition. There will always be divisions when Jesus begins to reveal himself and call disciples to follow him. This call will always draw men away from their place in the crowd with its preconceived notions. This doesn't imply that those in this smaller group have automatically forsaken all their ideas of how this movement will work itself out. They still have their notions of how it should happen, but they're separated from the crowd by their answer to this critical question: *"What do you seek?"*

## Five Hundred Favored

When we look at the other Gospels, Acts, and II Corinthians, we discover a compelling progression of discipleship. The crowd is everywhere and they receive physical blessings from the Lord. Out of that crowd Jesus finds five hundred disciples open enough for a post resurrection appearance (see II Cor. 15:6). I call this the '500 club'. Jesus blesses them with this experience because they're still looking for him after his death. They had not forsaken their brethren and joined the crowd.

## A Hundred and Twenty Waited

Out of that five hundred Jesus finds one hundred twenty committed enough to remain in the city until the Holy Spirit was poured out (see Acts 2:1-4). Many Christians have had awesome experiences of the presence of the Lord, but life gets busy and they're not around for the event that changes history. They may continue to go through life remembering that wonderful experience they had 'once upon a time.'

They have the promise of eternal life after they die and they're satisfied with that promise. But they'll not really be a part of the new thing God is doing in their generation.

They're satisfied with the 'once upon a time' and the 'some day over yonder.'

Are you seeking the Father's embrace again today?

## Seventy have Ministry

Among the one hundred twenty Jesus finds seventy committed enough for a mission (see Lk. 10:1). They went out in ministry healing and casting out demons.

Personally, I am not satisfied to be among the crowd who receive physical blessings. I want more. I am not satisfied to be among those who have experienced the presence of the resurrected Lord. There's more. I want to be a part of what he's doing in the earth. I don't want to be a fan in the stands. I want to be involved in promoting the Kingdom.

Jesus offers ministry to those who want more than an exciting experience. Are you ready to go out from the Father's embrace to embrace others with the embrace with which you are embraced, to comfort others with the comfort with which you have been comforted (see II Cor. 1:3-6)?

## Twelve are With Him

Out of the seventy Jesus finds twelve faithful enough "to be with him" (see Mk. 3:14). I'm not satisfied to have a ministry. I want to be with him. None of us can be a part of the original twelve, but we can be with him and we can have him with us. We can be with him in a more intimate way than merely working for him in ministry. In the final day there will be those who had a mighty ministry of prophesying, casting out demons, and working miracles. Nevertheless, Jesus will say to them, "I never knew you" (Matt. 7:23). He never had an intimate relationship with them.

What good is a ministry if he doesn't know you, if there's no intimacy with him in Daddy's eternal embrace? Ministry that doesn't issue from intimacy with the Father has no lasting value for the minister even if the ministry is valid. That's what Paul had in mind when he said, "If I give away all I have, and if I deliver my body to be burned, but have not love, I gain nothing" (I Cor. 13).

### Three are Trustworthy

Out of the twelve Jesus finds three he can trust enough to invite them to join him in delicate situations. Peter, James, and John were with him when he raised Jairus' daughter from the dead (see Mk. 5:37). Perhaps Jesus didn't trust the faith level of the others. These three were also the only ones present when Jesus appeared in the full brilliance of his glory on the Mount of Transfiguration. Jesus doesn't welcome just anyone to be present with him in the private places.

I don't have to understand what all the issues are. I just want to be trustworthy, that is, worthy of his trust in delicate situations. My heart cries for that. I'm desperately seeking that intimacy.

### Two Face the Trial

Of the three Jesus finds two courageous enough to stand with him at his trial. Peter and John were willing to follow while others ran into the darkness. When the trials come, many escape into the night to avoid confrontation. We know Peter denied the Lord that night; but he attended the trial. He faced it in the presence of Jesus—at a distance, yes, but in his presence.

I want to come to the point where I am willing to face the confrontations and stand in the presence of Jesus when he is on trial. Redemption is available when we fail in our ability to follow. I know I am redeemed, but I want to be an overcomer (see Rev. 12:11).

### Are You the One?

Jesus finds only one open and vulnerable enough to follow him all the way to the cross—that 'other disciple, whom Jesus loved.' That's John, the one who lay at the breast (in the bosom) of Jesus at the Last Supper and felt his very heartbeat.

Why does that disciple have no name? You can be that one! He beckons all of us to join the beloved disciple in that place where we can hear his heart. To the degree we find our place in the bosom of the Father and the Son, to that degree we'll be willing to go out from that place to share his love with others, even if it brings us to the cross.

The Church calls John "the Apostle of Love" because he is the "one whom Jesus loves" and because he speaks of love more than all the others. I want to be among that *'one-ified'* many—the many who are unified in him—who receive Daddy God's love and become apostles of love!

## *Commitment flows form Desire*

The level of our commitment flows out of our desire to be with him, to have him with us and to experience the love of the Father in Jesus. If we reach a place where we permit a mixture in our desire, we will be left behind in one of the groups that never make it all the way. What you seek will determine the distance you are willing to travel on this road from the multitude to the one. Why do you follow him? Is your heart crying for more? What is your answer? What do you hope to gain as you follow him?

I am not satisfied with merely going to heaven when I die. I want my life to make a difference for the Kingdom of God for the next generation. Embracing the cross is the only way to accomplish that.

We are on a journey into the fullness of what our Daddy God has for us 'here and now,' intimacy with the Father. On this journey we experience an ever increasing foretaste of what he has for us 'there and then.'

"Daddy God, are we there yet?" I won't be satisfied with anything less than the Father's embrace, even if it takes me to the cross. That's what I seek. Is your heart crying out for a place there with John in his bosom? Are you ready for a deeper walk with him?

What do you seek? We'll explore the answer of the two disciples in the next chapter.

# CHAPTER 4

# Where Do You Abide?

—◊◊◊—

We pick up where we left off with two of John's disciples following Jesus. John had identified him as the
Lamb of God when he saw him walking. His walk became a
sign pointing to the abiding place in the bosom of the Father.
From his relationship in the Father's bosom, Jesus made
love available to the world. When these two disciples began
to follow, Jesus asked them what they were seeking. Now we
turn to the disciples' response to that question.

## God Turns to Man

In John 1:38 we read, *"Jesus turned, and saw them
following, and said to them, 'What do you seek?' And they
said to him, 'Rabbi (which means teacher), where are you
staying* [abiding].'"

*"Jesus turned."* John records Jesus' second act; he'd been
walking, that's his first act, but now he turns. This isn't the
first time he's turned. As the eternal Word, he was with God
in the beginning and was the one through whom all things
were created. This Word, which is God, has been turning
toward man from the beginning of time. He was always
coming into the world (see Jn. 1:9). He turned to Adam and
Eve in the garden after they sinned. He turned to Abraham,

Isaac and Jacob. He turned to Moses in the burning bush. When the Lord spoke to the people at Mount Sinai, it was this Word turning to man. When the Word of the Lord came to a prophet in Old Testament times, it was this Word turning to man.

The trial and crucifixion were not his first experience of rejection by those he came to save. He was rejected by most people in every generation, yet he continued to turn to man. In every age he's looking for those who will respond to his love.

No law obligates him to turn; he turns because he is love. Love turns toward man. It never turns away. He has every right to remain within himself, but he turns. When we see Jesus turning, we see the Father turning. This act is a sign pointing to both the Father and the Son turning toward these two disciples who are following Jesus.

*"And saw them following."* He sees because his eyes are open; he's looking for something. The word translated 'to see' can refer to paying a visit. He comes over to our place to see us, to pay a visit, to dwell among us, to abide in our community, to make himself available as a friend and companion. The eternal Word is looking for a home here in our world. That's amazing. Why would he want a home here since he has a home in Father's house? He desires to find a home among us here so that he can bring us home with him into his Father's heart of love.

Will these two disciples of John the Baptist be willing to make a place for him to be at home with them? He has come out from his Father's bosom to his own people. He knows some will not receive him. Will these receive him and return with him into the Father's embrace? When he sees them following, he asks a question designed to discover what they are expecting to find by following him.

## The Question

"*What do you seek?*" We noticed in the last chapter that this question addresses disciples of every age who want to follow Jesus. Jesus has seen these men following. He knows why they're following and what they're after, but to draw out of them what they're seeking, he has to ask. The question is for their sake, not for his. By putting it before them, he makes them aware of something about themselves that he already knows. This is the beginning of a journey for them. If they're willing to stay on the path, they'll come to a destination far beyond the most impressive image in their bubble.

We often don't know what we're really looking for until someone asks the right question. Until we become aware of the answer to the right question, we're confused and frustrated; but that question comes! We may be somehow startled by it, but revelation dawns with the question: "What do you seek?" Suddenly we become aware of something we knew but hadn't noticed.

A good counselor knows how to ask the questions that bring his client face-to-face with reality. It's the same with teachers. If we just tell people the truth, we scratch the surface of their intellect with academic ideas without piercing into the heart with spiritual truth. Spiritual truth in the heart gives power to live. The right question can open the heart to receive that truth.

## Exposing the Real Problem

This point introduces a problem. We often think we are seeking one thing while we're really seeking something else. When we find what we thought we were seeking we're disappointed or disillusioned because we're not fulfilled; we're left empty and still seeking. This is where addictions find their power—we don't stop to consider that what we thought would give us freedom is actually holding us in bondage.

We were created to bond, but when we bond to things of this world we become bound.

We humans were created for love and intimacy and will never be fully satisfied until we find it in holding another who is holding us in an unconditional heart to heart commitment. God is Love. When we try to experience love from any other source we will always have a vague sense of emptiness. That's why we must take this question very seriously. "What do you *really* want? What are you *really* seeking? Is what you've found so far *really* satisfying in the deepest level of your person?"

The love of a fellowman is a good thing. It's also something we were created to desire. But human love will never be fully satisfying apart from the abiding presence of the Love who is God. When we find ourselves unfulfilled in a human relationship, we must step back and ask ourselves what we are really looking for in that relationship. Are we looking for something that can never be supplied by a human relationship? Are we really seeking a relationship with Divine Love? I think so.

We have developed images in our minds of what love would really look like if it came to us. Those images are often tied to the pain of not receiving the love we needed from our primary care givers in early life. That pain seeks comfort in some source that promises to fill the emptiness and soothe the discomfort. Nothing in this world can fill that void—nothing.

At the same time there's an image of Love deep inside all of us that's not tainted by all the trials of this world. It's there as a deep longing, as a hunger. We were created in God's image and that image is Love. Father God longs to have his creation in his bosom. That's why he sent his Son into the world. The image of God in man isn't a static image; it's not stationary. That would be an idol. The image of God in man is a movement, a dance, toward the peaceful joy of having a place in your heart for another who has a place in his heart for you.

The image of God in man is the dynamic image of the Love of the Father reaching out with longing for another— for his Son and for man. With that dynamic image deep in our humanity we will never be satisfied with anything less than a robust relationship with the inner life of the Father, Son, and Holy Spirit. Jesus' question, "What do you seek?" is designed to help us get in touch with our true humanity— our longing to belong to another in Love, a longing to abide where we were created to abide.

## *Following the Rabbi*

*"Rabbi (which means teacher)...."* The word *Rabbi* honored men who had distinguished themselves in the study and teaching of the Law of Moses and the traditions of the fathers. Those who learned under the rabbis were called disciples. A higher form, *Rabboni,* honored those who had gained even higher respect among the rabbis. They were teachers of other rabbis. The disciples have seen something (Rabbi), but they haven't yet seen him as the Teacher of teachers (Rabboni). Mary will recognize him in this way after his resurrection (see Jn. 20:16).

Since John is writing after many years of reflection, it may be more accurate to say he uses the signs to point every generation to the resurrected Lord. He's viewing the life of Jesus in the flesh through the lens of resurrection. He wants each successive generation to experience this Rabbi and come to know him as Rabboni.

Though these disciples didn't yet see fully, they did see something that prompted them to follow. They were becoming aware of a heart's desire that had been suppressed for a long time. They were no longer completely blind, but they weren't yet seeing the fullness of what is in Jesus Christ.

At that time they were perhaps seeing Jesus through the lens of their preconceived notions. But having engaged Jesus in this way, they've entered a way that will take them to deeper revelation—if they stay on the road.

## On the Way from Blindness to Seeing

This condition of "no longer but not yet" is the human predicament in light of what the Father has done in Jesus Christ. The world is *no longer* a world alienated from the Father, but it's *not yet* a world that's received reconciliation. The redeemed community is *no longer* ignorant of his saving grace, but does *not yet* know as they will know. We face an exciting future at the return of Christ; but we don't yet know what that means (see I Jn. 3:2). We don't even know what exciting thing the Lord may have for us later today.

We're all on the road from spiritual blindness to the full revelation of Jesus Christ, the love of God in the flesh. Even when we were totally blind, that blindness was a place on the road to this revelation. After a lifetime of ever-deepening insights into the things of God we will not have seen all there is to see. That too is a place on this road. We're all on the Way; none of us have arrived. The Way is a path, a road where the revelation of the Father unfolds as we go.

Deeper revelation is always available. No matter how far you go in God, God is farther yet. No matter how broad you become in God, God is broader yet. No matter how high you rise in God, God is higher yet. No matter how deep you go in God, God is deeper yet. What an exciting future we have in Christ Jesus!

Unfortunately many take a break on this road and do not advance in their journey. They're camping out beside the road because they've found something that pleases them there. It may be a special doctrine or a favorite way of worshiping. Those things are good but we must learn to move on toward the goal of the upward call of God, "forgetting what lies behind" (see Phil. 3:13).

Others backslide on the way. It could be some offense from a church member or some desire for the things of this world. These do not camp; they reverse their direction on the road that leads from death to life. That means they're going from life to death. Both the camper and the backslider are living and dying along this road that leads to the full revelation of Jesus Christ, but they're not moving toward the goal.

How can I move toward my future in him? I'm not only interested in his revealing the Father's love to me. That's very important. But how can I be involved in revealing my Daddy's love to my generation? How can I follow Jesus in his work of revealing the Father? How can I bear fruit for God? Jesus' response to Philip later provides a compass to help us find direction in our quest: *"The Father who dwells [abides] in me does his works. Believe me that I am in the Father and the Father in me."* (Jn. 14:10-11). Walking as Jesus walked, a walk of abiding in the Father and the Father in me, is the only way anyone can bear fruit for God.

## The Goal: Knowing the Father

Jesus' goal is that we come to *know* the Father, not merely to come to him. *"And this is eternal life, that they know thee the only true God, and Jesus Christ whom thou hast sent"* (Jn. 17:3). In eternal life we know God as Father, not in an academic way, but in an intimate and personal way. To know God is to have a fruit bearing relationship with the Father. "Now Adam knew Eve his wife and she conceived and bore Cain" (Gen. 4:1). That intimate knowing is what Jesus has in mind for us. Knowing about God and knowing *that* he is Father doesn't bear fruit. Knowing everything we ought to do doesn't bear fruit either. The law exposed that kind of knowledge as fruitless.

Even doing a lot of Christian activities doesn't necessarily bear fruit. To bear fruit for God and accomplish his purposes, we must *know* him and receive his wisdom and insight, his strength and direction. This can never come from us. It can only come through an abiding relationship, through knowing the Father intimately through Jesus Christ the Son, through receiving the word/seed (see I Pet. 23) that comes out from his bosom into our bosom. Intimacy precedes fruitfulness.

How can I *know the Father* in such a way that I can *bear fruit for God*? This is the bottom line of our quest. John introduces the answer to our query in the two disciples' response to the question Jesus put to them, "What do you seek?" The disciples responded to Jesus with their own question.

## Mutual Abiding is the Key

*"Where do you abide?"* Abiding is among the most significant themes in John's writings. It implies much more than being in a place to hang your hat before going out to make a contribution to society. In John 'abiding' refers to a dynamic relationship with the Father. Abiding is the Father/Son relationship that lets God determine all life activity. Abiding is the only condition that lets us bear fruit for God.

Even Jesus in his humanity was limited to this way. *The abiding of the Son in the Father made him the man he was. The abiding of the Father in the Son made revelation of the Father possible.* Abiding is related to both his *being* (sonship) and his *doing* (his response of obedience to his Father). To understand John's gospel, we must understand this mutual abiding of the Father and the Son. To gain what John is offering us, we must enter into this mutual abiding.

John introduces this theme of abiding in the first verse of the Gospel: *"In the beginning was the Word, and the Word was with God, and the Word was God."* The Word who became flesh was abiding in God long before he came to dwell among us. Jesus didn't cease to abide in the Father when he became flesh. His abiding relationship determined his teaching, preaching and healing ministry. He became the full expression of God in the earth because he was already the Word with God from the beginning. He was able to make the Father known because he lived his human life from his position in the Father's embrace.

The end of the prologue confirms this abiding theme: *"No one has ever seen God; the only Son, who is in the bosom of the Father, he has made him known"* (Jn. 1:18). Abiding in the bosom of the Father empowered his work of revealing the Father. He accomplished that mission by words and actions that issued from the Father's bosom. The life of the Son in human form displays the Father's faithful nature: He fulfills his promises.

Throughout both the Old and the New Testament God promises, "I will be with you." Through obedience as a Son, Jesus revealed the Father's faithfulness. All God's promises are 'yes and amen' in Jesus Christ (see II Cor. 1:20). The world can know the Father as a Promise Keeper because he was abiding, and still abides, in Jesus Christ to keep his promises to all men.

## *Abide in Love and Let Love Abide in You*

Combine this insight with I John 4:16, *"So we know and believe the love God has for us. God is love, and he who abides in love abides in God, and God abides in him."* God is love. Jesus in his humanity is in the Father. Jesus is in(side) Love. The Father (Love) is in him. He is in(side) Love and Love is in(side) him. When we're invited to follow Jesus Christ, we're invited by Love into Love. When Christ is in us, Love is in us to invite others to follow this Way to the Father's embrace. This is the inner life of the Trinitarian God, which is eternal life *in us*. I'm getting ahead of myself. Let's catch up.

Jesus points to this abiding relationship when he says to Philip, *"Do you not believe that I am in the Father and the Father in me? He who has seen me has seen the Father"* (Jn.14:9). Jesus follows with a statement that conveys the significance of this mutual abiding of the Father and the Son. *"The words that I say to you I do not speak on my own authority; but the Father who dwells* [abides] *in me does his works"* (John 14:10). His works are directly related to his abiding relationship with his Father.

The Son's work of revealing the Father is an outworking of the mutual abiding of the Father and the Son. In every situation you can ask, "Did Jesus do that or did the Father do it?" Because they are mutually abiding, you can simply answer, "Yes." Jesus did that. "Yes." Father did that.

## Seeking the Abiding Place

*"Where do you abide?"* The two disciples who were with the Baptist and followed Jesus asked this question. They'd also seen Jesus as he walked. John uses their question as a sign pointing to something even he apparently did not see until long after the resurrection. John wants us to connect the *walk* of Jesus with his *abiding place*. Mutual abiding released the work of the Father into the community and into the world through Jesus' walk.

*"He who has seen me has seen the Father"* finds its possibility and its reality in this Father/Son abiding relationship. John wants us to discover the secret of living a life of intimacy with the Father that will allow us to walk as Jesus walked—into the bosom of the Father and out from the bosom to the world with love for the world.

A true disciple follows Jesus in *this way*: he enters into the mutual abiding relationship. These two disciples become a sign of those who faintly perceive the connection between mutual abiding and the work of God. They probably don't understand, but they perceive something that arouses their deep longing and causes them to ask, "Where do you abide?"

Every true disciple needs to abide in this relationship with the Father and the Son in order to walk as Jesus did. Jesus did what he did for humanity because he was abiding in the Father and the Father was abiding in him. He was the Father's love incarnate by the power of this abiding relationship. We are invited to become little incarnations of the Father's love. In and through that relationship all things are possible to him who believes.

## Abiding Makes Love Effective: Healing the Paralytic

John chapter 5 illustrates abiding as the way of effectively loving people. In one of the five porticoes around the pool by the Sheep Gate, Jesus finds a paralyzed man among the *"multitude of invalids, blind, lame, paralyzed"* (Jn. 5:3). Jesus heals him and walks away. In the stories of the other Gospels, Jesus heals all who come to him. So why did Jesus heal one man and walk away? The multitude did not come to Jesus, but neither did the paralytic. What does John want us to see?

As we approach this story, remember the significance of signs in John's Gospel. The stories are written as pointers. John wants us to see what the sign points to. He doesn't want to impress us with the power Jesus displays in healing the paralytic. The healing is impressive, but that's not John's point. John wants us to notice the abiding relationship between the Son and the Father that makes the healing possible. That's clear from the teaching that follows the story. Let's unpack this story in John 5, phrase by phrase, and follow the sign to the Father abiding in the Son.

## The Pool and Our Paralysis

*"Now there is in Jerusalem by the Sheep Gate a pool"*
(Jn. 5:2). Water shows up in all of the first seven chapters of
John: We find baptism (Ch. 1), water to wine (Ch. 2), born of
water and Spirit (Ch. 3), living water (Ch. 4), the pool (Ch.
5), walking on the sea (Ch. 6), rivers of water (Ch. 7). In
chapter seven, the water is a sign of the Holy Spirit flowing
from the Rock. Later we find the pool of Siloam (Ch. 9) and
water poured in a basin (Ch. 13). We also find water and
blood issuing from Jesus' side (Ch.19).

So water plays an important role in John's stories. Here
in chapter 5, water reflects a popular expectation that healing
became available when an angel stirs the water. I suggest that
John uses the stirring water as a sign pointing to the movement of the Holy Spirit. The movement of the Holy Spirit
enables disabled humanity to get into the move of God. The
Spirit's movement is the flowing river of Love that enables
blind, lame, and paralyzed humanity to join in the Father's
movement into the world he loves.

When it comes to living in the abiding relationship with
our Father, we're all blind, lame, and paralyzed. We're blind;
apart from a miracle we can't see the Kingdom of God (see
Jn. 3:3). We're lame; like Paul, we can will what is right but
apart from a miracle we can't do it (see Rom. 7:18).We're
paralyzed; apart from a miracle we can't enter the kingdom
of God even if we're there when the angel stirs the water
(see Jn. 3:5).

This event isn't just about a physically paralyzed man
miraculously receiving the ability to walk in the streets of
Jerusalem; it's the offer of healing Love to a spiritually blind
and paralyzed human race. In his abiding relationship with the
Father, Jesus presents the Father's love to this paralytic and to
every paralytic in every age who seeks the abiding place.

## Paralysis and the Law

*"There is...a pool which has five porticoes."* Five reminds us of the five books of Moses. Even today in the Hebrew culture, mothers teach their children a song to help them learn their numbers: "There is *one* God, there are *two* tablets (of the law), *three* fathers (Abraham, Isaac and Jacob), and *four* mothers (Jacob's two wives and their maids), and *five* scrolls (the Torah, the Law)." John wants us to see this story in light of the Law of Moses and the condition of those under the influence of those five scrolls. Even a superficial reading of the Old Testament reveals that most of the people, the multitude of invalids, never received life under those five porticoes.

*"In these lay a multitude of invalids, blind, lame, paralyzed"* (Jn. 5:3) It's not that these people don't want to do the will of God. They're disabled. Most of the Israelite people under the influence of the five scrolls — represented here by the five porticoes — were simply incapable of entering into God's movement. Life with God — represented by the pool — was available under the Torah (law); and at least a few, like the prophets and women like Deborah and Esther, could get in the pool while the water was moving. The majority, however, were blind, lame and paralyzed spiritually. They could neither see nor enter the abiding place in the Father.

As it was for them, so it is for us; we can't enter the kingdom unless we are born of water and the Spirit (see Jn. 3:5). We must somehow get into the water while it's moving; but that's the one thing we can't do. In our humanity, we're paralyzed and lame. We can't even see how to get from where we are to where the water is moving. Our spiritual eyes are blind and our human intellect is darkened apart from a miracle of God.

## Victory over Paralysis

When Paul says, "I can will what is right, but I cannot do it," he wasn't in despair over gross sins as some interpreters think. In the context, he wants to bear fruit for God (see Rom. 7:4). "I really desire to do the will of God," Paul says, "but when I do what looks so right according to my human interpretation of the Law, the thing turns out so wrong that it's obvious what I did falls short of the glory of God. When I do what I think is right; the will of God is not accomplished. My good deeds do not serve the divine purposes because it's not in me to provide the divine power necessary to make it happen."

*None of us can do the will of God apart from God.*

His cry of victory is, "Wretched man that I am! Who will deliver me from this body of death [this blind, lame paralyzed body]? Thanks be to God through Jesus Christ our Lord" (Rom. 7:24:-25). He recognizes that the only way to bear fruit is to enter into the abiding relationship with Jesus Christ.

In this abiding relationship we have access to the Father who produces fruit through the Holy Spirit. "For this I toil, striving with all the energy which he mightily inspires within [breaths into] me" (Col. 1:29). Paul encourages us to depend on God who is "at work in you, both to will and to work for his good pleasure" (Phil. 2:13). He is speaking of the effective power of the abiding relationship that's available to every true disciple.

## We Can Only Wait

*"One man was there, who had been ill for thirty-eight years"* (Jn. 5:5). John seldom, if ever, uses words without a reason. He often uses numbers to draw attention to the point of the story. For years I wondered what the significance of these thirty-eight years could be. It came to me while reading Deuteronomy one day. Moses, recounting the journey through

the wilderness, mentioned that the journey from Sinai to the Jordan took thirty-eight years (see Deut. 2:14). The people were in the wilderness for forty years, but they spent the first two years in the Lord's presence at Sinai.

Perhaps John is connecting the time the man had suffered paralysis with the time the multitude spent in the wilderness after the 'water stirred' at Sinai. They'd been given a window of opportunity to enter the 'pool', but they chose to make the golden calf instead. In spite of that rebellion, God led them to the border of the land of promise during those two years and gave them an opportunity to enter. They refused to accept that invitation also. It was thirty-eight years before they got another chance to enter.

We can only wait on God to move. We can't make it happen ourselves. We might build a bridge over our 'Jordan', but that self-effort would be useless. Coming to the other side, we'd discover that geographical change isn't enough. Or we might get into the 'pool' while the water is calm and stir the water ourselves—that's what some pastors and evangelists do—but that isn't the same as God stirring the water.

The healing we need can only be accomplished when God is moving the water. *God alone can do the work of God.* The kingdom we can see apart from a move of the Spirit of God isn't the Kingdom of God. Any kingdom we enter apart from the energy he mightily breaths into us isn't his Kingdom.

## Another Significant Question

"*Jesus said to him, 'Do you want to be healed?*'" (Jn. 5:6). Like the earlier question "What do you seek?" this question has many implications. The answer exposes the inner attitude. At first it sounds unnecessary. Who doesn't want to be healed?

If he's healed, though, he'll lose his excuse for his lack of productivity. Some prefer their paralysis to the prospect of having to be responsible. Others would prefer to try and overcome their ineffectiveness with their own strength. If I can do it without help, the glory will come to me. Others like the special attention they get from being unwell; if they're healed, they'll have to relinquish their role as the imposed-on victim. An honest response exposes our secret underlying motives.

*"Sir, I have no man to put me into the pool when the water is troubled"* (Jn. 5:7). His answer surprised me. I expected him to say, "Yes, I want to be healed." Something in his answer is easy to overlook. Many seriously want to be healed so they can get on with a life of doing what they want. Their idea of freedom is life without restrictions. The multitudes have no interest in getting into the moving water and becoming involved with God's agenda. All they want is the freedom to do as they please. Anyone with this attitude would simply answer, "Yes, I want to be healed."

This paralytic's answer suggests that he won't be satisfied with a mere physical healing. He wants to get into the moving water. He wants to be involved in what God is doing in the earth.

John is using the pool in this story as a sign posted at the entrance of the abiding place: "All who would enter must answer this question—do you want to be healed?" It's posted at the place of entrance into the Kingdom with the promise of power to do the will of God. This paralytic's answer points out that our paralysis as such isn't the real problem. Our real need is to be in the moving water.

The paralytic's situation raises the question "How?" How can a paralyzed man enter into the moving water? How can a paralyzed heart become involved in the things of God? One must be born anew to see the kingdom, and to enter he must be born of water and Spirit (see Jn. 3:3-5). Nicodemus asks, *"How can this be?"* How can a man be born anew? When it comes to doing the works of the Father, either we're not yet born or we're invalids—blind, lame, and paralyzed. There's nothing we can do. We need a miracle.

## The Omnipotent Word

*"Rise, take up you pallet and walk"* (Jn. 5:8). But wait. Jesus just commands this man to do something that's impossible for him to do. How can a lame man get up? How can a paralytic carry his pallet? Here's a key to understanding Jesus as the Word of God. In John, the Word is God Himself and that Word has become flesh in Jesus (see Jn. 1:14). What's true of God is also true of his Word. When this Word became flesh, he didn't cease to be the creative Word of God. He merely clothed himself in flesh so he could abide with us and share our humanity.

We can illustrate the significance of this command coming from this man who is the Word of God by looking at the story of creation. God said, "Let there be light," and light came into being. Before that command came from the mouth of God, nothing was out there that could obey and become light. He spoke that command into nothingness. "So shall my word be that goes forth from my mouth; it shall not return to me empty, but it shall accomplish that which I purpose" (Isa. 55:11).

God "calls into existence the things that do not exist" (Rom. 4:17). When Jesus speaks, the creative Word of the Lord comes forth. God himself comes forth through the spoken word to accomplish what Jesus commands, and the paralytic receives power to walk and carry his pallet.

When Jesus comes to us, God's omnipotent Word is present to accomplish in us what he demands of us. The power to rise comes from Jesus' command to the paralytic, "Rise." The man hears the voice of the Son of God. He isn't reading a text from the Law. He isn't listening to a good teaching on healing from a paralyzed rabbi. He comes into contact with the reality that stirs the water in the pool by the Sheep Gate.

The reality is always more powerful than the sign. When this moving water comes to him—he doesn't go to the water, it comes to him—he is no longer the one he had been, no longer a paralytic. He is a new creature with ability to walk as Jesus walks, upright and free in the presence of the Father.

## *Be What you were Created to Be*

Jesus doesn't command this man to do anything other than what man was created to do. Man was created to walk upright. When Adam sinned, he became paralyzed and blind. In this fallen condition, he wasn't able to walk upright in God's presence. He could set his will to walk but couldn't follow through on his decision. Jesus came to set us free from our paralysis so we can walk in an abiding relationship with his Father of love.

*We were created for that love to flow into us and out from us.* Jesus came so that we can be what we were created to be and do what we were created to do. To be human is to be a receiver and dispenser of love. Less than that is less than human.

Those who believe in his name are given power to become sons of God (see Jn. 1:13). When our eyes are opened to see the Father while looking at Jesus, we're given the Spirit to enable us to walk as he walked. Those who hear this Word are set free by the command. Those who read only the written code apart from the Spirit find themselves in bondage to the Law. Those who hear only what the teachers of the Law have to say won't be able to walk upright under the porticoes. But Jesus says, "*If you continue in my word, you are truly my disciples, and you will know the truth, and the truth will make you free*" (Jn. 8:31-32).

## Sabbath Rest

*"It is not lawful for you to carry your pallet"* (Jn. 5:10).
Pharisees have a way of making the burden of the Law much
heaver than God intended it to be. In its original intention,
Sabbath law provided a way for us to enter into God's rest.
God created the world in six days; he created man as his
final act of the sixth day. Since the Hebrew day begins at
sundown, the Sabbath was Adam's first day. He entered into
Sabbath rest because God had already done all the work. He
was abiding in the presence of the Father, at rest in that place
God had prepared for him.

As Hebrews puts it, "Whoever enters God's rest also
ceases from his labors as God did from his" (Heb. 4:10). But
we can't enter the Sabbath rest until we are liberated from
the effects of sin in our lives; our paralysis and our blindness
must be healed.

To keep the Sabbath is to abide in that place where God
has already accomplished the work. We don't have to work
our way over to the pool or build bridges over the Jordan. We
simply rise and walk in response to the voice of the One who
utters the omnipotent Word of healing and liberation.

Contrary to the rabbinical interpretation of the Law, it's
not breaking the Sabbath to respond to the voice of the Lord
and walk. Paul puts it this way: "It is no longer I who live,
but Christ who lives in me" (Gal. 2:20). Paul was in Sabbath
rest while Christ was working in him and through him, just
as Jesus was at rest while his Father supplied all the divine
energy to accomplish his will.

This man's walk brought him into conflict with the religious leaders. "It's the Sabbath," they challenged him. "Why
are you walking and carrying a burden? Don't you know
the Law?" They don't understand that this walking and
carrying isn't a burden to this man. It's the manifestation of
the freedom for which Christ has set him free (see Gal. 5:1).
The walk of Jesus also brings him into that same conflict.

This man really is following Jesus in the way he's going—to the cross.

## Overcoming Sin by Hearing the Voice

"*See, you are well! Sin no more*" (Jn. 5:14). Here's another impossible command apart from a miracle. The command *Sin no more* relates to the earlier *Rise and walk*. Only Jesus can move freely under the Law (five porticoes). The rest of us are paralyzed by sin, and "the power of sin is the law" (I Cor. 15:56).

When the omnipotent Word of God joins us in our situation, he offers us a way out from under the power of sin. But it isn't a way of self-indulgence. He doesn't set us free to sin; *freedom to sin is bondage to sin*. He sets us free *from* sin. He liberates us from our bondage to sin so we can walk in the Father's presence. "For God has done what the law, weakened by the flesh, could not do; sending his own Son in the likeness of sinful flesh and for sin, he condemned sin in the flesh, in order that the just requirement of the law might be fulfilled in us, who walk not according to the flesh but according to the Spirit" (Rom. 8:3-4).

"*Sin no more*" is for us today, but we can never fulfill it by the flesh. Every fleshly attempt to avoid sin only brings us into deeper bondage to the power of sin—the Law. Walking in the flesh is simply relying on our human understanding of 'good and evil' and on our human strength to do what we think is good. When we attempt to overcome sin by our own strength and insight, following our bubble, we only prove ourselves paralyzed and blind.

We can only follow this command as we walk according to the Spirit. When our spirits hear the spoken command, power to walk in obedience comes through the energy that he mightily breaths into us at that moment. Now we can fulfill the "just requirement of the law." This abiding relationship is absolutely necessary to walk as Jesus walked. As we walk in response to the *voice* of the Father and the Son, we walk according to the Spirit. In this way, God accomplishes his will through our walking and we enter into his Sabbath. We're at rest in the Sabbath when God is with us providing the direction and energy for what needs to happen.

## The Significance of Voice

Voice implies the *presence* of the one speaking. Three things about hearing the voice of God in the presence of God disturb our flesh.

First, when we hear that voice, we're no longer in control of our own lives—really we never were. We must simply do what we're told or expose ourselves as rebels.

Second, we can no longer use our ministry to promote ourselves. Having done all, we can only say, "We are unprofitable servants" (see Lk. 17:10).

Finally, and perhaps the most serious, we *lose our excuse* for failure when we hear the voice with its command. We can no longer excuse ourselves with that 'I'm-only-human' cop-out. Our defenses are demolished if we ever really hear "He who has died is freed from sin," and "We have died with Christ" (see Rom. 6:7-8).

Do you want to be healed? Do you want to move about freely in an abiding relationship with Father God?

We need three things to hear God's voice.

First, we must be in God's presence. If he isn't present to us or we aren't present to him, then we'll never be able to hear his voice. If someone tells us what he said, we may hear he right words, but we'll hear their voice, not his.

Second, there must be a movement of God's Spirit. In both Hebrew and Greek, *spirit* and *breath* are actually the same word. Breath activates speech. You can't hold your breath and speak at the same time.

Third, God must be speaking. Sometimes the Lord breathes silently; sometimes his breath activates speech. We aren't free to make up words and claim he's speaking. If he's silent, we must simply wait in his presence until he speaks.

Notice that all three persons are involved in this speaking. The Father speaks the Word, and the Spirit brings it to its destination with the power that gives life to all things.

## Abiding and Doing the Father's Will

At the end of the story, the Pharisees stand ready to kill Jesus *"because he not only broke the Sabbath but also called God his own Father, making himself equal with God"* (Jn. 5:18). In Jesus' response, he reveals the secret of abiding. The story illustrates the way of the Son but doesn't explicitly state it. Once we uncover the secret, an element that seems confusing rises out of obscurity and we see how Jesus abides in the Father and the Father abides in the Son. We also see how we can walk as he walked. Let's uncover the secret.

*"My Father is working still, and I am working"* (Jn. 5:17). Jesus doesn't provide the energy for the healing. He simply expresses the Word and let his Father do the work by the Spirit. A person doesn't need supernatural powers to command a lame man to rise. Even I can do that. I can will the healing and I can put all my human energy into speaking the command. I can speak in a very authoritative voice. But I can't make it happen; doing the work is God's part.

In his humanity, the commanding is all Jesus does. He leaves the rest to his Father. I once commanded a healing and the person actually got healed, much to my surprise. Several times when I have commanded, nothing happened. *Why did the Father always do it for Jesus and only sometimes for me?*

*"My Father is working."* God is working on the Sabbath? When God established the principle of Sabbath in Genesis, he did not stop working; he just stopped his work of the first creation. His work of preparation for the New Creation began at the Fall of Adam, continued through the Old Testament, and made its way to this Sabbath day.

Since God created Sabbath for man, is it not appropriate that his work of liberation continue on a Sabbath? This Sabbath work is the work of healing and liberating mankind from what separates him from the move of God in the earth. All the promises of God are on their way to fulfillment as the Son follows the Father in what he, the Father, is presently doing. By the Spirit the Father empowers man to walk freely in Sabbath rest.

## Abiding and Sonship

*"The Son can do nothing of his own accord, but only what he sees his Father doing; for whatever he does, that the Son does likewise"* (Jn. 5:19). I thought Jesus, being God, could do anything he pleased. Here's a startling revelation. Jesus didn't say the Son *chooses* to do nothing on his own. He said he, as the Son, *can* do nothing on his own accord. Hebrews 4:10 speaks of this Sabbath rest in this way, "Whoever enters God's rest also ceases from his labors." The only way to experience Sabbath rest is to stop trying to do the work of God with your human strength.

Jesus enters into the completed work of the Father as he simply commands, trusting the Father to do on earth what he's already done in heaven. This gives us a definition of sonship. Jesus, as Son, can not follow his own agenda. He doesn't have an alternate plan in case the Father's plan might bring him to a place of discomfort. As Son, he let his Father determine his whole life and all his activities. He hasn't reserved the right to make the final decision for himself. He can do nothing on his own accord without ceasing to be Son.

*"But only what he sees the Father doing."* This shows the connection between the work of the Son and the work of the Father. This may well have been a proverb. In Jesus' day, fathers trained their sons in the family business by letting them watch and participate in what they were doing. The

father initiated and the son followed. Children weren't called sons until they could do what the father was doing.

Children haven't yet learned to work under the father's authority. We become children of God by being born of God; we become sons and daughters by obedient responses to the Father's voice. Sonship implies a level of maturity that has learned to submit to the Father. The word 'sonship' (as it's used in Gal. 4 and Rom. 8) actually refers to a ceremony affirming the child as a son in whom the father is well pleased.

In this story of the paralytic, the Father is doing something under the porticoes. Something is accomplished in the heavenly realm but not yet manifest in the earth. The Father wants the Son involved in his work. The Son on the earth sees what his Father is doing and submits to him by speaking the command from the Father's heart. Jesus simply does on earth what he sees his Father doing in heaven.

## *On Earth as in Heaven*

Jesus taught us to pray, "Your will be done on earth at it is in heaven." When he does *"only what he sees the Father doing,"* he shows us how to be involved in the fulfillment of that prayer. The Father's intention isn't simply for his sons to pray. He wants us to be partners in his work. Obedient sons provide a channel for the will of God in heaven to flow into the earth.

As we become obedient sons, God does his will in the earth through us. The sons of God actually do something, but it is not a work of legalism. They do what they see the Father doing. We can ask the question again, "Who did that? Was it the sons and daughters or was it the Father?" The answer is a resounding "Yes!" The Father is glorified in earth as the sons and daughters follow his voice.

The key is seeing. Trying to do what we think God *might* be doing doesn't work, and doing what we think God *ought* to be doing is presumption. That also doesn't work.

Without seeing, we just set ourselves up for embarrassment and failure. Trying to force God's hand only exposes that we have our own agenda and expect God to follow our lead. We're still children who haven't yet learned submission.

The Father is serious about maintaining the lead. To do the will of God on earth, we must first see what he's doing in heaven. To see what the Father is doing in heaven, we must have access to his heart. That access is available in the bosom of the Father. And Jesus came to bring us into that place.

*"For whatever he does, the Son does likewise."* The Son can *see* because he *abides in the Father* and he can *do* because the *Father abides in him.* This abiding makes his walk a vehicle for the Father to reveal himself and his love to the world.

John the Baptist had seen this walk that issued from the Father and said, "Behold the Lamb of God." A man's walk always says something about where he's at, where he's abiding. A man's abiding place relates to his identity. In the New Testament a man is a 'son of' whatever influences his behavior. Only the Son, the Lamb of God, abiding in the bosom of the Father, can walk the way this man walked—that is, only he and those who become sons of God by following him into and out from the Father's bosom.

## *Friendship with Father*

*"For the Father loves [phileo] the Son, and shows him all that he himself is doing"* (Jn. 5:20). The Father's love here is *philia*, friendship love. There's a friendship between the Father and the Son. *The Father enjoys showing* the Son what he's doing and *the Son enjoys doing* what the Father shows him. The Father and the Son delight in working together. *"And he who sent me is with me; he has not left me alone, for I always do what is pleasing to him"* (Jn. 8:30).

The Son lives to bring joy to his Father by joining him in his work. Friendship is never a drag. Friends don't do things together out of legal obligation. They want to be together. He has included us in this friendship; he wants to be with us and do things with us. When we become friends we enjoy our relationship with him. The joy in our daily walk reflects our friendship with him. A lack of joy indicates a lack of intimacy.

When Jesus said, *"These things I have spoken to you, that my joy may be in you, and that your joy may be full"* (Jn. 15:11), he was referring to the joy of doing the will of his Father. He desires to share that joy with us. We enter that joy as we do what we see him doing. This is the joy of sonship—Father and sons doing things together. This is the only joy that will fulfill us.

Jesus in his humanity could walk about under the law as a free man because he was neither blind nor lame. He was breaking the Jew's Sabbath, but he wasn't breaking the Father's Sabbath. He was ceasing from his own labor and entering into the Father's peaceful approach to the world. He could see what his Father was doing because he was abiding in his Father's love. He was empowered to do what he saw the Father doing because his life issued wholly from the Father's bosom. He could see because he was in the Father; he could do because the Spirit of the Father was in him and with him.

This is the secret of the mutual abiding for us as well. *"I am in Christ"* means I'm in the place of rest in the Father's embrace where I can hear his voice and see what he's doing. *"Christ is in me"* means he's doing for me, in me, and through me what he requires when he speaks to me by the Holy Spirit. It's no longer I who live, but Christ who lives in me.

## Out from Love into the World

Remember, John's concept of abiding doesn't refer to the geographical location of one's apartment. It's the dynamic concept of *Emmanuel, God with us*. God is Love, so abiding is a situation where a man's life is wholly determined by the decision, direction, and dynamic of the loving Father's presence—in his tummy pack. The reality of 'God with us' appears in the life of *this* man Jesus who does only what he sees his Father doing.

Following Jesus into the Father's friendly embrace will bring us into the place where our lives can also reveal the Father's love as we move out from his presence into the world. When we do this, we are in Love (God) and we go with Love (God).

When Jesus sees the multitude of invalids under the five porticoes, the need doesn't determine his response. His Father's love moved him. He didn't come to heal; he came to do his Father's will (see Heb. 10:7). He always responds to what he sees his Father doing. It's as though he looks to his Father and asks, "Are you doing anything here?" He sees the Father healing one man, so he heals that one man. Then he asks, "Father, are you doing anything else in this place?"

"No, Son, not today." So Jesus withdrew. Why remain if the Father is finished? He's ready to return any time he sees the Father returning. Being at rest in the Father's bosom, he has no need to try to do more than the Father is doing. The Father's love always knows when it's time to move toward a hungry heart, and he's willing to wait.

## Into the World with Love

This is the essence of the concept of abiding in John's Gospel. We are at rest while we're doing what Father is doing because it's all his doing. We peacefully and joyfully join him in the doing, as we leave all anxiety behind. By the Spirit he draws us back into the Father's love from which we came and sends us out with that love into the world he loves. By our obedient response to his voice we return to his loving embrace with others following us as we follow Jesus Christ. This is the true meaning of Sabbath rest. This is the way of sonship. This is the bosom of the Father.

Our God is a living, moving God. The image of God in man is a dynamic image reflected to the world as we follow him in the on-going history of his dealings with us and with our neighbor. This image can only be known and made known in the act of following Jesus in the way he walked—into and out from the loving Father's embrace.

*"He who has seen me has seen the Father"* (Jn. 14:9). The image of God we see when we look at Jesus is the image of the Father who loves what he created. His love is unconditioned and it's unconditional. The Father is committed to the redemption and sanctification of all he created. However, as we have noticed, love is not controlling. He will allow us to refuse his love, but he will not withdraw it.

*This is the place of active rest in the bosom of the Father.* All true disciples are called to abide here and walk this way. Have you come to this place? Can you see what Father is doing? Do you do only what you see Father doing? We all have a ways to go, don't we?

Where is the path? How do we get there from here? We'll focus on this in the next chapter.

# CHAPTER 5

# Come and See

—ɰɰ—

W e've noticed that true disciples are seeking the place where Jesus abides. Jesus' walk issued from his abiding relationship with his Father, and we can never truly follow him unless we also enter that abiding place. When we're in Father's bosom we can see what Father is doing. From that place we're empowered by the Holy Spirit to do what we see him doing. No other seeing can direct us in this way of discipleship. No other doing can accomplish Father's will in the earth.

We've also noticed that Jesus' walk made his life a revelation of Father's love. Through his walk he made his Father known to those who follow him in the Way. To know another requires time spent in their *presence*, time observing the other's acts and responses in many varied situations. Really knowing also requires listening to the other's heart, not merely his words.

In order to get to know someone intimately, we must also speak and act in his presence, noticing his responses to us. In other words, the joy of knowing Jesus Christ, and through him knowing the Father, doesn't come through mere familiarity with stories about him. Joy comes when we join him in his Father's bosom. From that position we do the work of

God, bear fruit for God, and experience Father's delight in us as his beloved sons and daughters. This seeing and knowing can only be experienced in the Father's bosom—in him.

## *God's Image in Man*

The true image of God is revealed in the history of the man Jesus Christ, who let his life and activity be wholly determined by his Father. Living his life in this way Jesus demonstrated the original intention of creation: "Let us make man in our image" (Gen. 1:26). The image of God is not a static idol; he is the *living* God. The image of God is the image of the Father, Son and Holy Spirit living together peacefully in intense intimacy and unified purpose.

Jesus, by living his life from his position in his Father's bosom, became everything God intended Adam to be. That's the reality and power of his humanity. That's why Paul called him the second Adam (see I Cor. 15:45-47). He succeeded where the first Adam (man) failed and became the firstborn of the new creation.

The first Adam failed because he tried to live independent of God. We'll discuss this failure and God's solution when we talk about the raising of Lazarus. Our focus in this chapter is on the place Jesus prepared in the bosom of the Father. That place is the same place he personally occupies.

Since Jesus Christ is the true Adam, the true man, we can assume that his model of following his Father in all things is the way God intended Adam to reflect his image. God wanted Adam to abide in his presence—in that place where God is working and man is participating in that work. God wants us to know him intimately as Abba Father rather than trying to know good and evil. He wants us to know him in the fellowship of his active love for the world. The true image of the true God can only shine forth in the earth as men and women live their lives out from this abiding relationship.

## Abiding Reflects the Image

Abiding in the bosom of the Father doesn't mean crawling up in his lap, sucking your thumb, and stroking your security blanket. It means active participation in his mission in the earth. The purpose of abiding isn't merely to produce right actions either. A legalistic system can do that. Many Pharisees produce right actions but the fruit of those actions isn't fruit for God. Self-righteousness based on a legal system never reveals the true image of God's righteousness. It's like knowing that God wants us on the other side of the Red Sea and building a bridge rather than waiting on God.

The ultimate purpose of abiding is for God's image to be reflected in the lives of men and women. Jesus is the only one who has ever fully reflected that image, but he isn't the only one called to reflect that image. "For those whom he foreknew he also predestined to be conformed to the image of his Son, in order that he might be the first-born among many brethren" (Rom. 8:29).

The writer of Hebrews put it this way, "For it was fitting that he, for whom and by whom all things exist, in bringing many sons to glory, should make the pioneer of their salvation perfect through suffering" (Heb. 2:10). Many sons will be brought—they do not go on their own strength, they are brought—to the bosom of the Father and from there will shine as the light of God's glory in the earth.

## Divine Hospitality

When Jesus says to the two disciples of John, *"Come and see"* (Jn. 1:39), it's an invitation to come over to his place and experience divine hospitality. It's more than an invitation to see the flat where he spends the night. The multitude can find that place without any special revelation. He's calling these men to come to the place where he abides in his Father. In that place and from that place Jesus reveals the true nature of God by the Holy Spirit that came on him at his baptism. Come and see means come and abide. Come and abide means come be an active part of his advancing Kingdom of Love.

The disciples who first heard this invitation didn't fully understand everything. None of them got it until after the resurrection. And the fullness of what is there in the life, death and resurrection of Jesus is still being filled out today as the church walks toward the consummation of all things when "creation itself will be set free from its bondage to decay and obtain the glorious liberty of the children of God" (Rom. 8:21).

None of us know what that means yet. We're still on the way toward the full revelation of Jesus Christ when every knee will bow and every tongue will confess. We're waiting for the "genuineness" of our faith to "redound to praise and glory and honor at the revelation of Jesus Christ" (II Pet. 1:7). Until then we can only follow the pointing signs.

## *A Place in the Father's House*

John develops this idea in chapter 14. Let's work through the passage, looking for insight into the 'place' as the necessary condition to develop God's image in man. We'll also be looking for insight into how we can abide in that place.

*"In my Father's House are many rooms"* (Jn. 14:2). The word translated 'rooms' ('mansions' in the King James) is a noun form of the verb translated 'abide' in John. We could say 'abiding places' and the idea would become clearer. Through the years people have offered many sentimental interpretations of this phrase—images of the "cottage in heaven" where I'll live when I die. We'll certainly live with him eternally on the other side of death. But Jesus isn't talking about life in heaven after death in this text. We learn from the fuller context of this chapter that he's talking about the life we're called to live here on earth as those who experience the indwelling presence of the Holy Spirit. He's

talking about the way of the Kingdom of God in the earth today through abiding.

## The Household of God

What is meant here by the Father's house, if not heaven? In Hebrews we find direction for an answer. "Christ was faithful over God's house as a Son. And we are his house if we hold fast our confidence and pride in our hope" (Heb. 3:6). *We are his house.* 'House' is used in the sense of 'household.' It isn't a place we can describe in terms of geographical location or architectural style. It's a people who abide with their Father. It's a people living life in an intimate relationship with the other members of the household.

Being a part of this household is what makes it possible for the "many sons" to be brought to glory (see Heb. 2:10). Through *fellowship with the Father* we participate in the glory of the *sonship of Jesus.*

Paul also spoke of a household. "So then you are no longer strangers and sojourners, but you are fellow citizens with the saints and members of the household of God" (Eph. 2:19). As he continued, it looks like he changed the image from household to house in the sense of an architectural structure. The change is only apparent, however, because in Paul's mind 'house' and 'household' are related. He continued, "...built upon the foundation of the apostles and prophets, Christ Jesus himself being the cornerstone, in whom the whole structure is joined together and grows into a holy temple in the Lord; in whom you also are built into it for a dwelling place of God in the Spirit" (Eph. 2:20-22). He's obviously speaking of the people, architecture is the metaphor.

The temple (house) is *in the Lord* and the Lord is *in the temple* (house). Here we have mutual indwelling from a different perspective. If the individual living stones (see I Pet. 2:5) aren't *in the Lord* then they can't be *in the house,* because the house itself is in the Lord. Some who gather regularly in church buildings may not be part of this house because they've not been born anew.

Some who are born into the household still choose to live outside their Father's house like the elder brother and the prodigal. Neither of those sons was in the house. One was in the field and the other was in a foreign country (see Lk. 15:11-32). These are "men of the flesh, babes in Christ" who "behave like ordinary men" (see I Cor. 3:1-4). They are in Christ but they don't act like it. They've not taken their place as an active part of the household. Household is a condition where mature sons and daughters are an active part of the Father's life and the Father is an active part of their lives.

## A Prepared Place

*"I go to prepare a place for you"* (Jn. 14:2). It's encouraging to know we don't have to prepare a place in the Father's house for ourselves. Jesus went to prepare a place for us. It isn't a place of rest, at least not in the sense of inactivity. It's a place of *intimacy* with the Father where we *hear his voice* and *delight to do* his will.

This place isn't merely designed to accomplish things for God. If the issue were getting the task done, the Lord could send angels with much less trouble. Our Father wants us in his presence; he wants to relate to us as sons and daughters. He wants to hang out with us. We don't need to be up-tight about the task. The work will get done as we enjoy his presence. The Father wants sons and daughters in the house, not servants out in the field apart from him. *It's all about being sons* not *doing things.*

Some children of God try to prepare their own place. Rather than simply listening to the voice of the Father, they use their natural abilities to promote themselves and their programs. Like Peter at the arrest, they do what they think is right. What they're building isn't the household of God. It may look good on the outside, but it's full of dead men's bones. It's a human house with a human headship; it reflects the image of fallen man partaking of the fruit of the tree of the knowledge of good (elder brother) and evil (prodigal son) rather than knowing God. They aren't abiding in the place Jesus prepared for them. They act as servants rather than sons, trying to earn the right to the good life in the Father's house. Or they act like rebels, trying to experience the good life by taking pleasure in unrighteousness. Both miss the joy of being with the Father in his house.

The idea of a place in the household is similar to Paul's concept of the Body of Christ and its many members. There is a place in the Body called "hand" and another place called "ear," for example. To abide in the place of the hand is to function as a hand under the guidance of the head.

None of us are called to be the whole Body or the complete household. Nor are we called to choose our own place. Each has his own place related to the *function* he's *called* and *gifted to fulfill* in the overall plan. Our place in the Body is the place Jesus went to prepare for us. We find our place by hearing his voice and walking in what he shows us. We have to come and see the place he's already prepared for us. When we come, we find joy in abiding with him in his active participation in the Father's life.

### Into His Presence

*"I will come again and take you to myself, that where I am you may be also"* (Jn. 14:3). This proclamation echoes God's announcement to Israel at the foot of Mount Sinai: "You have seen what I did to the Egyptians, and how I bore you on eagles' wings and brought you to myself" (Ex. 19:4). It's always the Lord's desire to bring his people to himself. Yes, he wanted to take the Israelites into the Promised Land; but the purpose behind the move was to have a people who would be a light to the nations. God wanted his people in a place where he could be with them and they with him. He

wanted to be with them in the land to show himself strong in the earth and shine his light to the nations through them.

We also find the importance of the voice in Exodus. "If you will obey [hearken to] my voice," God says, "You shall be my possession" (Ex. 19:5). We discussed the importance of hearing the voice in the last chapter. He desires a people who remain in his presence as the Spirit is moving, listening and responding to his voice. Only in this way can they become what they are destined to be—a light to the nations.

The land of promise became a land of curses when they tried to live as though God were not present to them. One of the most common rebukes spoken to Israel from the time of Joshua to the Exile was, "You haven't hearkened to my voice." Even at the foot of Mount Sinai the people said to Moses, "You speak to us, and we will hear; but let not God speak to us, lest we die" (Ex. 20:19). They preferred a human voice (the preacher) to hearing from God. Later in the Exile, they preferred a book to his presence.

When each man began to do what was right in his own eyes (see Jud. 21:25), Israel had already ceased to dwell in the Promised Land because they'd failed to abide in God's presence and hearken to his voice. They were still living in Canaan, but they weren't abiding in the place the Lord had prepared for them. He had brought them to himself. *He himself was the place he had for them.* But they walked away from him when they refused his voice. God allowed their enemies to harass them because they did not listen to his voice (see Jud. 2:20-21).

## Where Is He?

*"So that where I am you may be also."* To capture the significance of this, let's read between the lines and 'play' with the language. If I had been there I probably would have put my foot in my mouth the way Peter often did. "Wait a minute," I would've said, "What do you mean? Surely

you meant to say, 'Where I *will be*, there you may be also.' You don't have to go away for me to be where you are. I'm already where you are. I'm in your presence. You are here; and I am here."

Raising the question this way introduces the deeper insight that is in the *sign* of the text. Where was Jesus when he made that promise? Did he see himself as being somewhere other than where the disciples were? Jesus may have answered my blundering question like this:

"Fount, you don't understand at all. I AM (is) in a place you have not yet seen. If you had seen me where I AM (is), you would know that you aren't there yet. I've not yet prepared a place there for you. Where I AM (is), you can't come at this time because you're still blind and lame. But, though you can't come, I can bring you to myself in that place if you'll but hear my voice and respond when I return after preparing that place. Then I'll say to you, 'Rise, take up you pallet and walk.' Then you'll be where I AM (is)." By placing the '*is*' in parentheses I am drawing attention to the fact that Jesus is the "I AM" and that he IS in the bosom of the Father.

## The Place and the Way

"*And you know the way where I am going*" (Jn. 14:4). Thomas raises a question. "Lord, we do not know where you are going; how can we know the way?" Thank you, Thomas, for raising that question. But I still have a question of my own: "Jesus, I thought you said we're going to be with you where you ARE. Why don't you just open our eyes to see where you ARE? We're here and you're here. If being with you is the goal, wouldn't we find ourselves in the right place without moving from where we are now? *Why must there be a way?*"

Why is a journey necessary and what's the nature of the journey? Jesus has already come to us as Emmanuel, God with us. If God is here with us then aren't we also with him?

Consider: God was with Israel in the wilderness and in the land, but Israel wasn't with God because they didn't hearken to his voice.

In the Bible, to be 'with' implies being involved in a common pilgrimage. The Israelites weren't going the same way the Lord was going. God was with them on the path, but they were going a different way. He was going toward sending his Son for the world. They were going toward joining the Gentiles in killing his Son.

## *Radical Change begins a Radical Journey*

Even though the Father has come to us in Christ, a radical change still needs to take place before we can be with him where he *IS*. The necessity of this change comes from the fact that the call to *come and SEE* is also a call to *come and BE*—sons and daughters. We're called to be sons and daughters who are involved in what Father is doing. We're called to bear the image of the first-born Son in our daily conduct.

Apart from him we can do nothing. But when we experience this radical change we'll not be apart from him; we'll be with him where he *IS* and he will be with us where we are. He'll be with us in what we're doing because we'll be with him in what he's doing. There is an exciting future for those who hear and respond to this promise.

The radical change is what Jesus referred to as being born anew. But this is only the starting point of the journey. When we're born anew, we haven't arrived; we've only entered the Way and begun the journey. We've been predestined to be conformed to his image. Our *destination* is to be with him in eternity, but our *destiny* is to reflect God's image to the world through a life of obedience to his voice. That's the image of the Son. The Son does only what he sees the Father doing.

The journey is necessary because the radical change only brings us to that place of abiding where we see what he's doing and are enabled to join him in his work. In joining him we begin a radical journey of becoming mature sons and daughters of the Father.

## Jesus is the Way

"*I am the way, and the truth and the life; no one comes to the Father, but by me*" (Jn. 14:6). Here we have the first part of Jesus' answer to Thomas' question. He didn't say, "I'll show you the way." He didn't say, "I'll draw you a map." And he didn't say, "I'll give you a book of instructions and rules." He said, "I AM (is) the way." Just as Jesus is himself the abiding place, so he is also the way. *Jesus in me is his way for me*; he in me is *truth* for me and he in me is *life* for me. By the same token, Jesus' way is for me to be in him. Being in him is being in the *way*. Being in him is being in *truth*. Being in him is being in *life*.

Another way to say the same thing is, "*True life is truth lived*; and Jesus is *the way in* as well as *the way onward*."

The journey is a process of "being changed to his likeness from one degree of glory to another; for this comes from the Lord who is the Spirit" (II Cor. 3:18). It's a journey along a path none of us can discover on our own, for we can't see. Nor can we walk this path apart from the daily presence, direction and empowering of the Father's voice, for we are lame.

Having discovered the path (Jesus) and entered the way (Jesus), many think they've already arrived at the destination. But the concept of *way* implies going forward toward something ahead. *Jesus is the way to the Father.* Many fail to grow in their relationship with Father because they have been led to believe God's goal has been fulfilled in their lives when they accepted Jesus.

## The Way is a Journey to Sonship

"*No one comes to the Father, but by me.*" When Jesus comes to us and we come to him, we've entered the way into the Father's bosom. This means we've embarked on a journey where *the fatherhood of God* begins to work in us *the obedient sonship of Jesus.*

We're children now, but we'll someday *"be like him for we shall see him as he is"* (I Jn. 3:1-2). Sonship is a term that implies maturity in our ability to do only what we see our Father doing. Children are not yet there because they're not yet obedient. Children sometimes misbehave (like the adults who train them). They are on a journey from childhood to sonship.

The implications of entering this way are not merely future. There's a here and now aspect to this way. When we come to Jesus we've already come to that place of mutual abiding. *"In that day you will know that I am in the Father, and you in me, and I in you"* (Jn. 14:20). When we come to Jesus we're drawn into the mutual abiding of the Father in the Son and the Son in the Father.

He who is the way to the Father is also the place where the Father abides in the earth and does his work. If we are in him in this way, *we are the place* where the Father abides in the earth and does his work. When we look at ourselves collectively and individually this abiding relationship clearly hasn't yet had its full effect in our life and ministry. That doesn't mean we aren't abiding, just that we're still *on the way* while we are *in* the abiding place.

## A Place in the Active Body of Christ

Here again, it's a dynamic abiding. In coming to Jesus we have come to that place where *"my food is to do the will of him who sent me and to accomplish his work"* (Jn. 4:34). We've come into the Body of Christ. Our physical body is the instrument we use to accomplish things in the created world. The Body of Christ is in the world to do the works of the Father in the earth. We're not here for ourselves; we're here for one another and for the world. We are with him

146

and he is with us in the active intimacy of friends working together to bring love to the world.

From this place of mutual abiding we can say with Paul, "I can do all things in him who strengthens me" (Phil. 4:13). We must never define Paul's "all things" by the desires of our flesh. It must be the 'all things' our Father is presently doing in us and through us. We must continually hear the word our Father is presently speaking.

So, though we've arrived at the place of abiding, we're still on the way to becoming men and women whose lives bear the image and glory of God. We've already arrived at the place where the image of God is reflected. It's reflected in Jesus Christ; and we're in him. In another sense we have only entered the way because we do not yet fully reflect that image ourselves, not individually and not corporately.

This is the dialectic nature of the life we live as Christians. It can be stated thus, "already and not yet" and "still and no longer." This is the mystery of the abiding experience. It is no longer I who live, but I am often still acting as though the "old man" is alive. I am already in Christ where the image of God is reflected, but my behavior is not yet conformed to his image.

## *An Abiding Place for God in the Earth*

Before we look at the end of this dialogue, notice Jesus' two statements: "*I go to prepare a place*," and, "*I will come again*" (John 14:2-3). We'll try to understand these two statements by looking carefully at verses 12-21.

In John's Gospel the focus is on Jesus returning to the Father. One of the major issues in his returning to the Father is the path he took to get there: he went by way of death, burial and resurrection. As the old hymn says, "The way of the cross leads home." In his death he disarmed the principalities and powers. At the cross he purchased redemption and made a way for us to approach his Father. There his blood was shed, and from there it flows with forgiveness, cleansing, and healing for all who are unable to get into the moving water of God's presence by their own merits. He went to the cross to prepare a place for us in the bosom of his Father.

So far, we've focused on man coming to the Father through the Son. Let's shift our focus to the Son coming to us by the Spirit. When we come to the Lord, we can say, "I am in Christ." When the Lord comes to us, we can say, "Christ is in me." Through the cross and resurrection he prepared a place in the Father for us. He comes again looking for a place in us to continue his work of loving the world. He's looking for a home here.

## A Place Here for the Father and the Son

When we read, "*I will come again*," our minds usually jump to the rapture. Jesus is coming again just as surely as he came the first time: several passages in the New Testament establish that. But that isn't the point here in John's Gospel. Follow Jesus' next statements in John 14:12-21 as they shed light on the meaning and significance of his promise, "*I will come again*."

"*He who believes in me will also do the works that I do*" (Jn. 14:12). One of the main issues of the chapter 14 is doing the works of the Father here on earth. Just as the definition of 'Son' is 'doing what the Father is doing,' so the definition of disciple is, 'doing what Jesus is doing.' We can't legitimately claim to be true disciples if we're going our own way. If we're following our own agenda, we're not disciples. A disciple is one who follows another. Jesus and his Father are looking for a place to actively abide here and do their work in the earth.

"*If you love me, you will keep my commandments*" (Jn. 14:15). Our legalistic nature wants to interpret this in terms of rules that regulate our external behavior. We like that because we want to interpret the list in a way that makes us look good. That's what the Pharisees did. It's easy to take a written code into our own hands and run with it—away from intimacy with God. How many people and groups have given weird interpretations to Holy Scripture? Human interpretations only bring more division.

Jesus' basic command is to love, and it's really more like an invitation than what we generally think of as a command. Jesus calls us to love him and to love one another. We can only do that as we come to his abiding place and respond to the word which flows from the Father's heart. He alone knows what's required in any situation to fulfill the command to love. His voice will always lead us to do the loving thing. He desires us to live in his presence and respond to his voice as 'hearing' children. That's the only way the Father's work of love can be done in the earth.

## We Need a Helper

*"And I will pray the Father, and he will give you another counselor, to be with you forever... [and he] will be in you"* (Jn. 14:16-17). If we aren't painfully aware of our need of a Counselor, one who will be with us, it's because we've not yet taken seriously the challenge to do our Father's works. We may have tried to be religious and follow a system of rituals handed down from our earthly fathers. We may have experienced enough success to convince ourselves we know how to do the Father's will. But when we begin to recognize that we're called to work out the details of our daily lives in such a way that the Glory of God's presence is manifest in everything we do, then we know we need a Helper.

It isn't enough for us to be in him. We need God himself to work in us by the Holy Spirit, "both to will and to work for his good pleasure" (Phil. 2:13). That's what he promises with the coming of the other counselor, the Holy Spirit.

We often miss the implications of this promise because we fail to consider the relationship within the Trinity. We don't have three Gods; we have one God who is differentiated in three persons. When he offers us the Holy Spirit, he offers God himself in another person of the Trinity. The disciples weren't waiting for another God on the day of Pentecost. They were waiting for God to come in a way he'd not yet come to them.

The promise is that the Lord will be coming in a way that he can be *in* us as well as *with* us. This coming of the Holy Spirit is a key part of what Jesus meant when he said, "I will come again." But there's more here than a promise that the Holy Spirit will come on the day of Pentecost.

*"I will not leave you desolate; I will come to you"* (Jn. 14:18). He promises he will not leave us alone as orphans in our daily walk with him. The disciples weren't left to themselves to work out the details of obedience after Pentecost. It's the Lord who promised to come, and it's the Lord who did come. The Lord is the Spirit (see I Cor. 3:17). He came to be our daily Helper and he's well able to work out his will in our lives as we respond to him.

### Only Disciples will See

This promise is followed by the statement, *"Yet a little while, and the world will see me no more, but you will see me; because I live, you will live also"* (Jn. 14:19). He promises to come to the disciples in a form that the world won't see. But the disciples somehow will be able to see him in this form. The seeing here is a seeing made possible by the Spirit who will be sent to them. The world can never see apart from receiving this Spirit.

This understanding of his promise to come again seems necessary for another reason. The New Testament speaks of the second coming of Jesus as an event that all creation will see and acknowledge. Every knee will bow and every tongue will confess that Jesus is Lord (see Phil. 2:10-11). Until that time we can still stand in rebellion against his authority and deny his Lordship. The only conclusion I can draw is that Jesus isn't talking of the "second coming" here because he says the world will not see him.

He's speaking of the coming of the Holy Spirit on the day of Pentecost. For the coming of the Spirit is the coming of the Spirit of Jesus Christ. When he comes to us in this way, he comes to be *in* us so he can do the works of the Father through us. It's not a one time experience; it continues as we obediently walk toward the future Kingdom of God in the earth.

*When we find ourselves where he IS, we also find that he is in us where we are.* As we've said, we can't go to that place on our own strength; we're paralyzed. We can't see to walk in this way; we're blind. We need a Helper. He hasn't left us alone to enter or to walk in the Way. He has come to us by the Holy Spirit.

## He Empowers Us with His Life

He comes to us. He empowers us by his spoken word; we can now rise and walk. He opens our eyes; we can see what's there in the Spirit realm. What he enables us to see is what he's doing. He's been here all along, but, like the paralytic, we didn't know *who* it was (see Jn. 5:13). Like the blind man, we didn't know *where* he was either (see Jn. 9:12). As in the story of the blind man in chapter 9, if we ever really see him and if we really hear his voice, we can only bow at his feet and worship saying, *"Lord, I believe"* (Jn.9:38). We worship him because *we know who* it is who healed us and we now see him *where he is.* He is the Son: that's *who* he is. He is in the bosom of the Father: that's *where* he is. But he is also in us as well, and that's how we can live the abundant life here.

*"Because I live, you will live also."* We must hear this promise along side the preceding promise: *"I will come to*

*you.*" It's in his coming to us by the Holy Spirit that we receive his life.

The life he lived in the flesh was granted to him by his Father; *"For as the Father has life in himself, so he has granted the Son also to have life in himself"* (Jn. 5:26). If he received life as a gift, how much more must we receive life as a gift? The life we receive can never be an independent life. We have life only because he lives. He hasn't granted us a life we can take in our own hands and use for our own ends. Our way leads to death; his way leads to life. This life can only be walked out by the Spirit. "If we live by the Spirit, let us also walk by the Spirit" (Gal. 5:25). It's only by the presence and movement of the Holy Spirit abiding in us that we live our lives in the bosom of the Father.

## Knowing through Mutual Abiding
*"In that day you will know that I am in my Father, and you in me, and I in you"* (Jn. 14:20). This is the second time in the Gospel of John Jesus includes us in the mutual abiding. He included us when he said we must eat his flesh and drink his blood (see Jn. 6:56). In both instances he is speaking of the time after his resurrection. Before his death it was the Father abiding in the Son and the Son abiding in the Father.

In these texts he speaks of a time—*that day*—when we'll be drawn into the closed circle of the divine fellowship of the Father and the Son. I say 'closed circle' because "no one knows the Son except the Father and no one knows the Father except the son and anyone to whom the Son chooses to reveal him" (Matt. 11:27). If we hear his voice inviting us, he enables us to come and he enables us to see. In that place we can see because he welcomes us into his peaceful life with his Father.

## Knowing by Experience

*"In that day you will know."* In which day? In the day he comes to you. In the day you're no longer left desolate. In the day you're empowered to see him even though the world around you doesn't see him. When he's with you, opening your eyes to see and empowering you to do the will of the Father, then you'll know—you'll really know.

*What will you know?* Your eyes will be opened to see that *you are in him and he is in you.* You'll know because you'll be doing some of the greater works he promised you'd do. You will be accomplishing things that are impossible without the presence and working of God. You'll actually be accomplishing the Father's will, bearing fruit for God—fruit that issues from the Father's bosom.

We can only know as we experience the reality of the presence of God in our life. If we only have it in our heads, we don't have it. If we're not doing it, we don't know it. *If we know it, our lives will show it.*

For too long the Church of the West has been satisfied with head knowledge. We have even criticized those who talk about experience. We must move from simply being believers to abiding in his word. Remember that abiding means obedience to his word. Only through abiding in his word and walking as he walked will we become disciples. Only in this way will we come to know the truth by experience. Only in this way will we be made free (see Jn. 8:31-32).

The first step to this experience of knowing is to acknowledge that we are not yet free. In John 8 the Jews who had believed in Jesus were not willing to admit they were in bondage. Jesus came to set the captives free. If we're not in bondage, he didn't come for us. Our pride of thinking we already know can keep us from the knowledge of truth that makes us free. Theoretical freedom can't compete with the true freedom that comes from walking as an obedient disciple of the Son of the Father.

## A Word from His Presence

*"He who has my commandments and keeps them..."* (Jn. 14:21). We need to understand "commandments" here to mean a word presently being spoken—a *rhema* word. The root of the Greek word *rhema* is *rhea*. It has the basic meaning of *flow*. We have that root in English in the word rheostat. A rheostat controls the flow of electricity going to a light.

A *Rhema* is a word that is presently flowing forth from the mouth of the Father in the abiding place—a specific word for a specific moment. Any legalistic or systematic approach to this verse would cause a failure to grasp the meaning of what follows next. We must read it: "He who lives his life according to the commands that issue from the bosom of the Father in a given situation." In other words, to keep his commandments means to follow the guidance of the Holy Spirit moment by moment.

John's concept of the commandments is influenced by the Old Testament emphasis on the *voice* of the Lord. One of the major issues of the prophets was that the people were keeping the external forms of the law but were not hearkening to the voice of the Lord. This reference to the voice is found in many passages. God's original word at Mount Sinai was, "hear my voice and keep covenant" (Ex. 19:5). After 40 years in the wilderness the Lord warned them that, if they will not obey the voice of the Lord" (Deut. 28:15), they will eventually fall into the hands of their enemies. But he also promised that if they would return and obey his *voice* he would restore their fortunes (see Deut. 30:2).

When the prophets rebuked them, it was never for failing to keep a legalistic system; it was for failing to hear and obey the voice (see Jer. 3:13; 7:28; 9:13; 11:7 and many other passages in the prophets). We find this complaint against the people in every stage of their history. Our point here is that God has always wanted an intimate relationship with his people. He never intended to relate to them through a book apart from the Spirit, "...for the written code kills, but the Spirit gives life" (II Cor. 3:4).

## The Creative Word

The word (*rhema*) of God is creative. When he speaks, his word creates what he speaks. He speaks to what is not and it comes to be. He speaks to what is dead and it comes to life (see Rom 417). That's because his word is empowered by the movement of his Spirit, his Breath. (In both Hebrew and Greek the word for breath and the word for spirit is the same word.) If we know a command because we read it, or because someone tells us about it, we receive it as law. Paul tells us that "the power of sin is the law" (I Cor. 15:56). The commandments of God don't become life to us until we've heard his command as a *rhema* flowing by the Spirit into our human spirit.

There are some problems related to this walk. Some follow the impulses of their flesh and blame the Holy Spirit for their obnoxious behavior. Their presumption does not relieve us of the responsibility to hear from our Father. Others trust only their human reason to find their way on the path. They seem unaware that man's intellect is also fallen from grace. I grew up thinking God had given us a book and a mind and then went up to heaven and left us alone to figure out what he wants us to do. With this attitude we can only live as if he abandoned us to our own resources—as orphans.

He has not left us alone because he desires for us to rely on him. He has come to us and he is still with us as our Helper. As we remain in the abiding place, in fellowship with Father, he speaks to us and gives us direction (commandments) for our daily lives. This is how his will is done in the earth.

## Attached or Connected

Chapter 15 illustrates how we are using the word *rhema*. Jesus is the vine and we are the branches. He calls us to abide in the vine. On the vine, some branches are *attached* but not *connected*. They cease to bear fruit, wither, and die because *sap is not flowing* from the vine into the branch. Other branches are *connected* to the vine and have *sap flowing and that flow produces fruit.*

*"If you abide in me, and my words [rhemata] abide in you, ask whatever you will, and it shall be done for you"* (John 15:7). Jesus is saying, "If you'll hear the *rhema* word from the bosom of Father and allow it to be part of you, that word will produce fruit. It will produce fruit because your payer requests will be crafted by that word."

## In the Flow of Love

In this way we fulfill the command, *"Abide in my love"* (Jn. 15:9). We can abide in his love only as we allow his love to abide in us and flow through us.

*"If you keep my commandments, you will abide in my love, just as I have kept my Father's commandments and abide in his love"* (Jn. 15:9-10). None of us know what love really is. None of us know how to love apart from listening to Father's voice and responding to it. *"God is love, and he who abides in love abides in God, and God abides in him"* (I John 4:16). To abide (live) in love is to abide (live) in God. As we respond to his voice, his love reaches out through us to the world around us. This is how we abide in God and he in us.

*"He it is who loves me"* (Jn. 14:21). Our love for God isn't measured by how fervently we proclaim we love him. Neither is it measured by how deeply or how intensely we feel toward him. Our love for God is measured by how well we do what we see him doing, by how well we respond in the crucible of personal relationships.

Are we obedient to the *rhema* word from his mouth? Do we respond when he issues the invitation, "Come and see?" Those who walk in response to this invitation are the ones who love him. *Hearkening to Father's voice is loving God.* This is the way and there is no other way. At least there's no other way to life—no other way to the Father's heart.

There is another way, but it leads to a life of alienation and broken relationships with friends and family. It leads to death and separation from Father's love. It's the way of insisting that everything go our way.

If our goal is to have intimate fellowship with the Father, this is the only way: we must enter into Jesus' way of relating to his Father. Jesus came to those whom his Father loved and became neighbor to all of us. We must allow our Father's love to flow through us to his neighbors who are also ours.

## The Manifest Presence

*"And he who loves me will be loved by my Father, and I will love him"* (Jn. 14:21). But wait! I thought God loved the whole world. Does this mean we must work ourselves up to a certain level of obedience before he'll love us? Many believe they must earn God's love by doing all the right things. If John meant this, he would be contradicting other passages that insist on God's love for all his creation.

Here John is indicating a special manifestation of God's love that's waiting for the beloved who choose to enter into mutual abiding. There's no greater love than that demonstrated by the Father sending his Son. There's no greater love than Jesus laying down his life on the cross. *God doesn't love the obedient more; he simply loves them in a different way.*

There's a distinct and appropriate blessing waiting for the obedient sons. It's not earned; it's just the nature of things—like gravity. Those who respond to the invitation, "Come and see," will find this blessing.

*"I will love him and manifest myself to him"* (Jn. 14:21). The special blessing to those who keep his commandments is the *manifest presence of Jesus Christ*. God shows up when we do what we see our Father doing. That's what happened at the pool when Jesus healed the paralytic. Jesus did on earth what he saw his Father doing in heaven. When he did, his Father's presence was manifested in the paralytic's ability to pick up his pallet and walk.

The Father was with the Son before the paralytic walked. But that presence wasn't evident until it was demonstrated in the miracle. The Father abiding in the Son was doing his work of healing. One may miss the significance of the event, as the Pharisees did. But the Father's presence was manifested even though they didn't see it. The world never sees the manifest presence.

In the same way, when we walk according to the *rhema* word of the God who is present to us in Jesus Christ by the Holy Spirit, his presence is manifest in some tangible way in our situation. If the will of God is actually accomplished through our words or acts we will know he was really there in a manifest way. It will be obvious to us and to others who are in the abiding place; but the unbelievers may not see it.

We know he's always there: he is omnipresent. But most of us have tried to do his will in our own strength enough times to know that his presence isn't always obvious in what we're doing. Manifest presence means we can know it by observing the effect it has on us or on the people around us.

## How Will He Do That?

*"Lord, how is it that you will manifest yourself to us, and not to the world"* (Jn. 14:22). Jesus' answer to this question clarifies the dialogue that began in verse one. It's as though Judas, not Iscariot, had said, "That's a neat trick, coming to us in a way that we see you but the world will not see. How are you going to do that?"

Notice that Judas missed the point. He was centered on the sensational and curious aspect of what Jesus said. He hadn't really heard what needs to be heard. This is typical of all the disciples before the resurrection. John seems to have anticipated that his readers in every generation would do the same thing. He records the question and its answer to nail down the heart of the matter for us.

*"If a man loves me, he will keep my word"* (Jn. 14:23). In answer to the question Jesus simply repeats what he just said. It is obvious to him that his words hadn't found a place in the disciples' understanding. Jesus is saying something like, "Don't be overly impressed with the sensational aspect of this event of manifestation. Focus on your part as a disciple. If you concern yourself with hearing and obeying the *rhema* word that comes to you while you're abiding in Father's bosom, the rest will *flow* as a matter of course. It isn't a matter of how I am going to manifest myself; it's a matter of your hearkening to the voice. The rest is my responsibility, not yours, so let me handle it.'"

## A Place for God in the Earth

*"And we will come to him and make our home with him"* (Jn. 14:23). The word for 'home' here is literally 'abiding place.' This is the same word used in 14:2 referring to the room in Father's house. *We have a place in him; but he's looking for a place in us.* The Father and the Son come to abide in us and in what we're doing when we hear and obey his voice. Jesus is saying, "If you'll let your daily life be determined by what you hear as you abide in me, then the Father and I will show up in your daily life. We won't merely be present *to* you; we will be present *in* you. But there's more. We'll also be *present in what you do* so you can *bear fruit* in every good work."

As the Father was present in Jesus at the healing of the paralytic, so the Father and the Son will be present to those who hear the *rhema* word and enter into the flow (*rhea*) of what God is doing in the earth.

When we say, "Jesus is in my heart," the word *in* should imply a dynamic abiding. It doesn't mean a surgeon might find Jesus if he performed open heart surgery. It means that Jesus now lives his life through me. "It is no longer I that live, but Christ who lives in me." This was a possibility for Paul because God was with him. It's also a possibility for us because he hasn't left us desolate. He has come to us by his Spirit.

The question *"Does Jesus live in your heart?"* can never be fully answered in words alone. It must be answered by *a life lived in the presence* of the Father and in response to his daily direction. As the Father lives out his vision through the obedience of his Son, so Jesus lives out his vision through the obedience of his disciples. His abiding is dynamic; it thrusts us into the world as ambassadors and witnesses. The goal of our lives is that we might follow his lead and be able to say with him, "The works that I do are not mine; but his who sent me. Jesus who abides in me is doing his works." That's what it means to have the Father and the Son at home (abiding) in your life.

Is Jesus *'at home'* in you? Or does he feel out of place because of how you react to other people? If he abides in you, then love (God) abides in you. The Father and the Son have a home *here* in the lives of those who have found a home *there* in the shared life of the Father with his many sons.

## The World Can't See It

Finally, notice that the world never recognizes the reality of the presence of God in the Christian who walks in this way. When people get healed, the world attributes it to hypnotism or to white magic. The world sees only and emotional experience when someone receives the baptism of the Holy Spirit. When someone's life is turned around and he's delivered from his sin and bondage, the world thinks he's simply turned over a new leaf or had an existential experience.

If a person of the world sees more than a natural phenomenon it's because the Father is drawing him or her to Jesus who is the way to the Father. By that miracle, the person's eyes are opened and his or her paralysis is healed. That person is drawn into the abiding place and is no longer of the world. In this way Jesus manifests himself to the disciples, and the world does not see.

## A Command and a Challenge

*"Rise, let us go hence"* (Jn. 14:31). It's significant that chapter 14 ends with this command. 'Rise' reminds us of the command to the paralytic. The disciples are commanded and empowered to enter into the reality of what's been described in this chapter. They are called to a path they have never traveled. But 'let *us*' contains a promise of his presence on the journey. He's leading the way. No! He IS the Way. We have but to hear his voice and rise, take up our pallet and allow his life to flow through us. He is with us as the Way, and on the way, to our destination in Father's love.

The word 'hence' indicates both a destination and a journey. The destination and the journey are the mutual abiding of the Father, Son and Holy Spirit with us and in us in the sense we have described. By his abiding in us, he does his work through us and the Kingdom of God comes to those who receive the work

The command is also an invitation to intimacy with God. The command and invitation are issued to all who will hear and respond. Jesus returned to the Father from whence he came; now we may go with him hence—into the Father's bosom. On our way to the Father we reflect the image of God by doing what we see him doing. We abide in the bosom of the Father as we respond to his *rhema* word of invitation and command.

Have you entered the abiding place? If not, then rise, let us go hence. Come along with him, with the Body of Christ, and see.

In our next chapter we'll see that they did come; they did see and enter the abiding place that day. We'll focus on "Day" as a sign of light that shows what's really there. We'll ask the question, "What comes to light in the Day of our presence with him and his presence with us?"

# CHAPTER 6

# The Light of Day

—ॐ—

The two disciples who follow Jesus begin their journey in response to the testimony of one who was not the light but who came to bear testimony to the light. The journey to the abiding place would not have continued if they'd not also heard Jesus' personal invitation to come and see. They do hear and respond to that invitation. The invitation contains a promise: "You will see."

All of us who respond to his invitation are healed of our paralysis and receive the ability to 'rise and go hence.' Our initial response does not bring us to the fulfilled promise—we don't see immediately. Our blindness is healed after we wash in the pool of Siloam (see Jn. 9:7). We must begin the journey before we receive our sight. We have to come again today; we have to follow Jesus again today. As we follow, we begin to see.

John's Gospel is written so that each time we read it we see more than we saw before. As we continue to read and follow the pointing signs in the stories, allowing our daily relationships to be transformed by what we see as we follow, we receive the promise attached to the call. We see more clearly each time we read the Gospel. The end of the Gospel is the beginning of a new life of following the resurrected

Lord. The beginning of the Gospel is the end of the old life of going our own way. New life begins to grow as we go through the Gospel again—as we begin to follow again.

We now continue our meditation by returning to the two disciples who followed Jesus. When they asked where he was abiding he invited them to come and see.

## Coming Precedes Seeing

*"They came and saw"* (Jn. 1:39). They see. This seeing points as a sign to the disciples' experience after the resurrection. They see the significance of the life of the one they'd followed for three years. Their blind eyes are healed as they follow Jesus toward the place in front of the empty tomb and behind the closed doors. They don't see by their human insight. Their seeing is no longer limited to their bubble images. They see what *IS*. Dimly indeed, but they see. Unlike the priests and Levites of the first day, these two (and every true disciple) can see what those of the world can never see. Nor are they like the multitude that tries to force Jesus into the mold of their expectation.

They don't come to the place of seeing until the 'tenth hour.' They follow before the resurrection without seeing because they hear and trust the voice of the one beckoning them. They trust because they see something in his walk; but they haven't yet seen the abiding place that made that walk possible. They can confess, *"You are the holy one of God"* (Jn. 6:69), but they don't yet understand what that means.

At this point in the development of the Gospel they are probably still thinking of the Holy Hero who will swoop down out of the sky and do violence to those who are violating their notions of truth. When Jesus speaks of himself as the way to the Father they still have to ask, *"Show us the Father."* They are following, but they don't yet have a revelation of what they're looking at. The tenth hour of seeing has not yet come.

## Following Without Understanding

Even though the disciples don't fully understand what they see, they arrive at the 'place' (in the presence of the resurrected Lord) because they are willing to follow. Even meeting him as the risen Lord doesn't bring them to instant understanding. They still need to follow for some distance before they see clearly.

For example, Peter still needed Jesus to challenge him during the third appearance. Peter even needed to be confronted by Paul years later (see Gal. 2:11). They were (and we are) much like the paralytic who didn't know *who* had healed him until Jesus returned (see Jn. 5:13-14). Or like the blind man who was healed but didn't know *where* Jesus was until he came again and made himself known (see Jn. 9:12, 35). The disciples had been healed of their paralysis and blindness, but it took time for them to receive the full revelation of *where* he is and *who* he is as the Son in Father's bosom.

If anyone wants to come to this place and see, he must embrace this position of humility. He must admit he doesn't know and must stop trying to force reality to conform to his preconceived notions. The significance of the tenth hour is that few of us, if any, see clearly early in our life of following. We must walk with him over a period of time before we begin to discard our human expectations. Then we can begin to embrace the revelation of who it is we are following and where he is leading us.

This "following without full understanding" doesn't end when Jesus is raised. One indication is that the early church didn't begin any missionary activity to the gentile world until at least five years after the outpouring of the Holy Spirit. Even then it took a supernatural vision to convince Peter to go to a Gentile's house and speak to his family and friends about Jesus. It took several more years before the leaders in the church at Jerusalem made an official statement about accepting Gentiles into the fellowship without insisting they keep the Law of Moses (see Acts 15).

There's always more to behold in God than what we've seen so far. The destination of this journey is a more intense and ever increasing intimacy with the Father and the Son through the Spirit. The deeper we go into this abiding relationship, the more we realize it's eternal and can never be fully experienced this side of the consummation of the Kingdom of God. Even 'over there' we may continue to increase in the intensity of this intimate relationship.

## Hindrances to Seeing

The Pharisees and rulers fail to see because they refuse to humble themselves in this way. They prejudge everything according their human standards. They stay where they are. They don't come and they don't see. They prefer the place they already occupy because it makes them look good and gives them authority over others. They never see. And their guilt remains because they say, "*We see*" (see Jn. 9:41). This position of power and authority appears secure but it has no future. It leads only to death with no resurrection. The humble position that says, "I don't see clearly yet," is necessary to advance to the next level of seeing.

Other reasons keep some from finding the abiding place. Some stay where they are until full understanding comes. They want to follow but are not willing to move without first seeing; they're unwilling to enter the way until they understand where they're going. Their 'god' is unable to do anything for them until they understand. "How can I follow when I don't understand?" is their position. The first step of true discipleship is to respond to the call to come. *Coming precedes seeing.* When we insist on having answers before we follow, God moves ahead and we are left behind.

Others strive to fulfill their own vision without considering God might actually be going the other way. "How could

God go any other way?" they query. "He knows my way is right. God is as smart as I am, so he must agree with me." They don't take time to be still and listen for his voice.

## *They See the Place*

These two disciples, and those they represent, stay on the path until they see. But what do they see?

*"Where he was staying* [abiding]..." (Jn. 1:39). In my view this 'seeing' is a sign of the seeing that takes place after the resurrection. When the Baptist draws attention to Jesus and the way he walks, that prompts the first two disciples to ask, "Where are you abiding?" They ask because they want to abide with him and walk as he walks. They respond to his invitation to come, but the real abiding for them is not yet available at this time because Jesus has not yet gone to prepare that place. He will have to go away before he can prepare that place for them in the Father's house. He promises to return and bring them to himself. He wants them to be where I AM (is)—in Father's bosom (see Jn. 14:3).

What is this sign of seeing pointing to? It's pointing to the place Jesus prepared for them in Father's bosom. They see what no eye has seen, nor ear heard, nor the heart of man conceived. They see what God has prepared for those who love him. They see those things that are only revealed by the Spirit (see I Cor. 2:9-10). They see the Son abiding in the Father and the Father abiding in the Son in the fellowship of the Holy Spirit.

Their eyes are opened because they are willing to follow without first understanding. They're willing to follow because they answer the question, "What do you seek?" with their own question, "Where do you abide?" They are seeking the abiding place.

## Abiding with Him

"*And they stayed* [abode] *with him*" (Jn. 1:39). They enter into the abiding place. Jesus brings them to himself and in him they find themselves in the bosom of the Father of light. They remain (abide) in that dynamic relationship through which the will of the Father is done through the obedience of the Son in the power of the Spirit. They remain in that place—in the household of God—where the Son can do nothing on his own accord but only what he sees the Father doing. They become functioning members of the Body of Christ and let him move in the earth through their daily activity. Jesus welcomes them into the eternal fellowship of the Trinitarian God.

Yes, they *flounder* in that place, but it is *in that place* that they flounder. Yes, they make mistakes, but Father doesn't put them out of his tummy pack. They let Father pick them up when they fell. They continue to abide with him as those who blunder. Because of that abiding relationship, the Lord is able to do many mighty works through them in spite of, or better yet, because of their weakness. When we give our weakness to him in the abiding place, God's power is made perfect in our weakness (see II Cor. 12:9).

## In the Light of Day

"*They stayed* [abode]... *that day*" (Jn. 1:39). This brings us to this chapter's major theme. Which day? The phrase, *that* day, appears several times in John. It's the day when the spiritually dead "*will hear the voice of the Son of God, and those who hear will live*" (Jn. 5:25). It's the day when we "*worship the Father in spirit and truth*" (Jn. 4:23). It's the day when he promised, "*I will not leave you desolate*" (Jn 14:18)—the day he doesn't leave us alone in doing Father's will. It's the day when he manifests himself to us but the world does not see him (see Jn. 14:18-20).

This is the day of abiding. All these statements point to the day when they see him in his glory after the resurrection and receive the outpouring of the Holy Spirit. This is also the day when the Father and the Son come to us as we respond to him in obedience. It's 'Day' because the sunlight of the New Creation is shining—seeing is made possible.

The place of abiding is Jesus Christ himself. He is himself the place where the Father abides in the earth. He is himself the place where true disciples abide in Father's heart. He's also the way to that place in the Father. And he is himself the light that shines in that place in that day. He is the light of the world (see Jn. 9:5). To abide in him is to walk in the light of his Day. *This is the day that the Lord has made* (see Ps. 118:24). Let's rejoice and be glad in the light of this day. The Son is shining.

### *Light and Darkness in I John*

The motif of light and darkness, night and day, runs through John's gospel and his first epistle. Let's turn our attention to this theme of light and darkness. What does it mean to walk in the light or to abide with him in the Day when this Light is shining? As usual, some surprises are in store for those who have not yet followed the theme as John presents it. What do the signs of light and darkness point to?

Before we trace light and darkness through John's gospel, let's unpack key statements in I John, chapters 1-2. In my limited experience as a prayer minister, I've seen many Christians flounder in self-condemnation because they misunderstand the verses we are about to consider. John wrote this letter to comfort and encourage the community of believers, but these verses have discouraged and discomforted many. We feel condemned because we approach the verses assuming we already know what they mean.

### Walk as He Walked

We will limit our discussion to certain phrases related to walking and the light. We begin with I John 2:6. John says, *"...he who says he abides in him ought to walk in the same way in which he walked."*

*"He who says he abides in him."* This exposes the possibility of claims not based in reality. It's easy to present ourselves as abiding with Jesus Christ in the bosom of the Father. We can even convince ourselves we're abiding, but there's an 'ought' related to this claim. There's a way to test the validity of our claim.

*"Ought to walk in the same way in which he walked."* Our talk ought to relate to our walk. A specific walk is appropriate for those who say they're abiding in him. Jesus' walk caught John the Baptist's attention and evoked the testimony, *"Behold the Lamb of God."* If we're not walking in that way, we ought not to say we're abiding in him. If we *say* we abide, we ought to *walk* this walk. Abiding is directly related to walking.

So what is the nature of this walk in I John? For an answer, we turn to I John 1:5-9. *"This is the message we have heard from him and proclaim to you, that God is light and in him there is not darkness at all. If we say we have fellowship with him while we walk in darkness, we lie and do not live according to the truth."* As we unpack these verses we will be looking for the key that will allow us to read without feeling condemned by what we read.

### In God's Light

*"God is light and in him is no darkness at all."* Here John introduces the theme of light and darkness. *Light* often points to moral uprightness, ethical purity, or righteousness. *Darkness* often refers to wickedness, uncleanness, and corruption. These words certainly are used that way in scripture sometimes, but not here. God is upright and ethically

pure; he has no wickedness or uncleanness in him. But it's a mistake to assume John is using the words that way here; this mistake brings many Christians into self-condemnation. Follow John's thought and his meaning will become clear.

(In what follows I will attempt to bring to expression the turmoil that comes into the minds of those who have believed that walking in the light means being sinless. This is the religious tradition I was raised in. The discussion is especially for those who share the anxieties that come from this form of legalism.)

## *Our Dilemma*

*"If we say we have fellowship with him."* John uses *fellowship* here in a similar way that he uses the word *'abide'* in his Gospel. Fellowship implies a joint participation, a coming together, and sharing a common activity or experience. To have fellowship with God who is light means to walk in his light. We desire the reality of that joint participation. We can be involved in what we mistakenly think is fellowship with God when he's not with us in what we're doing. We may be in fellowship with our own vision and participating with many who share our vision. If so—if our vision didn't come from him—God isn't participating with us in what we are doing. There's no joint participation and no fellowship between us and God while we're following our own vision.

*"While we walk in darkness...."* If by darkness John means not living by an ethical code as well as God does, he's saying no one can have fellowship with God (who is light) if he fails to walk in perfection. How righteous do I have to be before I can have fellowship with God? John isn't talking about some internal, imputed righteousness that is somehow "in me" with no outward manifestation. He's talking about the way we walk in our daily encounters with our family, fellow-workers and neighbors.

If I have to be perfectly upright in my walk before I can have fellowship with God, I'll never make it. The only way any of us can be conformed to the image of the firstborn Son and walk as he walked is through fellowship with him. The fellowship must precede the growth. The problem is that this text is often interpreted to mean we must have perfect behavior before can we have fellowship. If perfection is necessary for fellowship we'll never have fellowship and therefore never grow into perfection.

*"We lie and do not live according to the truth."* Most of us are willing to proclaim to our neighbors and fellow Christians that we have fellowship with God. But if you examine my life in light of this "if clause" and find any weakness or uncleanness, my proclamation is exposed as a lie. I'm not living according to the truth. But if I confess that I have failures in my life, then I'm in another predicament: I'm exposed as one who doesn't have fellowship with God. What a dilemma! Beyond the social dilemma however, is the more serious threat of being out of fellowship with God

## Our Only Hope

John's discussion of light and fellowship continues: *"But if we walk in the light, as he is in the light, we have fellowship with one another, and the blood of Jesus his Son cleanses us from all sin. If we say we have no sin, we deceive ourselves, and the truth is not in us. If we confess our sins, he is faithful and just, and will forgive our sins and cleanse us from all unrighteousness"* (I Jn. 1:7-9).

*"But if we walk in the light."* Walking in the light is the very thing I can't do if this means being as righteous as God is. I can will what is right, but I can't do it (see Rom. 7:18). I don't always fail; but I do fail. How many failures does God allow before I'm out of fellowship with him? How many times may I stumble in the way before I'm thrust out of the

way? Have I already failed too many times? Perhaps I can rely on God's grace and only walk in partial light.

These thoughts reveal the insecurity of the believer who interprets the *light* as moral and spiritual perfection.

*"As he is in the light...."* Well, so much for that hope of being accepted if I only partially walk in the light. *"In him there is no darkness at all."* A person with this misunderstanding might despairingly feel like Jesus is requiring more than we are equipped to do—as though Jesus came to earth, boarded his private jet, flew around the world in ten hours (some jet, huh?), and then said, "Do as I have done. Here's a bicycle for you." How can I do as he has done when I don't have the equipment he had? How can I walk in the light as he is in the light as long as I am in my humanity?

*"We have fellowship with one another."* This promise comes with walking in the light—fellowship with one another. Does this refer to the disciples having fellowship with one another? Yes, but there is more. *"In that day* [in that light] *you will know that I am in my Father, and you in me, and I in you"* (Jn.14:20). We're also brought into the place where the Father loves the Son and the Son loves the Father in the fellowship of the Holy Spirit. He welcomes us into the Trinitarian Hug, if you please. All this is available if, and only if, we walk in the light as he is in the light.

In all this back-and-forth one thing presents itself to every believer as certain—we all know we have fellowship with God and we all know we have fellowship with other Christians. All the confusion that rises (at least in the tradition I was raised in) does not shake the inner certainty of our relationship with God. In the midst of the anxiety we know that we are known by a loving Father. We believe but, like the father of the demonized boy, we need help with our unbelief (see Mk. 9:24).

## Walking in Light Brings Forgiveness

If John had concluded his thought at this point we would have reason to confuse the issue. But John is not finished. He gives testimony to the help available to us through the shed blood of Jesus.

*"And the blood of Jesus his Son cleanses us from all sin."* Suddenly our legalistic line of reasoning no longer makes sense. If walking in the light means living a life without sin, then we would not need the blood of Jesus to cleanse us of anything. Follow the development. First we have: *"if we walk in the light,"* then we have the results of walking in the light: *"the blood of Jesus cleanses."* At this point those of us who have been influenced by this way of thinking must reevaluate our interpretation of the concept of light in this passage.

We must understand 'walking in the light' in such a way that it allows for failures because *walking in the light is the condition that brings forgiveness.*

*"If we say we have no sin, we deceive ourselves."* John is not engaging in double talk or contradiction. The person who's walking in the light must be willing to confess his sin. Otherwise he's self-deceived. What we're about to uncover should help those who can't stand under the pressure of the legalistic interpretation of this text.

Here's the situation that comes from the legalistic interpretation. Someone might claim to live without sin to avoid the trauma of being exposed to their friends as one who is out of fellowship with God. If deep down inside they know they're putting up a front, they are liars. If they really believe their claim, they're self-deceived. In either case, there is a serious problem.

The pressure to keep up the front doesn't allow them to be open and honest. Without this openness—without walking in the light—there's no real fellowship with anyone. It's like each is wearing a mask and the masks are having fellowship, but no one really knows the one behind the mask in an intimate way. Some don't even know who they are behind their own mask. If I don't know myself, I can't give myself to you.

*Without openness there can be no intimacy.* If we desire intimacy we must be open to ourselves, open to others, and open to God. Any attempt to cover ourselves takes us out of intimacy in all relationships.

## Acknowledging Sin is Walking in Light

*"If we confess our sins, he is faithful and just, and will forgive our sins and cleanse us from all unrighteousness."* Here we have another 'if clause'. Those who become clean and righteous before God are the ones who openly confess their sins. Those who try to hide their iniquity receive no forgiveness and no cleansing. The way into fellowship with God is "not because of deeds done by us in righteousness, but in virtue of his own mercy" (Tit.3:5). The way to the cleansing available through the blood of Jesus is not by working ourselves up to a certain level of righteousness to be acceptable. The cleansing comes to those who are open about what's inside and confess their failures. Walking in the light is allowing the light of God's presence to expose our sin and taking the humble position of confession and repentance.

## An Advocate with the Father

Now we turn to I John 2:1-2. *"I am writing this to you so that you may not sin."* In my early years of preparing for ministry I ran across this statement and the thought ran through my mind, "Oh no! It is too late, John. I've already sinned." The church of my early development gave me the impression that all the sins we committed before we were baptized were washed away, but woe to the one who sins after he's baptized. We were on our own to try to do enough good works to balance out the sins we committed. I am so thankful for the next phrase.

*"But if any one does sin, we have an advocate with the Father, Jesus Christ the righteous."* *The love of God is love for sinners.* The idea that sins after baptism are not covered is totally ridiculous. That would mean God loves the world and saves them by grace, but the Father becomes an ogre to his own kids. There's much freedom in knowing that he also forgives us even after we're saved. We—we Christians—have an advocate with the Father. We have an advocate *because we need one.* Knowing we have an advocate brings great freedom; but the freedom it brings isn't freedom to sin. Freedom isn't the absence of restriction. God forbid we should continue in sin (see Rom. 6:1-2). He gives freedom so that we might do our Father's will.

From I John we've learned that the *open confession of sin* is included in John's *concept* of *walking in the light.* Walking in the light puts us in a position to receive cleansing by the blood of Jesus. Confession of sin is walking in the light and that confession is answered by forgiveness of sin and cleansing of the tendency. With this insight we'll approach the theme of light and darkness in the Gospel.

## *The Woman Caught in Adultery*

We now turn to the story of the woman caught in adultery in John 8. In this story, the accent is on Jesus as the light that exposes the sinner in his or her sin. It's a sign pointing to the meaning of walking in the light. This is often missed in spite of the fact that this story is followed immediately by the proclamation, *"I am the light of the world"* (Jn 8:12). Even though many overlook this emphasis, it seems to be the main point of the story. Let's follow this story's development so we can understand how it relates to walking in the light as he is in the light.

## Dawning Revelation

*"Early in the morning..."* (Jn. 8:2). In the introduction to this story, the light is beginning to make its presence known. Day is dawning. The light is not shining in its full intensity yet, but as the light dawns in the early morning we begin to be aware of it. Creatures of the night that depend on darkness and obscurity to accomplish their work must now look for cover to hide their activity.

Cover-up and hiding can be effective as long as the light is not shining in its full brilliance. As the light increases in brightness, creatures of darkness must increase their attempt to hide. They'll soon be looking for caves and rocks to hide themselves from this light (see Rev. 6:15). But it's early; they need not rush. At least they haven't felt any urgency. The light that's beginning to shine is quite different from any human light that may have tried to expose them up to this point.

Actually this light had been dawning since the fall of man. The light making its debut here is that life mentioned in John 1:4-5: *"In him was life, and the life was the light of men. The light shines in darkness, and the darkness has not overcome it."* This light *"enlightens every man,"* and it was always coming into the world (Jn. 1:9). The coming of this light had not yet shown itself in a way that the night creatures were apprehensive. It's still shining in darkness. They still think they'll be able to hide.

## Light Exposes What's There

The phrase *"that enlightens every man,"* requires some comment. *Enlighten* simply means to shed light on or to illuminate. It doesn't refer to intellectual enlightenment here. Obviously every man hasn't been enlightened in that sense. When light is shining on an object, it's lifted from obscurity and shown to be what it really is.

This light—which is Jesus Christ himself—shines on all of us and exposes us for what we really are. Men and women who are spiritually blind can be exposed without even knowing they've been exposed. Their lack of awareness, however, doesn't change the fact that they've been exposed. They've been enlightened and illuminated and don't even know it.

*"All the people came to him"* (Jn. 8:2). Here we have the crowd, the multitude. Among them are some whose eyes have begun to be opened. But most of them haven't yet seen. They don't know into whose presence they've come. None of them have seen clearly, not even the disciples, because it's still early. But *seeing* isn't the point here. The real issue is being exposed by the light—*being seen*. He who is there among them has light in himself and can see clearly what's in front of him. He knows what's hiding there in the darkness behind cloaks of pretended righteousness. He knows what the night creatures are up to. He doesn't need anyone to bear witness about any man, for he knows what's in each one present (see Jn. 2:25).

## Exposing the Sin of Others

*"The scribes and the Pharisees brought a woman who had been caught in adultery"* (Jn. 8:3). Those who walk in the darkness—the creatures of the night—are always willing to use their own human light to expose the sins of others. These particular night creatures are a sign pointing to those who try to walk under the law by their own strength and human understanding. They're not lawless men; they're not the misfits of society or the outcasts and offscourings of humanity. They're actually the best this world has to offer. They're members in good standing among the chosen community of God. They take seriously a life of purity and righteousness according to the law.

Paul spoke of this group when he wrote, "Israel who pursued the righteousness which is based on law did not succeed in fulfilling that law. Why? Because they did not pursue it through faith, but as if it were based on works" (Rom. 9:31-32). Paul also recognized that this group's tendency to judge others was an indication that the judges are trying to obscure the fact that they're also sinners. "Therefore you have no excuse, O man, whoever you are, when you judge another; for in passing judgment upon him you condemn yourself, because you, the judge, are doing the very same things" (Rom. 2:1-2).

So these scribes and Pharisees bring the woman to Jesus. Their interest isn't in the woman or in the judgment Jesus might give. They're out to trap him, to bring him under the false light of their judgment. They think they can expose him by their human light. They want to make him look like a sinner in the eyes of others. They aren't aware that their light is actually darkness.

*"Moses commanded us to stone such. What do you say about her?"* (Jn. 8:5). These men are trying to use Moses as a veil to hide their evil intent. They're the sons of those at Mount Sinai who asked Moses to cover his face when they saw the light of the presence of God reflected there. Those who were 'his own' in the world, who received him not, have always wanted to veil this light. They secretly know that if they ever let this light shine in its fullness, they'll be exposed as sinners. Some tried to put out the light before it came to its full brilliance by killing the prophets—as though the prophets were the source of the light that came through their words.

These scribes and Pharisees move in the pale shadows of their human interpretation of the law as they try to accomplish their evil deed. Little do they know that the one they are moving against is himself the true light. He can see through their ill constructed veil.

## The Trap is Set

"*What do you say about her?*" They don't know this is really an appropriate question for Jesus. He's the one who can say, "You have heard it said...but I say." They're asking the only man who's ever been qualified to answer their question with authority. He's the only one qualified to add his own personal, "But I say," to the Law of Moses. He's the only one who knows what's in his Father's heart toward those who sin.

"*This they said to test him, that they might have some charge to bring against him*" (Jn. 8:6). There were two schools of thought in Judaism regarding the death penalty. One group taught that the law must be followed with ruthless strictness. If the law said, "Stone such," then the judge had a responsibility under God to carry out that penalty. There was no room for mercy. The other group taught that the law must be applied with mercy and concern for the individual case. If the defendant was a frequent offender then the death penalty might be considered.

These two factions actually join forces against Jesus. Later they'll even join Rome to accomplish their deed. Those who walk in darkness gladly join others in darkness when a crisis arises, even if they are arch enemies.

Follow the thinking of the scribes and Pharisees who bring this woman to Jesus for a verdict. "If he says stone her," they conspire, "we can accuse him of being merciless and cruel. He'll lose the respect of the multitudes following him. But if he says she should be released and given another chance, we can accuse him of rejecting Moses. In this case, the court will certainly hand down a death sentence for Jesus. Either way he answers, we've got him. He'll be exposed as a sinner." Thus the trap is set. They wait to pull the string when he answers.

As they wait they're only vaguely aware of the fact that they normally accuse one another of being merciless or too merciful in their response to other sinners. They know they are on opposite sides of this debate. Which ever side Jesus takes will condemn the other side. Which side will Jesus take?

"*Jesus bent down and wrote*" (Jn. 8:6). Commentaries usually emphasize the writing. They offer many interesting and fruitful suggestions about what he may have written or the meaning of the act of writing. There is value to those suggestions but text doesn't give us an answer. It seems to me that the accent should fall on the fact that he bent down. He stooped as he listened for Father's voice. He took a position below these men who set themselves up as judges. He has no insecurities to drive him to strive for the upper hand. He's not grasping for victory.

## The Trap is Sprung

"*Let him who is without sin among you be the first to throw a stone at her*" (Jn. 8:7). The trap is sprung and he's not caught. *But they are.* If any one should pick up a stone, he'd immediately lose the others' respect. He'd be claiming perfect righteousness in the presence of peers who know otherwise. They each know what the others are hiding and each knows the other is judging him. But if they don't pick up a stone, they're confessing themselves to be sinners and also subject to judgment.

What a dilemma! "How can I keep myself covered so the darkness in me will not be exposed?" Each has to make his own decision.

"*They went away, one by one*" (Jn. 8:9). They're not merely going away from a physical place. They're walking away from the light that has exposed them. "*This is the judgment, that light has come into the world, and men loved darkness rather that light, because their deed were evil. For every one who does evil hates the light, and does not come to the light, lest his deeds should be exposed*" (Jn. 3:19-20). Yet in walking away from the light, they didn't escape exposure—they revealed their deeds as evil by walking away from the light. Jesus, the light of the world, illumines every one of us and exposes what we really are. Darkness can't overcome this light and avoid exposure (see Jn. 1:4).

These men may have heard what Jesus said about adultery: "You have heard that it was said, 'you shall not commit adultery.' But I say to you that every one who looks at a woman lustfully has already committed adultery with her in his heart" (Matt. 5:27-28). If they did know of that statement, they may have expected him to pronounce the death sentence on this woman. At any rate, when Jesus asked the one without sin to cast the first stone each knew his own private thought life.

Sins of the heart are easy to hide from others. All you have to do is walk away from the light that exposes you. Just hide what you're thinking and doing in private. These Pharisees probably think Jesus will judge them if they admit they have lust. They probably have already judged themselves because they've done the same thing in their thoughts. That's why they walk away. They don't really understand the implications of the, "But I say unto you," statements in Matthew. Those statements weren't intended to make a law that's more difficult to keep than the one in Exodus.

Jesus came to reveal the Father's love, not his judgment. He was simply indicating that *we are all equally in need of his forgiveness and cleansing.* The one who did it and the one who thought it are equally qualified to receive forgiveness by walking in the light and confessing their sins. But the scribes and Pharisees walk away.

### Jesus Liberates the Woman

*"Jesus was left alone with the woman standing before him"* (Jn. 8:9). All her accusers have gone. She's there alone with Jesus the light of the world. Like the Pharisees she has also been exposed. She's "open and laid bare to the eyes of

him with whom we have to do" (Heb. 4:13). But since the accusers have gone away, she's legally free to go. Without witnesses there can be no day in court.

*"Jesus looked up and said, 'Woman, where are they? Has no one condemned you?"* (Jn. 8:10). Jesus had stooped. The woman is standing. I'm amazed at his humility. He doesn't make this sinful woman take a position below him. He's willing to look up to her. She represents the bottom of the barrel of society. He has stooped to a position beneath her, below the barrel if you please. He doesn't recoil at the thought of being under. For this the Father sent him into the world. From this position, he will be able to lift up every one above him when he is raised from the dead. This hope and promise is for all who come to the light and remain fully exposed in their sin. By walking away from the light the scribes and Pharisees have removed themselves from the barrel that will be raised up in the last day.

*"Has no one condemned you?"* There were none. She's free to go. No one can legally bring her to court except the Lord himself. Yet she chooses to remain in his presence fully exposed. Standing in that light she's uncovered, but she remains (abides) in the light. She isn't walking away from the light as the others have done. She has no way of knowing what his verdict will be. I can't help but wonder if she was tempted to walk away. But she seems to sense that this man is a friend of sinners. So she remains in his light. What will his judgment be? She waits for the gavel to fall.

*"Neither do I condemn you; go and do not sin again"* (Jn. 8:11). The one without sin doesn't condemn the sinner who remains in the light. *It's only those with something to hide that need to condemn others.* This keeps the attention away from them or makes them feel acceptable because they're at least better than others. Jesus has nothing to hide and nothing to prove. He is the light in whom there is no darkness at all.

We often put our fellowman in a bad light because we think it puts us in a good light and makes us look better. Jesus puts his fellowman in his own good light so his fellowman will *be* better. We don't look very good in his light at first. We are exposed. But his forgiveness and cleansing are available to those who are willing to walk in the light of his presence fully exposed. As we walk in the light, confessing ourselves to be the sinners we are, fully exposed in our wickedness, he is faithful to forgive and to cleanse, and we become sons and daughters of light (see Jn. 12:36).

## *Jesus Empowers Her*

*"Go, and do not sin again."* Jesus doesn't forgive us so we can be free to sin. He forgives us and cleanses us *from* sin. By that forgiveness and cleansing, he sets us free from the *power* of sin. When we excuse our sins or cover ourselves and hide from the light, we remove ourselves from the possibility of the exposure that will set us free. We remain in the darkness of denial and cover-up. In that darkness we try to do enough good deeds to balance out the evil in us. It's never enough, because we're still exposed as those who walk away from the light. Or we try to do at least enough good to convince others that we're free from sin. Their affirmation makes us *feel* better; but it does not make us *better*. Even if we can keep others in the dark about our secrets, we're still open and laid bare before the one who is the light.

Paul says, "The power of sin is the law" (I Cor. 15:56). As long as we try to please God by the goodness of our own doing—by keeping the law—sin continues to have power in our lives. Sin has power because rather than letting it be exposed, we try to hide it from the very light that would bring us freedom. The only power that can free us from sin is the light that exposes us. Like Adam, we hide behind our fig leaves because we're afraid. That which hides from the light is in darkness still. He who lives a covered life walks in darkness.

We try to hide because *we're not convinced the Father really loves us*. We think he will come down hard on us if he ever finds out what we have done (as though he doesn't know). *Hiding in the darkness is evidence of the lack of faith in a loving faithful Father*. At least we don't trust him to protect us form being exposed to other people.

On the other hand, when we let ourselves be fully exposed we can hear the omnipotent voice that says to us, "***Go, and do not sin again***." Hearing that voice empowers us to over-come the sin, it cleanses us from the unrighteous tendency in our hearts. "While we were still weak, at the right time Christ died for the ungodly" (Rom. 5:6). Jesus didn't come for those who are righteous according to a legalist system. He came for sinners. All you have to do to qualify for this forgiveness is to be an ungodly sinner who walks in the light of exposure.

When the light begins to dawn in your life and your sins are being exposed, don't walk away. Stand there and *trust the love that sent the light* into the world to liberate you. Boldly confess, "I'm the ungodly sinner you died for!"

## Hiding from the Light

"***Again Jesus spoke to them***" Jn. 8:12). To whom did he speak? To the scribes and the Pharisees, the ones who'd tried to trick him with their question. "But I thought they went away," you say. Yes, they went away. John is trying to call attention to something by telling the story this way. He wants us to notice that these men had withdrawn themselves from the threat of exposure. They went 'under cover' so the light would not be so bright.

They covered themselves with their self-righteous robes and missed the covering that Love makes available—the blood of Jesus. They didn't leave the vicinity; they only distanced themselves from the light. They still intended to find a way to charge him with some crime worthy of death.

*"I am the light of the world; he who follows me will not walk in darkness, but will have the light of life"* (Jn. 8:12). The woman had received the light of life. She had received because she was willing to face him as the sinner she was. Not so the scribes and Pharisees. They had too much to lose by open confession. (They really had much more to lose by refusing to confess. But one doesn't see that sort of thing when he's walking in darkness.) They would lose their chief seats in the synagogues. They would lose the glory they were accustomed to receiving from men.

They would also lose their sins. But that's the one thing they couldn't bring themselves to admit they had. The freedom that would come by confession would cost them more than they were willing to pay. They would lose their reputation among men if they were exposed.

## Seeking without Finding

*"I go away, and you will seek me and die in your sin; where I am going, you cannot come"* (Jn. 8:21). They will die in their sin because they refuse to admit they have any sin. Their guilt will remain because they walk away from the light that makes forgiveness possible. They cover themselves from the light of life by their long flowing robes of self-righteousness. Nakedness is too threatening to them because without their fancy fig leaves they look just like everyone else. Their manner of dress has become a substitute for an intimate relationship with God. They have come to identify with the clothes they use to cover their nakedness. As long as they're dressed right, they feel righteous. Proper dress and proper behavior both cover what's in their hearts.

From the other gospels we learn that there's a seeking that finds. "Ask, and it will be given you; seek, and you will find; knock, and it will be opened to you" (Lk. 11:9). In John, we learn that there's a seeking that doesn't find what really needs to be found. When we seek to establish our own righteousness we never find his righteousness. When we seek to establish our own way we never find Jesus, the true way. No amount of seeking will be able to find when we're walking in darkness.

This brings us back to the question of chapter three: *"What do you seek?"* Your own glory? Or his presence?

*"Where I am going, you cannot come."* He's going to the Father. He's going to prepare a place in the Father's house for sinners who walk in the light and receive forgiveness and cleansing. The whole world is invited to that place of intimacy in the Father's bosom. Those who join him on this journey will come to the Father. But walking with him requires walking in the light of exposure. It involves a willingness to remain in that embarrassing condition of being open and laid bare in his light.

Scribes and Pharisees aren't willing to be exposed, so they can't come to that place. Because of this unwillingness they'll never come, they'll never be healed of their spiritual paralysis. They'll never have their eyes opened to see the abiding place in the Father. They'll miss all this because of their unwillingness to face their sin when the light comes and exposes them.

### Will You Remain?

Are you walking in the light of exposure? If so, this is the word of the Lord to you, *"Neither do I condemn you, go, and do not sin again."* If you've tried to follow that command and discovered that you are not able to overcome sin by your own power and wisdom, then hear this word of encouragement: *"We have an advocate with the Father, Jesus Christ the righteous; and he is the expiation for our sins, and not for ours only but also for the sins of the whole world"* (I Jn. 2:1-2). Don't walk away or cover yourself with a self-righteous robe when the light shines on you. Walk in the light. Come to the abiding place and abide with him in the light of this day.

John tells us of another sinful woman: the woman at the well. We turn our attention to her in the next chapter.

# CHAPTER 7

# Living Water

—ⁿⁿ∿—

W e've seen that we must follow before we're able to see his abiding place. The two disciples came to that place and stayed with him that day. We understood the day to represent the presence of the Son who is the light of the world. Our sins are forgiven as we walk in the light of his presence, fully exposed, and confessing ourselves to be the sinners we are. We illustrated that with the story of the woman caught in the act of adultery. The Pharisees who were trying to expose Jesus walked away from the light of exposure. They weren't able to go where he was going—into the bosom of Father's love—simply because they weren't walking in the light.

## *Introducing the Woman at the Well*

There's another significant sinful woman in John. It's the woman at the well near Sychar, in Samaria. The impact of this story is profound once the reader follows the arrow and finds the real point. The impact comes when we realize the significance of the woman's response when she finally catches on to what Jesus is offering her.

This story also illustrates the integrity of the Gospel. As we noticed in the introduction, each of the stories and dialogues in John is related to all others. They play off one another. Each element of each story is echoed somewhere else in the Gospel. The structure in John makes it easier to see more deeply into the mystery of Christ each time you read through it. Once we recognize the significance of the way stories relate to one another we begin each new journey through the Gospel from a higher place on the 'spiral staircase' to the abiding place. Each time we go around to the same place on the staircase, we view the same stories from a higher level and we see our life in Christ from a new perspective as well.

John places this story in a parallel structure to the story of Nicodemus. John is contrasting the lowest member of the *religious* society with the most highly respected and influential Jewish leaders. The structure of chapters 2 through 4 connects the woman specifically with Nicodemus by placing the two on opposite ends of a 'teeter totter' with the testimony of the Baptist as the fulcrum. The Baptist's response to his disciples who were leaving him for Jesus is the center that balances the two opposite ways of responding to Jesus.

Nicodemus is a righteous man; she's a sinful woman. He's a ruler of the Jews; she's a Samaritan outcast. He comes to Jesus by night (that implies darkness); she comes at midday. He comes knowing who Jesus is, or at least thinking he knows. She comes without a clue. He's confused by Jesus' teaching; she comes to see him for who he really is. He goes away empty; she goes forward with living water.

The Nicodemus story is the obvious "mirror image" of the woman at the well, but rippled reflections of various elements of this woman's story ebb and flow throughout the Gospel. We'll notice some of them as we unpack the story.

## Some Keys to Understanding

To understand this story, it helps to understand where it took place. Jacob's well is in the valley between Mount

Ebal and Mount Gerizim. The Law proclaims both blessings and curses: blessings to those who keep the law, curses
to those who don't. God told the people to place the blessings on Mount Gerizim and the curses on Mount Ebal. The
Samaritans built the national worship center of their bastard
religion (as the Jews saw it) on the Mount of Blessings.
Sychar is on the Mount of Curses. The women of Sychar
would go down the slopes of the cursed mountain to the well
to get fresh water. When she went to worship she'd pass the
well in the valley on her way to Mount Gerizim.

Another fact helps us understand the development of the
story. What we call "running water" the Hebrews call "living
water." Living (running) water from a mountain stream is
fresh and satisfies thirst in a way that water from a cistern
(tap water) can never do. The term 'living water' isn't new
to the woman. But in the movement of the story from spiritual blindness to revelation, she discovers a heavenly reality
that's much more satisfying than running water.

## Setting the Mood

Let's observe the context of this story to get in touch with
the ambiance that surrounds it. Picture a woman dressed in
the traditional garb of the day—covered from head to foot
in black. No flesh shows except her eyes and forehead, her
hands, and, as she walks, her feet beneath her covering. Her
hands are callused from the hard labor required of women in
her time. As she walks down the dusty slope of the mount of
curses, notice her feet are bruised and scarred from stumbling
on the path she's followed for so long, the path of seeking for
love in all the wrong places.

Her eyes reveal disappointment and disillusionment.
Hopelessness covers her countenance like the black robe
that covers her body. On her forehead she wears guilt and
shame from the life she's lived. She can't cast her gaze down
to avoid eye contact because she must balance the jar on her

head, but her eyes hide deep in their sockets. She doesn't want to be seen.

She's coming down the slope to draw from the well Jacob gave to his son Joseph. Her thirst draws her. The well is hand-dug, about 100 feet deep. It taps into an underground stream flowing from the mountain toward the springs of the Jordan River. There's living, running water at the bottom. She probably has water from a cistern in the city, perhaps even a family cistern in her house—something like a rain barrel that collects water when it rains. But she's thirsty for fresh, living water. Still, stale water from the cisterns doesn't satisfy her.

She has probably been coming to this well daily for a long time. She's chosen the hour when the sun is at its peak because other women come in the cool of the morning. At high noon she can avoid their condemning looks and accusing voices. She's a reject and an outcast among them. She seems to be favored among men but for all the wrong reasons. Men don't normally come to the well to draw; that's women's work. So she feels relatively secure coming at midday. But today she's in for a surprise.

As she approaches the well, she sees a man sitting nearby. She knows he's a Jew by the way he's dressed. She proceeds cautiously, yet relatively secure because men don't speak to women in public. Jews don't talk to Samaritans at all unless absolutely necessary. When she arrives, he speaks to her. His voice startles her.

## The Journey

*"Give me a drink"* (Jn. 4:7). Jesus and the woman are both on a journey. Each has come to this well from a different place and for different reasons. Jesus is alone. His disciples have gone into the city to buy food. They weren't aware of the significance of his decision to come to this well. They left him to get natural food.

He's *"wearied from his journey"* (Jn. 4:6) and thirsty in the heat of the day. We hear an echo of a word spoken from the cross: *"I thirst."* The cross is the ultimate goal of his journey toward her, but the request for a drink is the first stage of her journey toward revelation.

Consider Jesus' journey to this place. Why is he weary? When did his journey toward this well begin? How did he happen to be here at the exact time she approaches? Earlier the text tells us that Jesus and his disciples *"had to pass through Samaria"* (Jn. 4:4). Passing through Samaria isn't a geographical necessity. To avoid soiling their feet with Samaritan dirt, many Jews went from Judea to Galilee by crossing the Jordan in Judea and going around to the Sea of Galilee. Jesus' need to pass this way came from the bosom of the Father. He is simply going where he sees his Father going. He's abiding in the Father and the Father is abiding in him. The abiding relation orders his steps to this place.

However, Jesus' journey didn't begin in Judea or in the synagogue in Nazareth where he began his public ministry, or even in Bethlehem where he was born. The beginning of this journey traces back to the Word of God in God and with God in the beginning (see Jn. 1:1). Through this Word the earth was created, and through him man was placed in the earth and given life.

When Adam fell, this journey began. The journey continued as this Word "came to his own" at Mount Sinai and was rejected by most of those he'd delivered from the land of bondage. The journey continued as he *"came to his own,"* when he spoke his word to them through the prophets. After millennia of coming toward a people who rejected him, it's no wonder he's weary. But he's determined.

At this stage of the journey—here at the well in Samaria—something significant is about to unfold. Let's follow the stages as Jesus gently draws the woman step by step to the place of seeing.

## *Awakening Curiosity*

*"How is it that you, a Jew, ask a drink of me, a woman of Samaria"* (Jn. 4:9). She knows a Jewish man would have to be desperate to speak to a Samaritan—even more desperate to speak to a Samaritan woman. She's probably thinking, "If he only knew who I really am. Not only a Samaritan, scum in the eyes of Jews, and not only a woman, the lowest class in this male society, but a *sinful Samaritan woman.*"

In this woman we have another representation of "the bottom of the barrel." But while the story of the adulterous woman focuses on Jewish society, this story focuses on world religions. The Jews considered the Samaritan religion worse than idolatry because the Samaritans claimed authority from Yahweh just like the Jews.

Jesus let's himself come to a place where he's at the mercy of this woman, at least in the natural. He has no jar to lower into the well. He's thirsty and he asks for water; but he has come here to *serve* this sinful Samaritan woman. This is typical of his way of coming to man: in weakness and vulnerability, ready to serve those who will receive. His Father's love for this woman brought him here. He's about to become a servant to the lowest rung of the religious order. Decent religious people wouldn't even let such a woman wash their feet.

## Who is this Speaking?

*"If you knew the gift of God, and who it is that is saying to you, 'Give me a drink,' you would have asked him, and he would have given you living water"* (Jn. 4:10). The woman is obviously thinking of running water at the bottom of the well. Before we discuss the living water, notice that Jesus speaks of himself in the third person, as though he were speaking of someone other than himself: *"He* would have given you living water." The water is the gift of God, but why would he speak as though he is not the one offering

the gift? He's obviously speaking of himself because in the next statement he speaks of "the water *I shall give.*" What does this unexpected way of speaking tell us? What does this sign point to?

John introduces this story with an interesting statement, **"Now when the Lord knew that the Pharisees had heard that Jesus was making and baptizing more disciples than John..."** (Jn. 4:1). Follow the words closely. (1) The *Lord knew* something; (2) The Pharisees had *heard* something; and (3) *Jesus* was making and baptizing disciples. Notice the relation between the Lord and Jesus and how the Pharisees missed something by failing to see beyond the surface.

Here's the point. We know *JESUS IS LORD*, but the Pharisees didn't know that. When they looked at Jesus, they didn't see the Lord, they simply saw his humanity. Jesus was fully human and fully divine but his divinity, his lordship, can't be seen apart from the miracle of opened eyes. The Pharisees hadn't heard that the *Lord* was doing anything at all. They'd only heard that the man Jesus was baptizing. They were totally unaware that the Lord was on the move in the person of Jesus.

This suggests a reason why Jesus unexpectedly speaks of himself in the third person. As Jesus speaks to this woman he knows that she only sees his humanity; as far as she knows at this point he's only a Jew. So he refers to his *divinity* in the third person. He is the one who brings the gift of God, but she doesn't know that yet. She's on the way to revelation; but she's not there yet. Will she stay on this path until it brings her to revelation or will she cloak herself and walk away like the Pharisees in the story of the woman caught in adultery?

## *Drawing and Pouring*

*"Sir, you have nothing to draw with, and the well is deep, where do you get this living water"* (Jn. 4:11). She's

staying on this path for now. Her understanding of living water is still limited to the fresh well-water. Living water as she knows it isn't available without the human act of *drawing* and a *container* to draw with. John uses the human act of drawing as a sign of our attempts to get our spiritual needs met by our own efforts. We can only draw from the natural well of natural water. This drawing requires a natural vessel, a water jar.

John's Gospel uses water to point to the Holy Spirit (see Jn. 7:37-39). The Father is ready to pour out his Holy Spirit through Jesus as a gift. This *pouring is an act of God*. In Acts 2, the Holy Spirit is *poured out* on all flesh. To receive what God desires to pour in, we must be empty and waiting to be filled. We must walk away from our water jars. We must forsake our human effort—the systems and programs we use to try to produce life for ourselves. Having left behind the jars of human effort, we'll be empty and ready to receive what our Father desires to pour into us. Only then can we have the living water Jesus offers.

*"Are you greater than our father Jacob"* (Jn. 4:12)? Jesus could've responded with a resounding "Yes, I am!" But he knows she isn't ready to hear that. He must bring her gently until she's ready. He's patiently leading her. She's following curiously, perhaps even sarcastically, but she's following.

*"Every one who drinks of this water will thirst again"* (Jn. 4:13). Jesus says, pointing to the well. The woman knows she always gets thirsty for *this water* as soon as she goes home. She'd put a jar of this water on the table for later. But when she returned to the jar, the water would no longer be *living, running water:* it would become *still water* on its way to becoming *stale water*. Even before she has emptied the jar, she's already thirsty for that fresh, sparkling water that flows freely at the bottom of the well. Yes, when she drinks of this water, she does thirst again. That's why she keeps returning to draw more.

## Beginning of Revelation

*"But whoever drinks of the water that I shall give him will never thirst"* (Jn. 4:14). Jesus begins to reveal himself to her as Lord. He no longer refers to himself in the third person. When he speaks of "the water that *I shall give*," he identifies himself as the one through whom the living water of God is given. *"The water that I shall give him will become in him a spring of water welling up to eternal life."* Many would walk away at this point. "How silly," she could've thought. "This man actually thinks he has access to a source of water that can always be springing up within you and flowing (living) in you eternally." But she doesn't walk away; she stays on the path. She may remain out of curiosity, but she remains.

## Eternal Life and Knowing God

The idea of eternal life is more than the idea of extended time. It certainly includes the 'for ever and ever' we usually think of. But forever isn't very appealing unless the life being extended is a really good, radically different life. No one I know would actually want to continue forever in the conditions that presently exist with its continual ups and downs.

Eternal life means life on the highest plain, the shared life of the Son in the Father's embrace, not only some day but even now. *"Truly, truly, I say to you, he who hears my word and believes in him who sent me, has* [not *will have*] *eternal life; he does not come into judgment, but has* [already] *passed from death to life"* (Jn. 5:24). Life in Father's embrace begins when we receive the living water and let it have its effect in us.

John indicates the nature of eternal life in his prayer. *"And this is eternal life, that they know thee the only true God, and Jesus Christ whom thou hast sent"* (Jn. 17:3). The word *'know'* is used to indicate more than knowing *about* God. Eternal life doesn't issue from knowing all the Bible says about God and his acts in history. You can know as much theology as Martin Luther or John Calvin and still not know the one they talk about.

The knowledge that *"is eternal life"* is an intimate relationship, the sharing of a common life. *It's a knowing that comes from being in the presence of God with your unveiled face facing him who is facing you in total openness.* It's embracing him who is embracing you. As we enter this intimate relationship with Jesus, Father welcomes us into his loving embrace. This is eternal life: welcoming the one who welcomes us.

We all have a deep desire to know and to be known by someone who accepts us as we are. We want to belong-with and to be longed-for by another. This is a longing to belong in the welcoming presence of one we desire to be with. When the Bible speaks of knowing God and being known by God, it speaks of the Father welcoming his Son and all those who are in him. He welcomes us into the inner life of God in the Spirit.

The other side of this is that, as we abide in Christ, the Father and the Son make their home in us. Eternal life also implies that the life of God is available to others as we follow the Son in inviting them into this new life in the Spirit. We know the Father and his Son as we abide in his love and allow his love to flow out to others by the Spirit. This is eternal life; this is living, flowing water.

## Increasing Revelation

*"Sir, give me this water, that I may not thirst, nor come here to draw"* (Jn. 4:15). Perhaps she's still thinking of natural water but she's staying with him. Perhaps she secretly hopes this Jewish man might actually have something she's been thirsty for all her life. The crowd in chapter six asks Jesus to give them the bread that brings life. They hope he'll provide what they're hungry for, but they end up walking

away when Jesus' answer doesn't fit their way of thinking. Will this woman go away?

*"Go, call your husband"* (Jn. 4:16). Here's another chance to just walk away. She thinks she knows what will happen if she brings the man she's living with to this Jewish man. She'll be exposed. She comes up with an answer that lets her avoid exposure for now.

*"I have no husband"* (Jn. 4:17). There. With no husband she won't have to expose her personal life to this man. But this man is more than a Jewish man. He's a prophet, one in touch with reality on the level of the Spirit. He can hear from his Father any details necessary to bring this woman to the next stage of her journey.

*"You are right in saying, 'I have no husband'; you have had five husbands, and he whom you now have is not your husband"* (Jn. 4:17-18). Now she's exposed. She can simply slip away just as the Pharisees had in the adulterous woman story. Like the women caught in adultery, she doesn't have to stay. Why does she stay? She has been seeking the fulfillment of her desire to know and be known by being with several men. Her experience with men has left her empty and guilty. When Jesus exposes her, he lets her know that he knows her and that there's no judgment coming from him.

She's experiencing being known by one who accepts her as she is. The fact that she remains indicates she's comfortable in the presence of this one who knows her better than she knows herself. Now she desires to get to know him and the one who sent him.

*"Sir, I perceive you are a prophet."* In this next stage of her journey, she recognizes he's more than simply a Jewish man. He's a prophet. But her level of perception isn't yet where it can go if she'll only continue on this path. The multitude in John chapter 6 also saw him as a prophet: *"This is indeed the prophet who is to come into the world"* (Jn. 6:14), but they didn't receive what he offered them.

Recognizing him as a prophet is not enough. She's begun to see the light. By acknowledging him to be a prophet she's also pleading guilty to his charge. By continuing the conversation, she indicates her willingness to walk in this light.

## Water, Worship, and the Father

*"Our fathers worshiped on this mountain; and you say that in Jerusalem is the place where men ought to worship"* (Jn. 4:20). She's pointing to Mount Gerizim. Some think she's trying to change the subject to avoid talking about her personal life, but that would be hiding from the light and removing herself from the path to revelation. In the context of this story, that clearly isn't what she's doing. Rather, John uses her response to draw our attention to a key point: *'living water' somehow relates to worship.*

It's in the act of true worship that we drink—that we know God and are known by God. C. S. Lewis noticed this in his book, *Reflections on the Psalms.* He wrote, "…it is in the process of being worshipped that God communicates His presence to men." He comes to us as we come to him. In daily, personal worship we enter into the continual flow of life in the Father's bosom and that flow enters us. In true worship we enter into the eternal life of Father and Son by the Spirit here on earth.

This woman lives on Mount Ebal where the curses were placed. The Samaritans have their worship center on top of Mount Gerizim. Jacob's well is in the valley between them. She's worshipped on Mount Gerizim all her life and never received any life from that worship.

It's as though these Samaritans go to their worship center—a broken cistern with no water—and sing about water, listen to messages about water, and talked in small groups about the value of water. But no one ever gets a drink. They all go away thirsty but no one is willing to admit their thirst. Each assumes the others are receiving because everyone puts up a front to avoid exposure. There's no intimacy with God and no intimacy between the worshipers, because one can't be intimate while covering himself.

The woman is asking the right question. Her journey from the Mount of Curses to the worship center on the Mount of Blessings is well worn, but she's still thirsty. In asking this question, she indicates her willingness to beat a path to Jerusalem and leave her family tradition behind if there's a promise of real living water there. If this prophet tells her to go, she's ready to follow him to Jerusalem for this water. She's really thirsty.

## The Woman Receives

"*Woman, believe me, the hour is coming when neither on this mountain nor in Jerusalem will you worship the Father*" (Jn. 4:21). What a surprising turn this is! She's ready to go to Jerusalem but Jesus says that's not the answer. The revelation in this promise is deeper than the geographical location. The promise to her is, "*You*, sinful as you are and being a Samaritan, *you* will worship the *Father*." It's impossible to worship God as Father if you aren't his daughter. You may worship him as *a* father, but that's not the same thing. Jesus offers her new birth and a relationship with his Father.

"*I know that Messiah is coming (he who is called the Christ); when he comes, he will show us all things*" (Jn. 4:25). She comes to the next stage of her journey. She began by seeing Jesus as a Jewish man. He is Jewish. Then she saw that he was also a prophet. Yes, he is; but there's more. She suspects he might be the Messiah but she isn't confident enough to say it outright. She hints with the hope that he'll confirm her suspicions. He'd told her all about herself. Since Messiah would "show us all things," this just might be the one she's been waiting for. If he is Messiah, she'll be even more ready to follow him.

*"I who speak to you am he"* (Jn. 4:26). Jesus' proclamation can be literally translated: *"I AM is speaking to you."* This translation does no violence to the text or to the Greek language. John's gospel contains several "I AM" statements like this. I don't mean statements like "I am the light of the world." The clearest "I AM" statement is his answer to the Jews in chapter eight, *"Before Abraham was, I AM"* (Jn. 8:58). Jesus identifies himself with the "I AM" (YHWH or Jehovah) who revealed himself by that name to Moses. YHWH simply means "HE IS." The name takes that form in the mouth of men. The form of the name in the mouth of God is "I AM." This name was on the mouth of Jesus when the band of soldiers came to arrest him. The proclamation—"I AM"—threw them all to the ground.

This woman isn't thrown to the ground because she's on the path to revelation. In fact she has arrived. She has met the LORD, YHWH. She now knows the one who knows her, and in knowing him she will come to know the Father by the Spirit.

## Controlling the Water Stops the Flow

In the natural it's obvious that when running water is put in a container it's no longer running water. When water remains still for a time it doesn't have the same zest as running water from a mountain spring. When we apply that to the living water of the Holy Spirit, several things come to light.

## Cisterns and Community Water

Let's broaden the concept of water beyond what John is doing so we can make a point. We noted earlier that water was available in the city in the community cistern as well as 'rain barrels' in some homes. There were also *religious cisterns*. Jeremiah faulted the people for forsaking the Lord, the fountain of living waters, and digging cisterns to sustain themselves (see Jer. 2:13). That's what the Samaritan religion had done and that's what the scribes and Pharisees had done. Any source of life apart from God's living presence is really a source of death.

A religious cistern is a place where the religious community gathers to teach and preach about water (life) and how to obtain it. Worship services are supposed to make the water available.

Some churches today are still healthy; living water still flows from the fountain of living water. But some religious traditions have dug cisterns and built dams to hold the water and bring its flow under the control of the cistern masters. By their doctrines, rites, and policies they've said to the water, "You can move here but not there. You may go this way but not that way." A cistern is nothing more than an attempt to control the water and its availability. Those 'cistern guards' in charge of the water can say, "You may drink if you follow our rules. The outsiders aren't worthy of our water even if they are thirsty."

When water from the rain comes from above (this happens when God comes to revive his people), it's living, flowing water. But when it comes to the walls of the man-made cistern of human tradition, it ceases to flow. Unless the cistern guards release their control it will become *still water*. Still water becomes *stale*. Stale water becomes *stagnant*. Stagnant water is dangerous if you drink it.

Stale water will sustain you but it will never fully satisfy your thirst. You'll thirst again. The cistern gives man the ability to resist what God wants to do and the ability to pretend God is in what man is doing. The pretense takes the form of preaching and singing about water you are not drinking. In either case—resistance or pretense—the source of life is separated from the water of the cistern and from those who rely on the cistern. If any group has water they can control, it isn't flowing from the source above; it's not living water.

### Rain Barrels and Family Traditions

Many houses with family cisterns caught rain while it was falling. Rain water is living water while it's moving. As long as the rain of revival (or renewal if you prefer) continues to fall, living water is available. But again, as soon as it reaches the borders marked off by the family cistern it ceases to flow. The family cistern can be used to control the movement of the water within the family. "Our family may do this but not that. They can go here but not there. They may receive this not that."

The family may've been involved in a time of the rain of God falling. When that happens, for the parents it brings life. For the children it becomes a practice. Children go through the motions because it pleases their parents and makes them feel accepted. For the grandchildren it becomes pretense or meaningless ritual. The water has become still, stale, and in danger of becoming stagnant. That's why revival seldom continues more than a few years.

The woman in our story is willing to walk away from family tradition to find living water at Jacob's well. She's even willing to walk away from the larger community and go to Jerusalem if that's necessary. She wants something fresh and life-giving. This is the attitude that receives living water.

When she approached the well she had a jar. Her plan was to use the jar to draw the living water from the bottom of the well. She would drink of that fresh, sparkling water as she had done for many years. When the water remained in her jar however, it would no longer be flowing, no longer living. It would become still, then stale. She would thirst again. That had been her life story.

### Personal Water Jars

Her jar is a sign of her own personal way of controlling the presence of water for herself during the rest of the day. She's developed her own way of relating to the water. Will she be willing to leave her personal cistern, her water jar, and trust that more water will be available when she needs it? Does she really believe the promise that this water will become in her a well springing up to eternal life?

*"So the woman left her water jar"* (Jn. 4:28). She came to the well because she was thirsty. She came with her jar to draw but never lowered it into the well. Now she's willing to leave her jar behind. She has received the real water.

All her life she'd been trying to draw water through her religious tradition. But human effort never comes up with water from the river that flows from the throne of the Father and the Lamb (see Rev.22:1). This living water flows on its own accord. One can't *draw* this water. It's the gift of God Jesus spoke about. It flows to the lowest place where it finds the humble sinners. It takes the path of least resistance.

Those who resist this water or try to control its movement discover that it flows around them and they're left with only a dry and lifeless form of the reality they desire. This woman didn't resist the water nor did she try to draw it by human effort. She didn't try to be worthy to receive it. She simply received. We know she was satisfied because she left her jar. She walked away from her attempts to control her personal religious experience.

## Sharing the Overflow

She *"went into the city, and said to the people, 'Come, see a man who told me all that I ever did. Can this be the Christ?'"* (Jn. 4:28). She didn't go to a place of seclusion to enjoy the fresh water she'd received. She returned to the city on the Mount of Curses. Like Philip in chapter 1, she didn't follow without bringing others to the river she'd discovered. She followed the way of Jesus who said, "Come and see." She followed the example of Philip who said to Nathaniel, "Come and see."

She understood that we can't give this water to others. We can only invite them to come to the one who gives this living water. This keeps the water flowing because it lets it flow out to others. The water makes a turn inside each individual and becomes a "*spring of water welling up to eternal life*" for others as well as for the one who receives.

This water stops flowing in some people's lives because they don't give it an outlet; they don't invite others to come and see.

## Comparing the Multitude and the Samaritan Woman

"*Rabbi, eat*" (Jn. 4:31). The disciples return after going into the city to buy food. Notice the contrast between this story and the feeding of the multitude. When Jesus saw the multitudes coming he asked Philip, "*How are we to buy bread, so that these people may eat*" (Jn. 6:4)? He was testing Philip because he knew he was going to miraculously provide food to point to himself as the "*Bread of Life.*"

There he didn't let them buy food. Here, he did; but there's no record of Jesus asking them to go purchase bread. Purchasing bread is also a sign of human effort (like drawing water) to gain what's needful for life in the Spirit. The true bread is a gift from God just as the living water. It can only be received as a gift.

### *Eating and Drinking*

In chapter 6 the major emphasis is on the bread and eating. Drink is mentioned in chapter 6 but almost incidentally when Jesus says, "*Unless you eat the flesh of the Son of man and drink his blood, you have no life in you*" (Jn. 6:53). Here in chapter 4, the issue is drinking; food is brought up almost incidentally. I say *almost* because it's not incidental in either case. Both stories are about eating and drinking and both point to the same reality.

It's significant that the feeding of the multitude and the teaching about the bread of life were on different sides of the sea. Jesus went to the "*other side*" to feed the multitude (see Jn. 6:1). No boat is mentioned. The absence of that detail may be a hint about how to read the walking on the sea after the multitude has eaten. The two different sides of the sea point as a sign to two different 'worlds'. On one side Jesus provides natural bread for the multitude in the natural world. On the other side Jesus offers the true Bread from heaven for those who would join him in the new world of the Spirit.

## *Bread from the Other Side*

In the evening after the feeding of the multitude the disciples were crossing the sea in a boat but they were not advancing. You might say they were trying to get over to the world of the Spirit in a row boat. "*It was now dark; and Jesus had not yet come to them*" (Jn. 6:17). It's always dark when Jesus hasn't joined us yet.

A boat to cross the sea is like a jar to draw water or money to buy bread. A boat is a human vehicle for crossing the sea just as a water jar is a human vehicle for drawing water. *Drawing, rowing and buying* represent human efforts to enter the life of God and accomplish his will. The concept of sea is distinct from water. The text tells us Jesus walked on the sea, not on the water. This is also the case in Matthew 14 and in Mark 6. Sea and water may be the same in the natural, but as *signs* they're different. The sea represents a barrier that must be overcome to get to the "other side" where the spiritual blessings are available. Jesus crossed to *this* 'other side' when he became flesh to dwell among us. On *this* 'other side' he provided natural bread as a sign for those who would follow him to the 'other side' of the Spirit.

As the disciples were attempting to cross to *that* 'other side' a strong wind was hindering them. There are contrary spirits (winds) that resist their attempt to get to the other side. Their human effort of rowing is without significant progress. Jesus then walks on the sea, back toward the Spirit side. When the disciples see him they are frightened. Jesus simply says, *"Fear not, I AM* (is)" (Jn. 6:20), and joins his disciples to make their journey successful.

*"Immediately the boat was at the land where they were going"* (Jn. 6:21). No one can come to *that* 'other side' unless Jesus is in his boat, and with Jesus in your boat, no rowing is necessary — you have arrived.

The many who were fed reach the other side (geographically) by the boats of human effort. However, human effort can never bring you to the 'other side' of the Spirit. They aren't really 'there' when the teaching is given. You could say they're in Church but they aren't in the Spirit. The disciples are really 'there' because they arrived by a miracle. The multitude is not really 'there' because they arrived on their own without the help of Jesus.

## Another Journey: Bread and the Father's Will

*"I have food to eat of which you do not know"* (Jn. 4:32). The water he offered the woman was water she knew nothing about until she continued to the place of revelation. The disciples begin a journey here to find the secret stash of food that sustained Jesus. Jesus had eaten and was satisfied by food they know nothing about. Their effort to buy food was wasted on him.

*"Has any one brought him food?"* (Jn. 4:33) they question among themselves. Buying is the natural way of acquiring food just as drawing is the natural way of getting water. But our way never acquires the realities indicated by the signs of water and bread. We can only receive the water of life as the Father pours it through the Son by the Spirit into the world. Real food can only be received from the Father as we hear the *rhema* word proceeding from the mouth of the Father.

*"My food is to do the will of him who sent me, and to accomplish his work"* (Jn. 4:34). This ties the stories of chapters 4 and 6 together. After feeding the multitude in chapter 6, Jesus went across the sea to Capernaum. The multitude followed him there and asked for more bread. Jesus challenged them with these words: *"Do not labor for the food which perishes, but for the food which endures to eternal life"* (Jn. 6:27). The parallel is obvious. In chapter 4, it's water that *springs up to eternal life.* In chapter 6, it's food that *endures* (abides) *to eternal life.*

The crowd's question in chapter 6 reveals another parallel. *"What must we do, to be doing the works of God"* (Jn. 6:28)? The spokesman connects the food which endures to eternal life with doing the works of God just as Jesus did with the disciples in chapter 4. These many points of connection make it is clear that John intends these stories to shed light on one another. Where shall we go for help understanding this connection?

## The Proceeding Word

In the other Gospels, the devil tempts Jesus by suggesting he change stones to bread. Jesus answers, "Man shall not live by bread alone, but by every word that proceeds from the mouth of God" (from Deut. 8:3). Jesus derives life from hearing and responding to the *proceeding word*, the word the Father is presently speaking. Jesus *lives* his life in the bosom of the Father and he *lives out* his life based on what his Father is saying to him daily. Daily bread is the *rhema* word that proceeds from the mouth of the Father.

We eat that bread by doing what's indicated by that word. Since he lived his life this way, he became the bread of life for all who follow him in the way he followed his Father, listening to the voice and responding in obedience. This is how to *eat* the bread that comes down from heaven.

Partaking of a wafer or broken cracker is only a sign and symbol of this reality. Have you eaten today?

In chapter 4 Jesus let his Father lead him to Samaria and linger at the well until the woman arrived. He'd listened carefully as his Father crafted his responses to the woman in a way to draw her to Jesus. Jesus proclaimed to the crowd in chapter 6, "*No one can come to me unless the Father draws him*" (Jn. 6:44). The Father was drawing this woman to Jesus. He simply heard and obeyed his Father and let his Father draw her. By responding to the leading of his Father, Jesus had been 'eating' while the disciples went to buy bread. On their own initiative, they'd *acquired* bread that perishes while Jesus *received* the bread that endures (abides) to eternal life.

Like living water, bread from heaven can't be purchased. It's a gift and must be received as a gift in the Father's presence and in the process of hearing and obeying his voice. In feeding the multitude, the disciples simply heard Jesus' instructions and distributed what he provided and the multitude ate to their fill. They were doing what they saw Jesus doing and responding to his *rhema* word. In this way they accomplished the Father's will in that situation.

There's another contrast between these stories. The multitude asked, "*Lord, give us this bread always*" (Jn. 6:34). They obviously didn't understand what the bread really was. Neither did the woman understand living water until she came to the full revelation. She'd also asked for the water without understanding what it was. "*Sir, give me this water, that I may not thirst nor come here to draw*" (Jn. 4:15). But she received and they didn't. The crowd "*drew back and no longer went about with him*" (Jn. 6:66). When he went a direction they didn't understand, they left him. She stayed on the path until revelation came and living water flowed.

Let's look at one final contrast before we move on. The crowd in chapter 6 was tied to the traditions of their fathers.

Their fathers had eaten manna in the wilderness. Tradition expected the 'prophet like Moses' to provide natural bread just as Moses had done. Their fathers had died in the wilderness because they weren't willing to listen to the voice (receive the bread of heaven) and enter the land of promise when the time came. In other words, the crowd at Mount Sinai and the crowd in John 6 ate the natural bread but they didn't eat the bread that was "doing the will of the Father."

The woman was also aware of the traditions of her fathers. But she knew death was abiding in that wilderness of traditions. She was willing to forsake her community and traditions to receive the water that issued from the Rock. In the context of the Feast of Tabernacles in chapter seven Jesus says, "He who believes in me, as the Scripture has said, '*Out of his heart* [belly] *shall flow rivers of living water*'" (Jn. 7:38).

The rock in the wilderness is a type of Christ (see I Cor. 10:1-5). The rivers of life flow from the throne of the Father, out of the 'belly' of the Rock, Jesus the Lamb. Anyone who comes to him and drinks will receive this water that becomes in him a well springing up (from his belly as well) to eternal life. Let it flow. Let it *rhea* (flow).

## Living Water and the River

Let's return to living water. What do we find when we follow the pointing finger? Our major clue is in the context mentioned above: on the last day of the Feast of Tabernacles Jesus says, "*If any one thirsts, let him come to me and drink.*" John answers our question: "*Now this he said about the Spirit, which those who believed in him were to receive; for as yet the Spirit had not yet been given, because Jesus was not yet glorified*" (Jn. 7:39). The Holy Spirit is the flow of the Father's life out of his bosom into the thirsty world. The Holy Spirit is the river that issues from below the threshold of the temple in Ezekiel 47.

## The Nature of the River

This Ezekiel passage describes a very curious river indeed. It gets deeper as it flows toward the east and then down the valley to the Dead Sea. There are no tributaries feeding this river; its only source is the presence of God in the temple. Yet it begins as a trickle and gets deeper the farther it flows.

How does it get deeper? As more and more people drink, and as this water makes its turn in them becoming a fresh spring flowing out from them to others, the river increases in depth and the current increases until it becomes a river to swim in.

If you go into the middle of this river the current is so strong that you go where the river is going whether you like it or not. I think you'll like it because this is the flow of the Father's love into the world. To be in this river is to be in the flow of that love that flows from the Father's bosom. This river brings life wherever it flows (see Ezk. 47:9). To be in this river of living water is to be in that place of mutual abiding—Father, Son, Holy Spirit and you.

This river of life is flowing from the heart of the Father through the life of the incarnate Son by the Spirit of life. It's flowing into the lives of those who hear and believe and it will continue to flow from them to others. This means we are participating in the very life of the Trinitarian God as the Father brings us into fellowship with himself through Jesus Christ by the Spirit.

To have eternal life is to know the Father and the Son in this intimate and intensively active way (see Jn. 17:3). Eternal life is entering into Jesus' way of relating to his Father and his way of relating to men and women in the world. *This is the Way that Jesus IS. This is the Truth that Jesus IS. This is the Life that Jesus IS. Knowing the Father intimately through the Son by the Spirit is Eternal Life. This is the River.*

## Come over to My Place

*"Many Samaritans from that city believed in him because of the woman's testimony, 'He told me all that I ever did'"* (Jn. 4:29). She invites them to "Come and see," and they believe enough to go where he is. They're on a path that will bring them to Jesus. They aren't there yet, but they are on the way. If they continue, they'll also receive living water as a gift from God.

*"So when the Samaritans came to him, they asked him to stay* [abide] *with them"* (Jn. 4:40). This shows they had heard with the ears of their hearts. Jesus invited the first two disciples who followed him to "Come over to my place and stay with me." Here the Samaritans invite him to come over to their place and stay with them. This is the mutual abiding that John speaks of—we in his place and he is in our place. These Samaritans received the living water; they entered into the place of mutual abiding.

*"It is no longer because of your words that we believe, for we have heard for ourselves, and we know that this is indeed the Savior of the world"* (Jn. 4:42). The evangelistic thrust isn't complete as long as people's faith is still tied to the evangelist. Eternal life doesn't come from believing and knowing what the preacher says. Each individual, and the community of believers as a whole, must come to know him personally. We must wean ourselves from those who first shared their testimony with us. Knowing what the woman said *about* Jesus is quite different from *knowing Jesus*.

To know *about* Jesus is academic and brings glory to the one who knows more than others. To know *Jesus* is intimacy with the Trinity. This intimacy brings the glory of God's presence into the lives of those who know him. Only by a personal experience do we come to his place and welcome him to our place.

## *Believing is Knowing*

*"We know that this is indeed the savior of the world."*
They don't say "We believe;" they say "We know." Here we have another glimpse into the meaning of "believe" in John. Believing isn't academic. It's personal. Believing is coming to see and coming to know in an intimate and personal connection. Believing is sticking to the path until you reach the goal. Believing is giving yourself to the other and letting him determine the direction of your life as he gives himself to you.

Through believing we come to the place of seeing. Believing is the biblical way of coming to know. We know by faith or we don't know at all. When we know by connecting ourselves to him—when we know intimately—we have life eternal because we're connected to the Eternal Life of the Trinitarian God himself. We share his life and he shares our life in community with other believers on *his* way into the world he loves.

Have you left your water jar? Are you willing to forsake tradition for a relationship with the Father? Have you entered the flow of the river that flows from the throne and from the Lamb?

In the next chapter, we'll notice Peter's floundering attempt to control living water. We'll explore the difference between the betrayal of Judas and the denial of Peter. Both were trying to control the water. Why does one become the chief apostle and the other fall into the pit of infamy?

# CHAPTER 8

# Betrayal and Denial

—m—

W e've seen the significance of the abiding place and the basic principles that help us seek and find that place. We also noticed that it's possible to be with someone on the same path while actually going to a different destination. Two pilgrims can be together on the path without being together in their vision of where they're going. It's dangerous to assume you will end up in the same place just because you appear to be walking the same direction as Jesus.

Let's explore Judas' betrayal and Peter's denial. They were together on the same path. They were both on the path with Jesus. Why does Judas fall out of the picture while Peter becomes the chief apostle? Our question in this chapter is: What's the core difference between these two men and their responses when Jesus makes a turn on the path? We'll begin with the changing of Simon's name to *Cephas* or *Peter* (Jn. 1:41-42).

## Simon's New Name
*"He first found his brother Simon"* (Jn. 1:41). John wants us to understand that Andrew *first* found his brother before he went to the abiding place. Peter was with the others when they followed Jesus that day. Others also joined them

on the way to that abiding place. Even Judas? Was he also on the way to the abiding place? We shall see.

*"So you are Simon the son of John? You shall be called Cephas (which means Peter)"* (Jn. 1:42) This day of transition began with John the Baptist seeing Jesus and identifying him as the Lamb of God. He publicly testified to what he saw, and two disciples followed. This day ends with Jesus seeing Simon as he's coming to follow. This isn't a man recognizing the Lord; it's the Lord recognizing a man.

When Jesus sees Simon, he first calls him by the name his earthly father had given him, Simon, son of John. In that name there was the potential inheritance of the futile ways from his ancestors (see I Pet. 1:18). But Jesus doesn't address him to affirm his fallen humanity and leave him with his human inheritance. He gives him a *new name* with a new *identity*, a *new inheritance*, and a *new future*.

## New Inheritance and New Destiny

The act of changing a person's name implies bringing them under one's authority and giving them a new destiny. A person who became a slave in biblical times was given a new name by their owners. They were given a task in life different from what they had chosen for themselves and different from the task given by their fathers.

Some of the kings and princes of Judah were re-named by the Babylonians when the captivity began. Daniel's name was changed to Belteshazzar. When the Lord took Abram under his authority and gave him the destiny of becoming the father of many nations, he changed his name to Abraham. In this text Jesus changes Simon's name and his destiny as he receives him into discipleship.

When we come to him he gives us a new name "which no one knows except him who receives it" (see Rev. 2:17). With the new name comes a new destiny.

*"You shall be called Cephas."* By changing Simon's name, Jesus is claiming Peter as his own and speaking creatively into his life. Peter (Greek) and Cephas (Aramaic) both mean Rock. Jesus speaks this name over Simon and establishes his future identity. He will be a solid rock among the disciples.

Simon doesn't fully embrace this new identity until after the Day of Pentecost (even after the resurrection Jesus addresses him as Simon, son of John); but the new name is given at the beginning of his journey. Between the promise contained in the new name and the fulfillment, we see that night in which darkness seems to prevail. That darkness obscures the inheritance and brings his identity into question, but it doesn't change Simon's ultimate destiny.

Simon—on his way to becoming Peter—needs the promise of this new name to have the courage to get up after he stumbles on his way to the abiding place. Simon can be encouraged in difficult situations knowing that the one who gave this new name is Lord of lords. The reality and depth of this confidence don't go untested. On the surface it appears he'll never become that solid rock he's called to be. When he faces the maid and the soldiers at the trial, Simon seems to lose his potential. Will he ever become Peter? He appears as a failure only to those who think the potential is in Simon's ability to understand and act properly.

## What's New?

The newness implied in the name-change reflects movement from a life relying on its own strength and direction to a life that receives direction and empowering from the Holy Spirit in the abiding place. Simon can never become Peter by acting in the power and wisdom inherited from his natural parents.

By this name-change, Jesus removes Simon from the place his father had chosen for him—fisherman—and from the place Peter may have chosen for himself as one of Jesus' disciples. By changing his name Jesus set Simon on a journey to the place he's going to prepare for him in the Father's house. The one who changed his name is committed to bringing Simon to his destiny by sending the Holy Spirit. This transition doesn't come from Simon; it comes from the omnipotent proclamation, *"You shall be called Peter."*

At this point, he's *no longer* the one he has been, but he is *not yet* the one he'll become. He's on the way to becoming the one Jesus calls him to be. "The old has passed away, behold, the new has come" (II Cor. 5:17). The reality of this promise is certainly tested beside the fire on the night of Jesus' trial. Did Simon fail, or is there something we need to learn through his denial?

## *Warning: Dangerous Intersection*

Before we approach the story of Peter's denial, let's notice a few things about the Last Supper just before the arrest. The conversation around the table was going something like this:

Jesus says, *"One of you will betray me."*

The disciples ask, *"Lord, who is it?"*

Jesus replies, *"It's the one I'll give this morsel to."*

Satan entered into him.

Jesus said to Judas, *"What you are going to do, do quickly."*

Judas immediately went out, and it was night (see Jn. 13:21-30).

As we unpack this, let's keep before us the question of what's different between Judas's betrayal and Peter's denial. Despite many similarities, there must be a difference. The difference isn't as clear cut as we'd like, but there is a significant difference.

## The Warning

"*One of you will betray me*" It isn't without warning that Peter approaches the High Priest's courtyard that night. Jesus had predicted that one of his disciples would betray him. The betrayer isn't obviously singled out to any except the beloved disciple. Peter may or may not have his own insecurities in this, as do the others. He tries to discover who will betray Jesus. He apparently senses that Jesus won't trust him with the answer, so he asks the beloved disciple to find out. His attempt is unsuccessful. John finds out but doesn't tell Peter.

"*Lord, who is it?*" In the other Gospels, each of the disciples ask, "Is it I, Lord?" Each is aware of his own weakness. Judas has already made plans, but each of the others has his own suspicions about himself. How comforting it would have been to receive affirmation at this point. But that comfort and affirmation isn't forthcoming. Peter has to face the next few hours armed with the promise implied when Jesus changed his name and the faith instilled in him as he believed the promise and trusted Jesus to fulfill his word. He has to walk into the night trusting the one who has proven himself faithful over a period of several years.

If we're not seriously asking, "Is it I," we may be on our way to a denial or even a betrayal. We need to ask when it's dark outside—when it's night. We must be careful lest we assume we've already become the one he called us to become. Simon could've fallen into that trap when he tried to become 'Rocky' by attacking those who came to arrest Jesus.

When things aren't going the way we think they should, when Jesus isn't leading the way we expect him to, we need to ask in all earnestness, "Is it I? Please tell me now. Don't let me fail." But as the seriousness of the question dawns, don't forget who has called you by name.

## Covenant Implications

*"He to whom I shall give this morsel...."* Earlier that night, Jesus had quoted from Psalm 41: *"He who ate my bread has lifted his heel against me."* Sharing a morsel of bread had serious covenantal implications in that culture. The offer of a morsel is the offer of a covenantal relationship. If a person accepts the bread he's accepting the stipulations of the covenant and agreeing to remain faithful to the relationship from that time forward. A covenant is binding and there are serious consequences to breaking covenant. Marriage is a covenant; we all know the consequences that come to the lives of the couples and children when couples break covenant. Breaking covenant with the Lord has eternal consequences.

When he offers him the morsel, Jesus offers to Judas all of the blessings available to covenant partners. Judas performs the most serious of all breaches of social relationships when he betrays the Lord. He breaks covenant. But he couldn't have broken covenant if the covenant hadn't been offered or if he hadn't accepted the bread. In offering the morsel, Jesus offers Judas a place in the bosom of the Father. By receiving it, Judas appears to accept that place.

Judas isn't the only one who receives a morsel that night. All participate in the meal and eat of the covenant bread. Jesus makes the offer to all; and they all eat the bread. Do the disciples break covenant when they flee in the night? Does Peter break covenant by his denial?

On that night Judas removes himself from the possibility of arriving at the abiding place. But how is his betrayal any different from what Peter does? Why are the covenantal promises still available for Peter but not for Judas? For that matter, how is Judas's action fundamentally different from the others running away in the night? Or from what we do when we inwardly cower instead of boldly testifying of Jesus' work in our lives? When we deny him by our silence?

## Satan's Part and Man's Part

"*Satan entered into him.*" We can blame it on the Devil now. But wait. Matthew records a situation where Jesus addresses Peter this way: "Get behind me, Satan! You are a hindrance to me; for you are not on the side of God but on the side of men" (Matt. 16:23). Jesus speaks to Peter but addresses Satan. Or is he speaking to Satan but addressing Peter? Satan's name simply means adversary. It's Satan who's on the side of men. But Peter is also on the side of men (meaning 'in the flesh'); and Jesus is talking to Peter. Peter is also a hindrance because he is unknowingly taking an adversarial role.

Somehow—because he is on the side of men—Peter's stand is directly related to Satan trying to hinder Jesus. We place ourselves in that relationship with Satan any time we set ourselves on the side of men and walk in the flesh, resisting what God wants to do. When we criticize those he's using we're not abiding in the Father's embrace.

Yet, though Peter is rebuked in this way, he isn't rejected. So the question is this: How can I make sure that when I stumble (as Peter did and as we all do), I won't fall headlong as Judas did (see Acts 1:18)? How can I stay in covenant with him when my humanity fails? The gravity of the question is almost overwhelming. We must discover the difference between betrayal and denial. One lets us remain in the abiding place, somehow or other. The other leads to death without resurrection.

"*Satan entered into him.*" This indicates that Judas is deceived. He's under the influence of the Arch-deceiver. Some scholars suggest that Judas actually thought he was doing the right thing in betraying Jesus into the hands of the Jewish leaders, that he expected Jesus to work some miracle at the last moment and make his move for political power. If that's so, and I think it is, then Judas is also unaware of his adversarial role. Even though Jesus had said, "*One of you will betray me*," Judas doesn't appear to take it personally. He may be the only disciple who isn't asking himself, "Is it I, Lord?" He considers his deed an act of loyalty to the cause.

He's confusing loyalty to his bubble with loyalty to Jesus. Was Peter's loyalty to his own bubble also? Where's my loyalty? Where's your loyalty?

## *Permission Granted*

*"What you are going to do, do quickly."* Jesus knows what Judas has arranged with the High Priest. As Judas leaves that night he follows Jesus' instructions. He's doing it quickly in obedience—so it seems. Jesus tells him to go in the direction he's chosen. Judas hears what he wants to hear; he enters totally into his bubble and Satan joins him there. He thinks Jesus is going to conform to his human image of the Christ. Judas thinks he is helping Jesus advance the Kingdom. He sincerely believes he is doing what's right. That's the nature of deception. You really believe you're right.

Demonic forces are always ready to help you maintain your deception. I once knew an unmarried couple who were in a bedroom becoming very passionate. They prayed that God would have someone knock on the door if he wanted them to stop. No one knocked. You can finish the story.

How often does Jesus release us to do what we've already planned to do? We tend to think we're favored disciples when we feel a 'release in our spirit' to do what we've set out to do. What a danger—to move in the permissive will of God! Our Father often permits us to do what he actually disapproves of (like the prodigal son) because he knows our minds are made up. Judas has permission to go ahead in his deception. From one perspective it looks like he's acting in obedience. Jesus told him to go do it.

What we do under such circumstances never frustrates the ultimate will of God, but it can certainly put us on a path of personal destruction that leads to the place where death abides (see Pro. 14:12). The stone is never rolled away from that grave. Whoever enters there abides in outer darkness and eternal night.

## Judas and Simon at the Crossroad

Judas and Simon both face that night, but each in a different way—one way is betrayal and one is denial. What distinguishes these two men?

### Judas Makes His Move

*"He immediately went out."* He doesn't merely leave the upper room. He leaves the place of fellowship with the other disciples; he leaves the household of God. He returns to the state of being separated from Christ, having no hope and without God in the world (see Eph. 2:12). He walks away from the light of the world, the light that shines in darkness, the light that darkness can't overcome. He's exposed and doesn't know it.

*"And it was night."* How dark it must be for Judas to do what he does. My heart goes out to Judas. "Wait, Judas. Don't go. Can't you see where you're going?" But he can't see; it's night. How can he possibly see while he's walking away from the light? Jesus had given the invitation, *"Come and see."* Somehow Judas had followed without coming to the place of seeing. Later that night Judas comes with lanterns and torches.

You need that human light when you walk into the night. But the light of your own kindling never lets you see the realities of the Kingdom of God.

This is sobering—that God actually gives permission to those walking according to their own dreams. He may even send a "strong delusion to make them believe what is false, so that all may be condemned who did not believe the truth but had pleasure in unrighteousness" (II Thes. 2:11-12).

*The real issue is where we find pleasure*: Do we find plea-sure in going our own way and establishing our own agenda? Or do we have pleasure in responding to the voice we hear from the bosom of the Father?

## *Jesus Identifies Peter's Role*

After Judas leaves, Peter and Jesus talk.

*"You can't follow me now,"* Jesus says to Peter, *"but you shall follow afterward."*

*"Lord,"* says Peter, *"Why can't I follow you now? I'll lay down my life for you."*

*"Will you lay down your life for me?"* Jesus asks. *"Truly, truly, I say to you, the cock will not crow, till you have denied me three times"* (Jn. 13:36-38).

Judas did what he did in response to permission granted by Jesus. In contrast to Judas's apparently submissive atti-tude, *Peter resists Jesus*, even challenging his direction. Earlier in the evening when Jesus wanted to wash his feet, Peter refused. *"You'll never wash my feet"* (Jn. 13:8). And now Peter questions Jesus' decision that he'll not be able to follow now. He's called *Simon* Peter throughout this context. The transition from *Simon* to *Peter* isn't yet completed.

*"You cannot follow me now."* He didn't say, "You may not," he said "You cannot." Jesus is on his way to die for the sins of the world. Simon can follow him to the spot where the trial and crucifixion take place, but neither he nor anyone else can go with Jesus in the actual fulfilling Father's plan. Father is about to give the life of his Son for the reconciliation of the world. Peter simply can't join Jesus in the actual doing of this deed that brings forgiveness and cleansing to the world.

*"You will follow me afterward."* We can take up our cross and follow but only after Jesus has completed *this* work on the cross. A disciple doesn't lead; he can only follow after-ward. We can lay down our lives for one another (see I Jn. 3:16), but that has value only because Jesus has already done

what only he can do. Only the Son of Man can go where Jesus went. Only the Son of God can do what Jesus did. Our longing to enter the shared life of the Father and the Son can only be fulfilled by following afterward. We can't do his work but we can follow—afterward.

## Simon's Commitment is Challenged

*"I will lay down my life for you."* Simon doesn't want to follow afterward. He wants to be involved in the doing of the deed. He wants to be on the front line. Simon really wants to be Peter. He exposes his impetuous human nature here. He wants to be the number one disciple. This is much more than an overly enthusiastic cover for his insecurities. He really is willing to give himself totally to the messianic vision *as he understands it.* He really desires to be a part of what God is doing. We have to give him that.

*"Will you lay down your life for me?"* It's as though Jesus says to him, "Peter, I know you're *willing* to lay down your life. Your commitment is commendable as far as it goes. But if you lay down your life tonight, it won't be *for me* that you lay it down. You'll be giving it *for your own concept,* not for the Kingdom I've come to establish.

"Your act of giving, no matter how courageous, can be meaningful only in following after me. Any attempt to force my hand (as Judas is doing) or to join me in the act (as you want to do) can only put you in a position of denying all that I am and all that I stand for.

"No, Peter, you may follow later by laying down your life for others. I don't need you to lay down your life for me. I have come to lay down my life for you. Until that's done, both your living and your dying are meaningless."

*"You will deny me three times."* This must have really hit Peter. "If you keep following your own dream (and you will), you'll end up denying me." Jesus' response to Peter's commitment must have cut deeply. "Will you?" Jesus seems

to questions Peter's ability to follow through on his commitment. Then he predicts Peter will deny him before morning light dawns.

*"One of you will betray me,"* doubtless still echoes in his ears. He has more than personal anxiety to deal with now. Jesus has singled him out. "Could I be the one to betray the Master? No! I could never do that. Not me. What is Jesus thinking?"

### The Confrontation

All the disciples follow Jesus into the night, at least for a time. Finally we come to Jesus' arrest in the garden. Here we find the same two men, Judas and Peter, each playing leading roles in the unfolding drama. As Judas brings the soldiers to the place where Jesus is praying, remember that he's acting in response to the permission Jesus gave. Let's follow the story in chapter 18.

*"Now Judas, who betrayed him, also knew the place"* (Jn. 18:2). I can't help but wonder if John wants us to understand that Judas knew the abiding place. John obviously is thinking of a particular location—the Mount of Olives. The question is whether he's also thinking of this place as a sign of the abiding place. The 'place' is where Jesus often met with his disciples—where he is with them and they are with him. It's the Secret Place. Is it too far fetched to ask whether John is indicating more than a geographical location? It's the garden of prayer according to the other Gospels.

Matthew speaks of the Father as one who hears prayers in the 'secret' place because the Father *is* in secret (see Matt. 6:6). That's the place of communion in the bosom of the Father. That's the place where the reality of the bread of covenant is offered and received. Does Judas know that place? We shall see.

## The Secret Place

Every previous attempt to arrest Jesus had failed because he has this secret place. He was able to withdraw himself into the Father's bosom. He was hidden under the shadow of his Father's wings. The temple guards came to arrest him and repeatedly returned without him. The people tried to stone him and he talked his way out of that. That's impossible if you know anything about mob violence.

The Gospels make it clear that this hiding place isn't like a cave or some room behind a secret panel. It's his abiding relationship with his Father that protects him until his hour comes. Even a disciple who knows the place can't lead a band of soldiers to that secret place.

It's obvious from what follows that neither Judas nor the soldiers arrived at the abiding place. Our answer to the question above is an unequivocal NO; Judas did not know the secret place. How can a disciple, one who's actually been in this place, betray his Master? By this deed Judas proves himself to be a false disciple who doesn't know the place.

Somehow he has *been* there without being *there*. He has seen the *place* without *seeing* the place. Having eyes he doesn't see; having ears he doesn't hear; neither does understanding come into his heart. Judas becomes a sign pointing to disciples in every age who resist the way Jesus is going and who, when Jesus doesn't play by their rules, sell him (or his disciples) out to the prevailing system.

## Lanterns and Torches

*"Judas…went there with lanterns and torches"* (Jn. 18:3). The presence of Jesus as light in the world exposes the sin of mankind. Those who walk away from the light are exposed as trying to cover their sin. Here we see light from another perspective. It illumines the path so one can see where he's going and know when he has arrived. Coming with lanterns and torches shows they're depending on their

own human light to find their way in the darkness and to recognize the one they've come to arrest. Torch light only shows what's available for natural observation. Lanterns never provide the revelation of the Holy Spirit. They never reveal the Father in Jesus.

Isaiah spoke about this situation: "Who among you fears the Lord and obeys the voice of his servant, who walks in darkness and has no light, yet trusts in the name of the Lord and relies upon his God?" (Is. 50:10). Isaiah spoke of those who can't see; but they hear the voice. They're in close enough proximity to the Lord to hear his voice even though they can't see. This verse relates to disciples who hear and respond to the invitation to come and see. They follow without seeing where they're going. They trust in the name and obey the voice.

The next verse in Isaiah describes Judas' situation. "Behold, all you who kindle a fire, who set brands alight! Walk by the light of your fire, and by the brands which you have kindled! This shall you have from my hand: you shall lie down in torment" (Is. 50:11). Those who don't trust the voice while on this journey—who don't rely on their God—will kindle their own fire for light in the darkness. The frightening thing is that God permits them to continue in this self-deception.

### The Light of His Presence

Jesus and his disciples are in the garden, but John makes no mention of any of them having lanterns or torches. The absence of this detail in John's report of that night may be intentional. The *sign* is that the disciples didn't need the light of torches because they were with the true light of the world. They'll later receive that light *in* them on the Day of Pentecost.

Even then they will not understand the fullness of what they see in Jesus Christ, but they will see by his light, albeit as "in a glass darkly" (see I Cor. 13:12). They're simply following the one whose light enlightens every man. As they follow they have the expectation of seeing him face to face at the end of their journey.

Jesus has been among them for some time as the light shining in the darkness. They've been walking with him without seeing the fullness of that light. Jesus says to Philip, *"Have I been with you so long, and yet you do not know me?"* (Jn. 14:9). There had been moments when they'd seen glimmers of the light, as when Martha said, *"I believe you are the Christ, the Son of God"* (Jn. 11:27). And Peter had seen something when he declared, *"You are the Holy one of God"* (Jn. 6:69). But none of them had seen that light clearly. If they had, that night and the following three days would have been different.

Judas and his band are walking by the only light they know. Because they have torches, they're not stumbling on rocks or fallen branches, but they're stumbling over the Rock that will become the cornerstone of the Father's household (see Eph. 2:20). Judas has been walking by his own light all along. He continues to rely on his own torch even when following the light of the world.

That explains how he's been able to come toward the *place* without even a glimmer of the true light to help him see what was there to be seen. He knows Jesus, but only with his own human understanding. He's seen, but only with the human light of the torches he had kindled. He's a prisoner of his own bubble.

The choice is clear: walk by the light of his presence (the only light that lets us to see what's really there) or walk by your own light (the light that lets us cover our own sin but won't let us see the Father in the one who's there in the darkness with us). Walking by the first light leads to participation in the peaceful life of the Father and Son. Walking by the second light leads to death and torment.

When you're in that dark place of not fully understanding, don't strike a match. Call on the name of the Lord, listen for his voice, and abide in his presence.

### Illustrated by the Blind Man Story

The story of the blind man helps us. The Pharisees are walking by their own light when they say to Jesus, *"We see"* (Jn. 9:41). Depending on the light of their torches, they can say with confidence, *"This man is not from God"* (Jn. 9:16). In their darkness, they lift their lanterns in Jesus' presence and say, *"We know this man is a sinner"* (Jn. 9:24). That kind of self-assurance isn't available to those who walk in the light of the Father's presence in Jesus Christ.

The blind man sees, but he isn't self-confident. When Jesus asks if he believes in the Son of man, he doesn't come up with a pat religious answer. He asks a question—an indication of a seeking heart: *"And who is he, sir, that I may believe in him?"* (Jn. 9:36). Even though Jesus has opened his eyes, he doesn't assume he can see clearly by his own light. He's willing to ask. He's walking in the light of dawning revelation.

### Seeking and Finding

*"Whom do you seek"* (Jn. 18:4)? Let's return to the story of the arrest. Jesus takes the initiative even in his own arrest. This question is similar to his question to the Baptist's two disciples who'd turned to follow him: *"What do you seek?"* The question here is also significant. He isn't wondering which of the men in this small group these guards are looking for. Perhaps the best way to uncover the significance of this question is to consider how a true disciple would answer. To Jesus' earlier question, the disciples answered, "We're seeking the abiding place that lets you walk upright." Every disciple's answer to *"Whom do you seek?"* should be, "We're seeking the Father who abides in the Son."

*"Jesus of Nazareth..."* (Jn. 18:5). These men aren't seeking the Father and they aren't seeking the Son. They're seeking Jesus of Nazareth. Their focus is on the *man* who is threatening their world view. Who would knowingly come to arrest the Lord God? By the same token, what man earnestly seeking the Lord would come to arrest Jesus of Nazareth? Jesus is Lord.

As we noticed in the story of the Samaritan woman, there's a distinction between his humanity and his divinity. We can see his humanity without seeing his divinity. That should be obvious after reading this far. These soldiers are blind to the divinity of the one they've found by their torches.

To seek Jesus of Nazareth is not necessarily to seek the Lord, but to arrest him is to bring God under the judgment of your own human tribunal. The soldiers don't know the fullness of deity is pleased to dwell in him (see Col. 1:19). Jesus is Lord.

*"Judas, who betrayed him, was standing with them"* (Jn. 18:5). Judas hasn't been standing with the Lord during this encounter. He's positioned himself with those who kindle a fire, who set brands alight. He's standing with Satan and with those who aren't on the side of God but of men. During his time with the other disciples, he probably said all the right words and did all the right actions (like many today), but he wasn't standing with them.

## Jesus Is the "I AM"

*"I am he"* (Jn. 18:5). There's revelation in Jesus' response. The phrase can be translated simply, "I AM." It echoes the name by which God revealed himself to Moses at the burning bush: "I AM THAT I AM" (Ex. 3:14). Jesus is identifying himself as the God who appeared to Moses in the burning bush. He'd previously identified himself in this way to the Jews: *"Before Abraham was, I am"* (Jn. 8:58). We

can expand his response in this way, *"The Jesus of Nazareth whom you seek is the 'I AM' whom you do not seek."*

**"They drew back and fell to the ground"** (Jn. 18:6). They were in the presence of the coming King with no eyes to see. They were under the power of the coming Kingdom with no ability to stand, much less enter. They were lame and paralyzed. The simple act of uttering his divine name puts them to the ground. Under the power of the presence of the Father in Christ Jesus, these men fall to the ground just like the priests when the glory of the Lord entered he temple (see I Kings 8:11). It seems like this kind of experience would get their attention. But just like some religious people today, they discount it as an odd phenomenon, dust themselves off, and continue on their mission.

## Substitution

*"If you seek me, let these men go"* (Jn. 18:8). Jesus is Lord even in his arrest. Here he's telling the soldiers what to do. One can't find a clearer statement of Jesus' work of substitution. *"Let these men go."* The only person in the garden that night that doesn't deserve to die is letting himself be taken in the place of all others.

Father is providing the true Passover Lamb for his house-hold. The Lamb is being led to the slaughter without opening his mouth in resistance. Because of him we're delivered from the Evil One who comes to kill, steal, and destroy. Here is the offering of the Day of Atonement as well. He's taking on himself the sins of the world. He'll take all sins outside the gate and deposit them permanently in the grave.

Because of him we can live. Because of him we're free. We're free to take this journey to the Father and abide in the place Jesus went to prepare for us—Father's bosom. Because of him we can love our neighbors and bring them to the Father.

## Simon Peter's Boldness

*"Simon Peter, having a sword, drew it* and **struck the high priest's slave and cut off his right ear"** (Jn. 18:10). Here again Peter moves without listening for the voice. He doesn't wait for instructions. He wants to lead. Judas is likely encouraged. Probably both he and Peter think Jesus will now follow their lead and make his move to establish himself as King of Israel.

Jesus is already making his move toward receiving his crown. None of these disciples know the way to the place of coronation. If he'd let them lead, they'd have gone straight for the golden crown. They don't understand that the way to glory is through suffering, not through self-assertion. They can't even suspect that the crown waiting for this King is a crown of thorns. Nothing like that has ever entered their bubble.

*"Simon Peter...struck the high priest's slave."* We noted earlier that 'Simon' refers to this man with his human heritage and inclinations. 'Peter' refers to the new man he will become with a heritage from his Father in heaven. He's no longer merely Simon; he's Simon becoming Peter. The additional element here is that he's Simon trying to be Peter, the Rock, in his own human strength and human wisdom.

Probably he's trying to prove to Jesus that he's willing to risk everything and fight for the kingdom. He's showing how far he's willing to go to avoid denying Jesus. *Simon is a sign of disciples in every age who're willing to wound others to establish their identity and leadership.* How is this any different from Judas walking by the light of his own lantern? Human light, human strength, human wisdom—it's all human. What really distinguishes Judas from Simon?

A major point of interest is Simon Peter's boldness and confidence. He knows he's the only disciple with a sword and he knows they're outnumbered. He knows they have no chance of victory unless Jesus backs him up in this attack. His boldness is exemplary. His confidence in Jesus' ability is well founded. Jesus could have overcome the crowd with a word. But Simon's understanding of the way of the Kingdom is based on human wisdom. "Defeat violence with violence" seems to be his motto.

Any study of Peter's denial must keep this boldness in mind. He won't back down just to save his own skin. He's no coward. He isn't fearful. He's willing to risk everything to defend the cause as he understands it.

## *The Most Significant Intersection*

*"Put your sword in its sheath"* (Jn. 18:11). This command must've come as a shock to Peter. He puts his life on the line for Jesus and Jesus rebukes him. Judas is probably shocked as well. It's now clear to both of them that their ideas and plans are contrary to the direction Jesus has chosen for himself.

Both have tried to force Jesus' hand. Both are now faced with a decision about their future. Will they continue to follow this man Jesus as he obviously goes in a direction contrary to their preconceived notions? Or will they choose their own way against his? Will they walk in the light of their own torches, in their own strength and wisdom? Or will they continue to follow this light even though it's shining very dimly? Will they believe in the light, that they might become sons of light (see Jn. 12:36)?

Here's the most significant intersection on the discipleship road. The roads aren't marked, there are no natural signs. Such experiences don't come with a label: "This is a test," though there are warning sings along the way. The absence of any spoken word from Jesus intensifies the darkness.

He doesn't invite Simon to follow nor does he ask Judas to come stand with him. He leaves each to face this decisive crossroad without a word, without the voice. Their choice will expose what's inside. Has the light found an opening to enter their heart? Let me explain the significance of this question.

*"If any one walks in the day,"* Jesus says, *"he does not stumble because he sees the light of this world"* (Jn. 11:9). The light of this world can keep you from stumbling in this world as long as it is day. But day has ended. It's night. Actually it's been night for centuries. The dawn of the New Creation is at hand. The night is darkest just before the dawn.

*"But if any one walks in the night,"* Jesus continues, *"he stumbles, because the light is not in him"* (Jn. 11:10). The opposite is also true: if one has the light *in* him he won't stumble in the night. If these men have the light *in* them, they won't stumble by choosing the wrong road at this critical dividing point. Since all the disciples stumble that night, we conclude that the light was not yet in them, at least not fully.

## The Great Divide

Up to this point we've emphasized the similarities between Judas and Peter. Here we see the key differences that really matter. Along the path, walking with Jesus, Peter has been open to receive a glimmer of the light into himself. He will stumble momentarily and he will even fall. But because he's willing to receive more light, he'll be able to rise again. "A righteous man falls seven times, and rises again; but the wicked are overthrown by calamity" (Prov. 24:16).

Judas clings to his torch and doesn't let the light from the new world penetrate. He'll fall, never to rise again. In John this is the last we hear of Judas. He's no longer there. He's exposed as one who's been on a totally different journey all along.

Peter follows—yes, at a distance, but follows still. He could've walked away and sought another Messiah who would appreciate his strength and wisdom. Here's the key difference between true and false disciples. True disciples follow even when they don't understand where Jesus is leading. False disciples go their own way.

The *basis* of true discipleship is the *presence* of the Lord. The *motive* of true discipleship is *to be with him* no matter where it takes you or what it costs in terms of reputation or comfort. What should we do when Jesus doesn't go our way? Peter illustrates one option; Judas illustrates the other. Are you still with us?

*"So the band of soldiers...seized Jesus and bound him"* (Jn. 18:12). I stand in awe at this event. A group of men arrest the Lord, the 'I AM'. They're actually able to bind him. How can a creature put his maker under constraint? Can a man put God on a leash? But the real wonder isn't that they do that. They could've done nothing if Jesus hadn't given himself in love, if he hadn't chosen to become flesh and dwell among us, if the Father hadn't loved the world enough to send his Son.

## Simon Peter's Denial

*"Simon Peter followed Jesus, and so did another disciple"* (Jn. 18:15). Full of disillusionment, Peter follows Jesus. Renouncing his own idea of how this journey *ought* to end, he follows. He follows without knowing what to expect, without knowing what might be required of him, without knowing where Jesus is going. In total abandonment, expecting nothing in return, he follows. *He follows Jesus*. Is that not a picture of true discipleship?

*"And so did another disciple."* John presents himself anonymously again. John and Peter are the only disciples who follow Jesus into the court of the High Priest's house. The others flee and scatter in the night. John follows quietly and at peace. Peter follows also but confusion churns within him because Jesus rebuked him when he tried to be a good disciple. Even though it's dark and the light of Jesus' presence isn't discernable, he follows. He remains at a distance, but not so far away that he can't see Jesus.

*"This disciple was known to the high priest"* (Jn. 18:15). John apparently comes from a family of significant social standing. Only upper class people, or people with a lot of money, are known in the court of the High Priest. Yet the

maid at the door and those in the court know John. He's allowed to enter with no questions asked. (This probably means that John's family was very successful as fishermen.) But Peter can't enter until John speaks to the maid.

*"So the other disciple spoke to the maid"* (Jn. 18:16). The maid, the official door-keeper, must see that no trouble-makers enter the court that night so she isn't willing to let Peter in. But John is not only known there; he's respected enough that, when he wants to bring a friend, he's not refused. The maid trusts John and she's willing to trust his friend at his request. As Peter enters, she wants to know if he's a disciple.

### The Unexpected Question

*"Are not you also one of this man's disciples"* (Jn. 18:17). She knows John is a disciple of Jesus. The word *'also'* tells us that. She wouldn't have stopped Peter from coming in because of this; she'd already let John enter. She simply wants to know. The question comes as a surprise if we're expecting Peter to deny Jesus as the Christ (and he will). She doesn't ask, "Do you believe this man is the Son of God, the Christ?" She doesn't ask about his belief; she asks about his discipleship.

Since Jesus had predicted that Peter would deny *him*, I would've expected her to ask if Peter believed that Jesus was the Messiah. The lordship of Jesus wasn't in question here, at least not in the mind of the maid. Perhaps there's something we need to learn from this curious turn of events.

### Peter is Not

*"I am not"* (Jn. 18:17). The insight from this response is profound. Peter didn't say, "He is not," referring to Jesus. He said, *"I am not."* Jesus had said, *"I AM."* Simon can only say, *"I am not."* John the Baptist's reply to those who asked if he was Elijah was the same: "I am not." Jesus is the light; John

is not. When we compare ourselves among ourselves we can say, "I am this," or "I am that." But when we compare our being with the great "I AM," we can only say, "I am not." On the other hand, when the Lord speaks into our nothingness we are what he says we are. Peter is denying that he is what Jesus called him.

There's more. Let's paraphrase this to capture its significance. "You ask me if I'm this man's disciple. Until tonight I thought I was. I tried to be his disciple. I wanted to prove myself as his disciple. I even put my life on the line trying to be the Peter he's called me to become. When he rebuked me and told me to put my sword away it suddenly occurred to me that I've not been following him; I've been following my own dream. No, even though I wanted to be and tried to be, I'm not (yet) Peter, this man's disciple. I'm only Simon, the son of John."

These are the obvious implications of his answer in light of her question. She asked about his discipleship, not about his belief in Messiah. He has finally come to accept himself as one who is not (yet) the one Jesus called him to be. In his denial, he's walking in the light of exposure.

*"This man's disciple?"* The maid asks, pointing a finger at Jesus who is at the mercy of his accusers. Let's read between the lines again. "No, I'm not *this* man's disciple. If you'd asked me last year, I'd have confessed my discipleship with pride. The man I was following had an answer for every accuser. He left them speechless and dumbfounded. One time they came to arrest him and returned to those who sent them saying, 'No man ever spoke like this man.'

I was *Thatman's* disciple. *Thatman* was my leader. I would follow *Thatman* even into the jaws of death. But *this man* has given himself into their hands and has done nothing to defend himself. This is *not* the man I was following."

*"This man's disciple?"* She points to this man whose life is obviously near its end. She's been at other trials of this

nature; she knows he's going to die. "No, the man I was following has life in himself and gives life to whomsoever he wills. When he speaks, his words are spirit and life (see Jn. 6:63). To be with him is to be in the presence of eternal life itself. But *this* man? There's death in the air. No! I'm not *this man's* disciple."

## The Lord of Glory Is the Suffering Servant

We can identify ourselves with Jesus' power and authority while refusing to identify with him in his weakness and vulnerability. But, *to fail to follow him in his weakness is to fail as a believer.* It exposes that we're not following the one who was on the way to the cross. To turn from him in his weakness is to turn from him in his real strength, because he is the same one in his strength as he is in his weakness.

There's not one Jesus who's strong and another who's weak. There's only one Lord. And he's Lord precisely in his weakness, for it's on the cross that he disarmed all the principalities and powers (see Col. 2:15).

We can't be a disciple of the Lord of glory without being a disciple of the Suffering Servant, for there is no Lord of glory who isn't also the Suffering Servant. If we try to follow the Lord of glory apart from his suffering, we're following a lord that exists only in our imagination. There are gods which are "no gods" (see Deut. 32:17) who promise power without weakness and glory without suffering. But the power they offer is weakness and their glory is shame. Their message comes from the father of lies and their disciples are deceived by that lie. Their end is death with no resurrection.

Jesus had said to Peter, "**You will deny me three times.**" As it turns out, *Peter really did deny the Lord.* He may have thought he was denying his discipleship, and he was. But at the same time he was denying that *this man* on his way to the cross is the Lord of glory. To deny that the one who appears in weakness is the same one who appears in power is to deny the Lord.

We make a false claim when we say we're following Jesus in his miracle ministry while refusing to take up our cross and follow him in his Suffering Servant role. By that false claim we're denying that Jesus is Lord of our personal life.

*To deny one's discipleship at this intersection is to deny the Lord.*

## This Man's Disciple

When we consider the rest of the story, we can see why Judas isn't given the leading role on the Day of Pentecost. He withdrew himself from the race. Taking his case into his own hands he judged, condemned, and executed himself. It isn't yet clear, however, why Peter was chosen to take the lead. He hadn't run away in the night, true; but Peter wasn't the only disciple who had followed Jesus to the trial.

John was also there and he continued to follow Jesus even to the cross. Peter didn't. The maid who asked Peter the fatal question knew John was a disciple; and John didn't try to cover himself by denying his discipleship. He didn't deny the Lord in his hour of trial as Peter did. Why is Peter chosen to lead rather than John? The answer isn't found in Peter's badness or in John's goodness. The answer is only in the gift and calling of the one who called Simon and changed his name to Peter.

Peter probably experienced some of what we call self-condemnation, but he didn't take judgment into his own hands. Having followed Jesus, he remained in the vicinity of his presence. He followed "afar off," but he followed. Even though he followed as the one who denied the Lord, he still followed.

In following Jesus, he came to the place of being fully exposed in his self-directed discipleship. But he experienced that exposure in the presence of the one who forgives the sins of those who don't hide from the light. Judas walked away from the light and experienced his exposure outside the realm where grace operates, away from the presence of the Lamb of God who takes away the sins of the world. Are you being exposed?

## *Abiding in His Presence is the Key*

We need to learn from this. When we find ourselves exposed as sinners it's critical for us to remain in his presence. When we grovel in self-condemnation and self-pity we're behaving as though the one we follow isn't the one who died in our place. By condemning ourselves we deny that Jesus is the one who has taken our guilt on himself. We deny that Jesus is both the Lord of glory and the Suffering Servant. On the other hand, when we remain with him in the light of exposure—when we're willing to say, "I am not,"—we become true disciples, walking in the light.

When we go to him with our sin, rather than trying to deal with it ourselves, we acknowledge that he is Lord over death, hell, and the sin that would take us there. We acknowledge that we're his disciples in spite of our weakness. We live our life as the weak who need his strength, as the sinners who need his grace, as the sick who need his healing. We follow him as those on their way out of death into life.

Our discipleship isn't a result of our insight or ability. *If I'm a disciple of this man, it's not because of my courage to stand but because of his commitment to be with me.* When I come to him with my shortcomings (which are very short and always coming), it's still into his presence that I come. In that presence there's exposure but that exposure brings healing for my paralysis and sight for my blind eyes. Now I can follow him, stumbling and rising again with his help. In him I have a Helper. I can follow him into the Father's embrace because he helps me in my weakness. From that position in the Father, he will thrust me into the fulfillment of his will in the earth.

Are you *this man's* disciple? Will you follow him in his trial and crucifixion? Or do you only want to be identified with his glory? Are you willing to die for him? Will you live for him?

In our next chapter we will see the significance of the washing of the disciples' feet and will find the standard by which true discipleship is measured.

# CHAPTER 9

# Do As I Have Done

—⁕—

U p to this point we've focused on the abiding place and the way to get there. Jesus is the abiding place and the way; the Father is the destination. Our *destiny* is to be conformed to the image of Jesus Christ. Our *destination* is to be in the bosom of the Father. We made a distinction between our abiding in him and his abiding in us. To the degree that we abide in Christ we are already in the Father's bosom. As we do what we see him doing he abides in us and his will is done in earth as in heaven.

Now we turn to the practical question: How can I know I'm abiding in him and he in me? Let's begin with Jesus' activity on the fourth day of chapter one (see Jn. 1:43-51). We will not find our full answer in this text, but we will find pointers. One of our purposes is to continue to demonstrate the integrity of John, how he introduces a topic early and elaborates on it later. After noticing how Philip followed, we will discuss the story of Jesus washing the disciple's feet. There we will find our answer.

## *Finding and Following*
*"He found Philip and said to him, 'Follow me'"* (Jn. 1:43). This is no chance encounter. Jesus seeks him out.

Philip isn't looking for Jesus. He may be looking for the Messiah, but he has no way to know this man Jesus from Nazareth is the one he's looking for. Jesus hasn't performed any miracles. He hasn't taught any profound teachings. Philip isn't there because he's heard John say, "Behold, the Lamb." He doesn't know who Jesus is. But Jesus knows who Philip is and he knows his Father is drawing Philip to himself. So Jesus seeks him out and finds him.

I can't help but wonder when I hear, "I found the Lord." I'm not opposed to describing our encounter with God like that, but our language may betray our self-centeredness. God wasn't lost. We were lost, blind, and paralyzed. Even if we were looking for him, he was looking for us long before we even thought about him. We may have been looking for 'God' in some sense, but when he finds us there's usually an element of surprise on our part. Where would we be if we'd found the 'God' we were looking for? I'd probably be involved with some form of eastern religion or the New Age movement. I'm glad the true God sought me out and found me.

### Is there a Standard?

"*Follow me.*" We've already asked, "What does it really mean to follow Jesus?" If it means to get behind him and go the same way he is going (and it must mean that if it means anything), then it's important to discover which way he's going. We emphasized the importance of following him in what he's presently doing rather than trying to follow a map or written instructions. We must be present to him in the moment to follow him in what he's doing today.

In this chapter we'll explore whether we have any concrete standard by which we can discern what he's doing today. Is there anything like a general scenario we can use as a paradigm of the way of abiding in the Son on the way to Father's bosom? Some pretend to hear from God. Others are deceived, thinking they're following God when they're not. The danger of self deception is always present unless we have something to tie our confidence to. Without an anchor we can only drift with the current or be blown by winds of doctrine. *So what distinguishes genuine hearing from presumption or deception?*

### An Emerging Pattern

"*Philip found Nathaniel*" (Jn. 1:45). When Jesus calls Philip, he says to him, "*Follow me.*" Before he actually joins the band of men who were with Jesus, Philip does something that indicates he's entering into the way. Philip first finds Nathaniel and says to him, "*We have found him of whom Moses in the law and also the prophets wrote, Jesus of Nazareth, the son of Joseph.*" On the surface it might look like Philip is delayed in responding to the call to follow. But he's actually following Jesus in this act. Jesus had found him and called him to himself; Philip follows by finding Nathanial and inviting him to come along. This isn't yet the security we're looking for but we're beginning to see the direction the arrow is pointing. *Following is doing what he does.*

We find further indication that Philip is following Jesus in Philip's words when Nathaniel responds negatively: "*Can anything good come out of Nazareth?*" Philip's answer is simple and to the point. "*Come and see*" (Jn. 1:46). Like Jesus, he doesn't try to convince Nathaniel with logic. He doesn't list prophecies and try to show how Jesus fulfilled them. He simply issues the invitation, "*Come and see.*"

This invitation comes in the same form as Jesus' invitation to the first disciples. Philip is following in the way by bringing others to path toward the abiding place with him. He may not understand—in fact, he probably doesn't—but he's following. We still haven't found the security we're looking for. Even those who are deceived invite others to join them in their deception.

The Samaritan woman went into the city and called others to Jesus in this same way: *"Come and see"* (Jn. 4:29). She also seemed to know that bringing others to the place of revelation and obedience does not involve convincing arguments or prescribed steps of action. To see Jesus in the abiding place one must come *to him*. It's possible to follow a philosopher without ever knowing him personally. One can be a disciple of a great teacher by reading his books. To be a disciple of this man Jesus however, one must be where he is and do what he's doing. There's no other way to follow this man.

Each man must see for himself and this seeing can only occur in the presence of Jesus. I can't depend on someone else's seeing. Even if they've seen clearly, I must see for myself. Others who have seen can only invite; they can't take you there. You must come. I must come. We can't follow the living Jesus and accomplish the Father's will unless we're being led by the Holy Spirit. Others can invite, but we must follow Jesus.

Prescribed steps can't bring us to this place. That's a legalistic system. These steps may reflect the way Jesus has led someone else, but the question remains: "Is that the way he is leading me?"

## Abiding and Following

This leading is available and possible in the place where the Father abides in the Son and the Son abides in the Father. Jesus Christ is himself that place and that way. To walk in this way we must simply come to Jesus daily, see what he's doing, hear what he's saying today, and walk in obedience. But many of us have tried to hear his voice and walk this way only to discover we can want it desperately, but we can't do it alone. "The spirit is willing but the flesh is weak" (Matt. 26:41).

Judas and Simon were both with Jesus (the right place) and following him (the right way) as he moved through

Galilee and Judea. Neither of them was *in* Christ and neither of them was able to follow him faithfully. That only became a possibility after the resurrection when the Holy Spirit came upon the disciples.

To be in his presence is not enough; we must also walk in his way. To do this we need power beyond ourselves. That power comes through the Holy Spirit. As the Spirit of him who raised Jesus from the dead abides in us, his Spirit empowers our mortal body to produces fruit for God (see Rom. 8:11). The words he speaks to us become *"spirit and life"* to us as we rely on the Spirit that gives life. The flesh can never accomplish the will of the Father (see Jn. 6:63).

This returns us to the practical question: Is there any concrete content to this concept of abiding? Are there any trustworthy principles that help us recognize the way and know those who walk in it? Anyone can claim to be in this place and tell us he knows the way. But it's an open question whether he's really in *this* place. He may be 'abiding' in the vain imaginings of his bubble. If he's in some other place, then his directions and guidance will lead in a direction I don't want to go.

Is there a standard that we can judge such claims by? Can I know whether the way I'm going leads to life or death?

## Washing the Disciples' Feet

Jesus said something to his disciples that points us in the right direction. *"I have given you an example, that you also should do as I have done to you"* (Jn. 13:15). Taken alone and out of context, we can easily misinterpret this. Some suggest we try to live by some ethical system which they assume Jesus followed. The content of such a system might be something like: "Don't drink, don't smoke, don't chew and don't go with girls that do." Jesus did not focus on these externals. He focused on the heart of man as he relates to his fellowman and to God.

Another approach might be to recognize the context of foot-washing and insist that we wash each other's feet when we come together. After all, Jesus did say, *"If I then, your Lord and teacher, have washed your feet, you also ought to wash one another's feet"* (Jn.13:14). There can be value in a foot-washing ceremony. I've been part of several, and the Lord moved in a beautiful way among his people as we humbled ourselves before each another in this way. But, at the same time it's possible to do the external deed and miss the point so that the ceremony becomes just another ritual. It's also possible to fulfill the deeper intent of this command without actually washing feet.

As we look at the context of the washing of the disciples' feet, we'll see the standard by which all discipleship can be judged. We can't discover this standard merely by looking at the elements of the story without following the line of the pointing finger. Jesus' acts are signs pointing beyond themselves to something much deeper in Father's heart. They're also signs that point us in the direction we should go as we follow Jesus into the heart of God. That's why he said, *"Do as I have done."*

## Setting the Stage

John set the stage in the first three verses of chapter 13. He wants us to read the story in light of its introduction where he gives the keys to interpret it. Behind every movement of the unfolding drama, he wants us to see certain things in the background and let this backdrop interpret the story. Let's look at the arrangement of the stage.

*"Now before the feast of the Passover..."* (Jn. 13:1). The events occur before the Passover, and John wants us to see the details of the story in their relationship to that feast. Passover is the feast where an innocent lamb is given over to slaughter so the household might be protected from death and delivered from bondage by applying the shed blood.

The father of the household provides the lamb, and the lamb goes to the slaughter without lifting up its voice in protest or resistance.

At this Passover feast, the Father will provide his Son, Jesus, as the Lamb for slaughter; and the Son will go that way in submissive obedience to his Father.

*"When Jesus knew that his hour had come to depart out of this world..."* (Jn. 13:1). Throughout the Gospel, Jesus refers to this hour. It's the hour when both the Son and the Father will be glorified. It's also the hour of his departure from this world, the hour of his death. John wants us to see that the glory of the Son and the glory of the Father shine most brilliantly through the obedience of the Son, even to the point of death on the cross. Seen through the lens of the resurrection, the death of Jesus is the hour of his greatest glory. His love is most clearly manifested there.

## *The Basic Scenario*

John also outlines the basic scenario of the way of our obedience. The details he includes help us recognize the basic elements of a life abiding in the Father's love.

*"Having loved his own who were in the world..."* (Jn. 13:1) The ones who are his own in this story may only be the believers who keep his word and enter into the abiding place, those *"you gave me out of the world,"* the ones who *"have kept your word"* (Jn. 17:6). But this phrase may also include his own who received him not as well as those who believed in his name (see Jn. 1:11-12). In other words, the deed about to be prefigured in the washing of the disciples' feet may be for the whole world, or it may be only for disciples.

All men are his—he created them. No man or woman has any other origin. Some live as though they aren't his. But they remain his, even when they don't receive him. Man's rejection of God doesn't override the fact that he created them and they are his. Show me a man who created himself and I'll show you one who doesn't belong to God.

Someday the Son will deny many before his Father, but that doesn't alter the fact that he's their Creator and he loves them. He retains the right of ownership even when they illegally sell themselves to the devil. It's his right of ownership that gives him the right to judge them. If they belonged to another, he wouldn't be their judge. When he brings some to judgment that doesn't imply he doesn't love them. The judgment is simply the fruit of their rejecting his love.

## *The Question of Judgment*

Notice the development of the theme of judgment in John 3:16-17. (1) *"For God so loved the world that he gave his only son, that whoever believes in him should not perish but have eternal life."* This makes it clear that God loves the whole world, not merely those who believe. (2) *"For God sent his Son into the world, not to condemn the world, but that the world might be saved through him."* God's ultimate intention is salvation, not judgment. (3) *"He who believes in him is not condemned; he who does not believe is condemned already because has not believed in the name of the only Son of God."* Judgment and condemnation do not originate in the will of God, but in man's rejection of the Father's gift of love.

So the question before us is whether this phrase 'his own' refers to all mankind or only to those who become believers. We'll keep the question before us as we continue. The story itself will provide an answer for us. However, we do have a preliminary indication of the standard we're looking for. *If we're judging and condemning others, we're not following him in the way.*

## The Extent of His Love

*"He loved them to the end"* (Jn. 13:1). The familiar translation of "to the end" is misleading. It sounds like it implies that he loved them (and us) all the way to death. For a natural human being, that would indeed be the maximum expression of love. But we know that Jesus continues to love even after his death.

This phrase indicates the *extent* of the love expressed rather than the *duration* of that love. The NIV translates it *"the full extent of his love."* "He loved them to the end of loving," is a good way to say it. "All the love that's in the Father comes to full expression in this deed," might even be a better way to capture the meaning. Behind this unfolding drama of foot-washing is the backdrop of all the love that is God himself. All the love resident in the Father is available to us in the event this story points to. No segment of God's love is held in reserve. It's all poured out for those who are *his own.*

## The Covenant Meal

*"And during supper…"* (Jn. 13:2). John is the only gospel that doesn't record the institution of the Lord's Supper. The details make it clear that John is recounting events that took place at the Last Supper. The other gospels reflect the significance of the Lord's Supper in the breaking of the bread and the drinking of wine. John has already connected the Bread to the Body of Christ in the feeding of the multitude and he referred to the Blood of Jesus as the drink that brings life.

Here John wants us to see the significance of that night through the details of the foot-washing. The reality this sign points to is the same reality that the sign of the Lord's Supper points to. However, we'll see it from a different perspective.

*"When the devil had already put it into the heart of Judas Iscariot, Simon's son, to betray him…"* (Jn. 13:2). For some reason, it's important for us to know that Judas has

already made his decision and that Jesus is aware of his plan. We need to see that Jesus doesn't reject him even though Judas has rejected the way Jesus is going. Jesus doesn't withhold from him the benefit of the deed prefigured that night, even though he knows what's in Judas' heart.

Judas fails to receive what's offered, but *Jesus doesn't fail to make the offer.* If Judas is no longer one of his own, the separation is an act of Judas, not an act of Jesus. Jesus hasn't come to judge, he's come to save whosoever will. Judas removes himself from the place of abiding where that blessing is available; but that blessing is still available to him if he will only choose to receive it now.

Here's another preliminary indication of the way. *If we're excluding others we're not following Jesus in the way.*

## The Head of the Household

*"Jesus, knowing that the Father had given all things into his hands..."* (Jn. 13:3). The act Jesus performs that night is with the full knowledge of his position as the Son of the Father. He knows he's heir to the throne. He's aware that the whole estate—heaven and earth—is his. He's not ignorant of his position as the one who "reflects the glory of God and bears the very stamp of his nature, upholding the universe by his word of power" (Heb. 1:3). As we follow the drama, we mustn't forget who the principal actor is or lose sight of the extent of the estate he's head of.

*"And that he had come from God and was going to God..."* (Jn. 13:3). He not only knows what belongs to him, he knows where he came from and where he's going. He knows he'd been in the beginning with God and that he is himself God (see Jn. 1:1). He's aware that he'll soon return to the glory he had with his Father from the beginning. He's on the way to being exalted at the right hand of the Father (see Eph. 1:21) and the Father will shortly bestow on him the "name which is above every name" (Phil. 2:9).

A person who knows he's a dignitary and that he's about to be exalted doesn't normally do what Jesus did that night. But Jesus knows there's only one way to come to the glory that's eternal, and there's only one way to take others back with him into the Father's bosom—it can only be accomplished through radical servant-hood. The greatest of all is the servant of all.

## *This is the Way*

John isn't merely interested in the fact that Jesus knew these things about himself. He wants us to see them as the backdrop that gives meaning and significance to the various acts as the drama unfolds. It's not enough to notice what he did; we must recognize *who* did this and *where* he was going when he did it. We must notice, because *this is the way* of those who are on the way into the Father's bosom.

Washing feet alone doesn't express the fullness of what John wants us to see. It points in the right direction, but it's not the point. There's no deep significance to the fact that the disciples' feet were clean that night. This is one of the signs that was written "that you may believe" (Jn. 20:31). We must follow the line of the pointing finger to find the way of abiding in the bosom of the Father.

It's good for the church to know that Jesus washed the disciples' feet. He was willing to humble himself to the position of the lowest slave of the household. But if we close our study there we'll miss a greater point. How can we see the Passover Lamb in his act of laying aside his garments? How can we see the full extent of God's love in his filling the basin with water?

In this unfolding drama we must see Jesus on his journey from his eternal position with the Father through his earthly experience. We must see him returning to the Father's bosom with many brothers and sisters. We must see because this is the way we're called to walk. Our journey begins from the

Father's bosom when we are begotten by the seed which is the living and abiding word (see I Pet. 1:23). Our journey continues as we go to our neighbor and return to the Father's bosom bringing them with us.

This is the background we must approach the story with. With the stage set in this way we'll be able to see what John wants us to see. With this backdrop in full view we'll be able to hear what he wants us to hear. If we really see and really hear, our faith will be rekindled and we'll find ourselves in the abiding place on the way out of death into life. And we won't be alone on the journey—He'll be with us, and we will be in a peaceful community of believers intimately connected to one another and to our Father.

## *Paul's Contribution*

Let's look at one more thing before we look at the story more closely. The 'backdrop' that gives meaning and significance to the story of the foot-washing is the incarnation, crucifixion, resurrection, and exaltation of Jesus. John presents the theology of the cross in story form. What Paul presents in logical fashion in his epistles, John presents in the stories and dialogues of his Gospel. In other words, John's supreme interest is in the theological and practical implications of Jesus' life, death, and resurrection. This biographical sketch points to the truth of who Jesus is as the Son of God and what we must do to follow him.

We can understand the theology of this story most clearly by looking at Paul's logical presentation of the gospel side-by-side with John's story. For this purpose we'll look at Paul's synopsis of the life of Christ on his way out from and back into the Father's heart. Philippians 2:5-11 reads:

> *"Have this mind among yourselves,*
> *which is yours in Christ Jesus, who, though*
> *he was in the form of God, did not count*

*equality with God a thing to be grasped, but emptied himself, taking the form of a servant, being born in the likeness of men. And being found in human form he humbled himself and became obedient unto death, even death on a cross. Therefore God has highly exalted him and bestowed on him the name which is above every name, that at the name of Jesus every knee should bow, in heaven and on earth and under the earth, and every tongue confess that Jesus Christ is Lord, to the glory of God the Father."*

## The Acts of that Night

Paul's statement portrays Jesus as coming from the Father into the world and going back to the Father. Let's compare Paul's synopsis step by step with John's story of the washing of the disciples' feet.

## The Servant's Position

Jesus *"rose from supper"* (Jn. 13:4). That's his first act. This relates to Paul's statement that Jesus didn't count equality with God a thing to be held on to. Jesus rises from supper in the full knowledge of his position as the "crown prince" into whose hands the Father had given all things. He knows the Father is abiding in him as he approaches the fulfillment of the Passover feast. In Christ Jesus the Father is present at this feast. God was in Christ reconciling the world to himself (see II Cor. 5:19).

In that culture, reclining at a meal is the privilege and prerogative of the father and sons of the household along with their guests. Servants stand and serve during the meal while the privileged recline and eat.

In rising from supper, Jesus demonstrates his willingness to lay down his right as the Son. As heir of all things, he isn't counting his privileged position as something to be grasped. He's giving up his right to be served at table and condescending to the position of a servant—standing.

This act is *a sign pointing to the incarnation.* When the Word of God became flesh he gave up his rights as God and took the position of a servant of God, as a human being.

## The Son's Identity

"*Laid aside his garments…*" (Jn. 13:4). His second act corresponds to Paul's statement that Jesus emptied himself. The garments people wear at a feast identify their social status. Both masters and servants are recognized by the clothes they wear. The guests will still recognize the master if he rises from supper and keeps his status symbols. Jesus' condescension doesn't end with his taking a common position with the servants. He also removes the recognizable marks of his divinity.

When a person divests himself of the uniform that reflects his rank, he doesn't cease to be the one he is. He simply puts himself in a position where his rank won't be recognized and respected by those who don't know him apart from the uniform. When he joins us in our humanity he doesn't cease to be God, but he puts himself in a vulnerable position. In that standing position and with his garments laid aside, he is among other servants as one they can resist and defy; they can even crucify him.

There could've been no effective resistance to his ministry and authority if he'd come into the world fully clothed in the power his divinity.

Jesus didn't come as "the angel of the Lord" when he entered the world in the first century. He didn't appear as a cloud by day or a pillar of fire by night. His coming wasn't attended with thunder, lightning, and a loud trumpet blast as at Mount Sinai. He appeared as a common man from

Nazareth. Nothing about him was intimidating. He was too meek to frighten or command respect from anyone.

## The Servant's Identity

*"Girded himself with a towel..."* (Jn. 13:4). His third act points to his willingness to take not only the position of a servant but also the uniform of a servant. A master who has risen from supper and laid aside his garments still isn't obligated to take on himself the markings of a servant. There will always be servants who recognize him and continue to offer their services to him, even though he's not wearing his expensive clothes.

This Master, Jesus the Son of God, put on the vestments of a servant when he began his ministry. It wasn't enough for him to be found in human form. He became a servant of servants.

To be human is to be a servant of God and a servant of other men and women. That's the design of creation. Since the fall there've been good servants and bad servants. Good or bad, rebellious or submissive, to be found in human form is to be a servant. By girding himself with a towel Jesus was "made like his brethren in every respect" because he "partook of the same nature" (Heb. 2:14, 17).

Even at Jesus' birth we see this. He wasn't born in a king's palace, but in a stable and placed in a manger. If Mary had come with a halo over her head, as many artists depict the story, the innkeeper would have found room for her. After Jesus' birth he wasn't placed in a cradle draped with purple; he was wrapped in the swaddling cloth of common folk and laid in a manger. He came wrapped in the flesh of humanity—poverty stricken humanity at that! The flesh he bore wasn't the flesh of a proud ruler but the flesh of a humble, oppressed member of society. He girded himself with a towel.

"Being found in human form, he humbled himself," is Paul's way of saying it. The towel is a sign of a servant even today. In a restaurant, servants are recognized by a towel over their arm. But in Jesus' day, to be girded with a towel was a mark of the lowest servant in the household. There's a hierarchy among household servants. The personal valet of the master has more status and privileges than the slave who is responsible to wash the feet of guests when they arrive. Jesus girded himself with the markings of the lowest of all servants.

## *Water and Blood in John*

*"Poured water into the basin..."* (Jn. 13:5). His fourth act requires a little more explanation. John plays with the concepts of water and blood, drinking and washing, as they relate to the work of redemption. He does this in his Gospel as well as in First John.

He brings the Holy Spirit into play in the context of water. *"If anyone thirst, let him come to me and drink"* (Jn. 7:37), is spoken of the Holy Spirit the disciples were to receive. In First John, the Holy Spirit is connected with both water and blood: *"there are three witnesses, the Spirit, the water, and the blood; and these three agree"* (I Jn. 5:8).

John is the only evangelist who draws attention to the fact that water and blood came forth from the side of Jesus at his crucifixion. This is a key in John's thinking—it's the only place where he insists on the trustworthiness of this witness (see Jn. 19:34).

The water and the blood coming forth from Jesus' body had a profound effect on John's thinking. This conjunction of blood and water at the most crucial event in all history alerted John to a deeper meaning. Blood and water are important in many Jewish rites and ceremonies. This connection helps us notice what John is drawing attention to when he tells the particular stories in which water and blood are significant. We'll look at several examples to see the trend.

## At the Beginning and the End

For the perceptive reader, blood and water are together at the beginning of the Gospel when Jesus changes the water into wine (see Jn. 2:1-11). Wine is an unmistakable symbol of the blood of Jesus for the early Church. After John witnessed the flow of both blood and water from Jesus' side, he could look back to the event of the changing of the water to wine and see it as the *"first of his signs"* in which Jesus had *"manifested his glory"* (Jn. 2:11). John's Gospel begins and ends by bringing the water and the blood together in a single event.

It's not easy to discover everything John saw in this water-to-wine story, but some things are clear enough. The six stone Jars used for purification rites connect the event to cleansing. The jars were apparently empty, signifying that Jewish rites had nothing more to offer. The Jars are filled with water, the element used in the Jewish right as well as in Christian baptism. Jesus adds the element of wine (for drinking). Wine can refer to the blood that cleanses us (see Rev. 7:14) as well as the Holy Spirit which the disciples were to be filled with (see Eph. 5:18) and which they would drink (see I Cor. 12:13).

Jesus replaced John's baptism with a baptism that included both water and the Holy Spirit. Both cleansing (water) and new life (wine) are available through the ministry of Jesus.

The blood of Jesus is clearly the effective cleansing agent (see I Pet. 3:21). Water is the element where baptism takes place. In our foot-washing story the water poured into the basin was for washing, so John uses this story to point to the water and the blood that flowed from Jesus' side at the cross. But, as we'll see, he's not thinking of the initial cleansing of baptism (or, more accurately, the justification baptism points to). He's thinking of the cleansing ministered to those who are already clean (see Jn. 13:10).

## Both Cleansing and Drinking

The water made into wine wasn't used for washing but for drinking. The second part of Paul's statement in Titus 3:5, the "washing of regeneration and renewal in the Holy Spirit," shows that it was common in the early Church to bring together the washing of baptism and the coming of the Holy Spirit to the individual. The metaphor of drinking refers to the Holy Spirit several times in scripture. For example: "For in one Spirit we were all baptized into one body...and all were made to drink of one Spirit" (I Cor. 12:13).

The reference to baptism and drinking is not a mixing of metaphors but an indication of how the early Church understood their entry into the Body of Christ. They understood themselves to be washed from all contamination as well as filled with new wine, which is the new life in the Spirit.

John does the same in his Gospel: living water is offered as drink to the woman at the well. There it relates to *"worship in spirit and truth"* (Jn. 4:24). Again, Jesus says, *"My blood is drink indeed"* in the context of the feeding of the multitude (Jn. 6:55). In the context of the Feast of Booths he says, *"If any one thirst, let him come to me and drink"* (Jn. 7:37). John tells us that Jesus refers to the Spirit when he speaks of this drink. So with the image of drinking, we have another way in which John brings into conjunction water, blood, and the Holy Spirit.

The water Jesus pours into the basin in our story of the foot-washing points to what is made available through his death. In this story it's not for drinking but for washing feet.

## The Acts of the Servant

*"And began washing the disciples' feet..."* (Jn. 13:5). His fifth act marks the lowest point of his condescension. Although he's divested himself of all the external markings of his divinity, he's still God. Although he's taken on himself the form of a servant, he's still Lord. He doesn't have to serve.

Wasn't it enough for him to humble himself *like* a servant? Hadn't he made his point by humbling himself to the point of looking like a servant? Can't we learn from him that we should humble ourselves before one another by simply noticing that he was willing to gird himself with a towel? Perhaps, but John's point is not merely some internal humility but actual service rendered.

*"You shall never wash my feet"* (Jn. 13:8). Apparently Peter thought it was enough for Jesus to dress like a servant. He didn't actually have to *act* like one. His response is similar to John the Baptist's when Jesus came to be baptized: "I should be baptized by you." (Matt. 3:14) John's reluctance was due to his understanding of baptism as related to the forgiveness of sin. But Peter's resistance comes from his failure to understand: *"You don't understand what I am doing now, but you will understand later"* (Jn. 13:7). Peter's resistance doesn't come from defiance but from misdirected devotion. He wants to protect Jesus from humiliation, just as he does at the arrest.

*"If I do not wash you, you have no part in me"* (Jn. 13:7). One aspect of the significance of the *foot-washing relates to having a part in Jesus Christ.* By the time John's gospel was written, the Church was familiar with Paul's concept of the body of Christ: "Now you are the Body of Christ, and individually members of it" (I Cor. 12:27). To be a part of Jesus Christ is to be a part of the Body of Christ. Being a part involves more than having your name on the church roll. It means being a functioning member of the Body as it "upbuilds itself in love" (Eph. 4:16). Each of us must do our part in building one another up.

*"Lord, not my feet only, but also my hands and my head"* (Jn. 13:8). Simon on his way to becoming Peter reacts in his typical fashion. He isn't willing simply to accept what Jesus offers. He either wants less or more. In saying *"You'll*

*never wash my feet*," or "*wash my hands and my head also*," he's refusing the offer as Jesus presents it to him.

## Bathing and Washing Feet

"*He who has bathed does not need to wash, except for his feet, but he is clean all over*" (Jn. 13:10). Here we see another significance of the washing. It's a ministry to those who are already 'clean all over'. It's for those who've received justification by faith. This answers our earlier question about those who are "*his own who are in the world.*" Those who are 'his own' in this story are the true believers. The reality indicated by this foot-washing is available for baptized believers.

We've seen that there's an aspect of God's love reserved for those who keep his word. To them, Jesus promises that he and the Father will come and make their abode in them. So the love which Jesus offers in the washing of feet is the love of the intimate relationship within the bosom of the Father. That love is received and ministered in the context of being a part of Jesus Christ, being in Christ as a part of his Body. All the love that is in God is available in one way to wash us all over. And it's available in a special way to those who are already clean all over.

## From the Bath House Home

The key to understanding this act lies in the distinction between bathing and washing feet. Most people in that culture didn't have a place for bathing in their homes. They either went to a river or a public bath house to be clean all over. But on the way home, their feet got dirty again. Foot-washing was regularly ministered to anyone who came into the house from a journey which brought their feet into contact with the dirt and filth on the streets. That ministry of washing was administered by the lowliest of servants, the one who girded himself with a towel.

When we come to the 'bath house' of justification by the blood of Jesus, we're cleansed from all our sins—we're clean all over. But we're called to begin a journey toward home. The one who cleansed us doesn't want us to stay at the bath house. He's gone to prepare a place for us in the Father's house and has called us to come abide with him in that place.

When we begin to walk from the cleansing to the abiding place we come into contact with the things of this world. We are sometimes defiled by what we walk through, but only on our feet. We become defiled by anger, resentment, various lusts, selfish ambition, and the like. We need on-going cleansing. We can rejoice because he has provided cleansing for the sins we commit after we're converted as well as those we committed before we turned to him. He has filled the basin with water to take care of any daily contamination while we're on the journey. Glory to God, we're cleansed.

*"And you are clean, but not every one of you"* (Jn. 13:10). Judas, the betrayer, isn't in a position to receive what's really being offered. He hasn't received the initial cleansing of the bath house. But Jesus doesn't single him out in a way that's obvious to the other disciples at this time. Jesus washes Judas' feet also. The offer isn't withheld from him. He does receive the external form of this washing, but apparently without its full internal effect. He has clean feet that night, but he's not clean within—he isn't clean all over.

## Returning to His Place

*"When he had washed their feet, and taken his garments, and resumed his place..."* (Jn. 13:12). In these two final acts, taking his garments and resuming his place, we see the second half of Paul's scenario. Jesus became obedient even unto death, even death on a cross so that he could pour water in the basin. Because of that obedience, God has highly exalted him and bestowed on him the name that is above every name (see Phil. 2:8-9). He resumed his

place at the right hand of the Father and was fully clothed in his divinity once again.

This is the glory the disciples recognize after his resurrection. It's the glory the Church may recognize today. The Hebrew writer puts it this way: "When he had made purification for sins, he sat down at the right hand of the Majesty on high, having become as much superior to angels as the name he has obtained is more excellent than theirs" (Heb. 1:3-4). This glory will be acknowledged by all creatures when he returns. Every tongue will "confess that Jesus Christ is Lord, to the glory of God the Father" (Phil.2:10).

## Washing One Another's Feet

*"If I then, your Lord and Teacher, wash your feet, you also ought to wash one another's feet"* (Jn. 13:14). Now we come to the crucial point of the story. What Jesus has done here points to something we should be doing for one another as members of his Body. We can't make this journey alone. It's an affair of the covenant community. Having received this ministry, we ought to make it available to other believers on a daily basis. It ought to become a part of our journey as we walk in the way he walked. It's not enough to receive it from him. We're to offer it to others who are on their way from the bath house to the place of abiding. None of us have fully arrived.

Not one among us fully abides in him and does only what we see him doing. We're all on our way from 'here' to 'there'—from the bathhouse home—and we all get our feet dirty from 'stuff' that's on the path.

Jesus' journey made a full circle from the Father into the world and back to the Father. And he picked us up on the way back. This is the way he walked—out from the Father's Love with Love, and back to the Father's Love with others in(side) Love with him. (You may need to spend some time meditating on that statement.) We follow him by walking in Love from Love received at the bathhouse. As we walk, we're in(side) Love drawing others into Love as we journey to Father's bosom of Love.

This is the concrete manifestation of love within the community that will convince unbelievers that the Father sent the Son into the world (see Jn. 17:21-23). The world has a right to conclude that the Father did not send the Son if we're not unified in this way. Their conclusion isn't right, but they have no evidence to the contrary.

## The Mind of Christ

*"I have given you an example, that you also should do as I have done to you"* (Jn. 13:15). Peter heard what Jesus was really saying. Later he wrote, "For to this you have been called, because Christ also suffered for you, leaving you an example, that you should follow in his steps" (I Pet. 2:21). After the resurrection Peter recognized that Jesus had filled the basin with water by his willingness to suffer for the welfare of others whose feet are dirty. The grace of God is evident in our lives as we, "mindful of God," endure pain while suffering unjustly (see I Pet. 2:19), so that the other person, "though they do not obey the word, may be won without a word" (I Pet. 3:1).

This is one of the sure ways we can recognize those who are following Jesus' example: they will be laying down their self-life for the brethren (see I Jn. 3:16). *The love of the Father in them covers the multitude of sins they see in others.*

This aspect of following Jesus was in Paul's mind when he presented the picture of condescension that we've compared to the foot-washing story. He'd said earlier, "Only let your manner of life be worthy of the gospel of Christ" (Phil. 1:27). A life "worthy of the gospel" is a life lived in conformity to the self-emptying of Jesus Christ. When he said, "Have this mind among yourselves, which is yours in Christ Jesus" (Phil. 2:5), Paul charged us to make ourselves available to one another as Christ made himself available to us.

The mind that's ours in Christ is a mind that condescends to serve, that does "nothing from selfishness or conceit" and "looks not only to his own interests, but also to the interests of others" (Phil. 2:3-4).

## *Grace for One Another*

Paul doesn't call it foot-washing, but he refers to the same reality when he says, "Let all bitterness and wrath and anger and clamor and slander be put away from you, along with all malice. And be kind to one another, tender-hearted, forgiving each other, just as God in Christ also has forgiven you" (Eph. 4:31-32). The word translated 'forgive' in this text is a verb form of the word 'grace'. Paul is telling us to wash one another's feet (grace one another) even as God in Christ has washed our feet (graced us).

He gives the reason behind this call to forgiveness earlier: "for we are members one of another" (Eph. 4:25). We're to lay aside our robe of self-importance, gird ourselves with the servant's towel, and wash one another's feet. In this way we demonstrate that we're his disciples. In this way we do as he has done. When we do this right, the world will know that the Father sent the Son. The world will also know that the Father loves us even as he loves his Son (see Jn. 17:21-23). They'll want to be a part of such a community—if they ever see it.

Within the body of Christ, there's an on-going need for forgiveness. This forgiveness is always available to each of us from the Father. This forgiveness is available because Jesus is the expiation for our sins (see I Jn. 2:2). The water in the basin is available for us to use for one another to cleanse the daily contamination that may comes from contact with the world. Do I allow love to cover the sin of others?

This forgiveness from God the Father is the basis of the "unity of the Spirit in the bond of peace" (Eph. 2:3). But this unity in the body of Christ can only be maintained if we make the water in the basin available to others who have been exposed in a weakness or who have offended us personally. The reason there's a lack of unity in the Church is that we do the opposite. When we see a brother overtaken in a fall, we sling more mud on him rather than humbling ourselves and girding ourselves with the servant's towel.

## *Cleansing and Communion*

Now let's look at how this foot-washing relates to the Last Supper. Paul gives us direction when he discusses the division in the church at Corinth. This division manifested itself around the Lord's Table. "Therefore when you meet together, it is not the Lord's Supper that you eat. For in eating, each one goes ahead with his own meal, and one is hungry and another is drunk" (I Cor. 11:20-21).

In the Church at Corinth, there was no receiving of one another. The rich weren't humbling themselves to 'wash the feet' of the poor by making their abundance available. Instead they were counting themselves superior to the poor who'd received a dirty deal from the financial community. The rich weren't taking the position of serving those who were unable to make it in the financial world.

Paul indicates the seriousness of this kind of division when he says, "He who eats and drinks, eats and drinks judgment to himself, if he does not discern the body" (I Cor. 11:29). The Lord's Supper is a sign of the unity of the Body of Christ. "Since there is one loaf, we who are many are one body; for we all partake of the one loaf" (I Cor. 10:17).

If we partake of the external sign of that unity without washing one another's feet, we imitate Judas who received only the external washing. We're receiving the external form but we ourselves aren't clean because "if you do not forgive men, then your Father will not forgive your transgressions" (Matt. 5:15). It's not that the Father doesn't make forgiveness available. Those who don't forgive others are giving evidence that they haven't received God's offer.

## The Primary Act of Love

The primary act of love in a fallen world is forgiveness. It's not the only act of love, but it is the primary act. Doing nice things for people isn't love if you're harboring resentment in your heart. The nature of love is that, if you've received it freely, you'll let that love spill over on others. People who know they're loved are easy to be around because the love they've received overflows into their environment. The same is true of forgiveness. If you've received it freely, you'll let the forgiveness spill over onto others.

Let the body of Christ hear this, "*If I then, your Lord and Teacher, washed your feet, you also ought to wash one another's feet.*" In the hearing and keeping of this word we'll find ourselves in the abiding place where the Father and the Son come and make their abode in us. As Andrew Murray wrote, "Doing the will of the Father is the bond of union with Jesus." This is true communion with him and with one another. As we humble ourselves to serve one another, we're following Jesus. Anyone who's not walking in this way hasn't come to the abiding place. "*Beloved, if God so loved us, we also ought to love one another*" (I Jn. 4:11).

## How Can I Know?

How can I know if I abide in him? "*All who keep his commandments* [to love] *abide in him, and he in them.*" And again, "*God is love, and he who abides in love abides in God*" (I Jn. 4:16). How can we know if he's abiding in us? "*And by this we know that he abides in us, by the Spirit* [of love] *which he has given us* (I Jn. 3:24).

Arrogance and pride are the opposite of condescension. A judgmental and critical spirit isn't the Holy Spirit. Anyone who hates his brother (not in the sense of bitterness, but in the sense of unwillingness to wash their feet) has neither seen him nor known him who is Love. *"He who says he abides in him ought to walk in the same way in which he walked"* (I Jn. 2:6). If we aren't washing the feet of those around us who have been contaminated by their contact with the world, we aren't abiding in Love—we aren't abiding in the Father.

As we see one among us who lays down his self-life for the brothers, who has a spirit of forgiveness and sharing, we know we're in the presence of one who's with the Father in the abiding place. From this abiding place, Jesus continually forgave the sins of those around him. He didn't walk through life criticizing those who failed to do everything right. The Pharisees did that. He didn't come to judge the world; he came that the world might be saved through his willingness to forgive and cleanse.

After the resurrection he came to the disciples and breathed the Holy Spirit into them and said, *"Receive the Holy Spirit. If you forgive the sins of any, they are forgiven; if you retain the sins of any, they are retained"* (Jn. 20:22-23). The receiving of the Holy Spirit directly relates to forgiving the sins of others—to washing their feet. The Holy Spirit is the Spirit of God's love; it's the love of the Father who sent his Son to forgive sins. Failure to forgive another's sins doesn't make God hate us, but it causes disunity in our relationship with others and with God. It causes a breach in the Body of Christ.

How can we say we've received the Holy Spirit if we don't walk in a spirit of forgiveness—if we don't show love for those who have failed in some life situation? Their feet are dirty. How can we say we abide in him if we don't wash their feet? Is your relation to him obvious in the way you relate to your wife? Or to your husband? Are you following him as you relate to your family and other Christians? Is his love for the world around you flowing through you?

In our next chapter we'll look at the raising of Lazarus from the dead. We'll follow another unfolding drama where Jesus makes the Father's love available to Adam's race. We'll discover that we too have a part to play if we choose to accept the role he assigns to us.

# CHAPTER 10

# The Great Exchange

—ᴍ—

The raising of Lazarus in chapter 11 of John has many points of interest for us to consider as we pursue the way Jesus walked. Remember that John is a book of signs pointing beyond themselves. This story signifies much more than the raising of a particular man from the grave. To follow the pointing finger in this story, we must read it in the larger context—the Son of God demonstrating his Father's love to those who are his own—just as we did with the story of Jesus washing the disciples' feet.

*Lazarus* is a Greek form of the Hebrew name *Eleazar,* a name that means "God is my Helper." This name seems to be significant to the meaning of the story. "Man-in-need-of-a-Helper" describes our condition as humans from the beginning of time. Adam wasn't created a sinner, but he was created weak—one who needed God's help to become what God created him to be. God intended for Adam to live in his presence and in total dependence on him.

Adam was indeed a man who needed a Helper. We inherited this need, this weakness; but God didn't leave us desolate and helpless. Adam had God as his Helper. Every descendent of Adam has this God as his Helper. Like Adam, many today choose not to avail themselves of this help. Our choice doesn't nullify the availability of help, but it puts us outside the Helper's household.

The story of Lazarus is pointing to Jesus coming to humanity's village to make himself available as our Helper.

## Lazarus and His Significance

*"Now a certain man was ill, Lazarus of Bethany, the village of Mary and her sister Martha"* (Jn. 11:1). Bethany means 'house of sorrow.' In this story, Bethany is a sign pointing to the dwelling place of those who haven't yet received help from this Helper. Lazarus' illness is a sign pointing to the condition of those who haven't yet experienced a visitation of the Helper.

The basis of all sin is attempting to live apart from this Helper. When Adam ate of the tree of the knowledge of good and evil, he was trying to find a way to live by his own knowledge. He discovered the truth of what Paul articulated much later: "...I can will what is right, but I cannot do it" (Rom. 7:18). In choosing to walk by his human knowledge, Adam removed himself from intimacy with God where help is available. But God was still his Helper.

There can be no true intimacy for those who abide in different places. Intimacy requires being together in the same place. Adam was no longer in the place (the garden) prepared for him. He was in a different place and on a different path now that he'd chosen his own way. He became ill and was on his way to death because he was separated from the tree of life in the place of intimacy with the Father.

*"It was Mary who anointed the Lord with ointment and wiped his feet with her hair, whose brother Lazarus was ill"* (Jn. 11:2). John records Mary's anointing Jesus' feet later in chapter 12. It seems strange that John introduces her here with a deed she hasn't yet performed in the sequence of his narratives. Anyone reading the Gospel for the first time will wonder who he's talking about. We'll talk about this again

later as we draw insights from this story as it relates to the stories of chapter 12. Attention to this inverted sequence will help us discover the reality this story points to.

## The Purpose of the Illness

"*So the sisters sent to him, saying, 'He whom you love is ill'*" (Jn.11:3). Jesus and his Father love all Adam's race. We've already noticed that the Father and the Son have a special love for those who respond to the voice within the abiding place, but that's not the love he's referring to here. He's referring to his greater love that's willing to lay down his life for the beloved. God loves the whole world—all those who need his help—and he sent his Son to be their Helper. The Son died for the whole world. There's no greater love than that. The one the Father and the Son love, the one the Father sent the Son for, the one the Son is willing to die for, the one whose name means 'God is my Helper', is ill.

He's ill because he, along with all the sons of Adam, hasn't yet experienced the presence of the Helper. The Helper hasn't yet come to the House of Sorrow. In his weakness, Lazarus can will what is right, but he can't yet walk in the way of intimacy with the Helper because the Helper hasn't yet arrived in Bethany. The Great Physician hasn't yet come. When the Helper comes, he will not come to judge but to heal and bring fullness of life for all who are willing to receive him.

"*This illness is not unto death; it is for the glory of God, so that the Son of God may be glorified by means of it*" (Jn. 11:4). The illness will result in death, but it's not *unto* death. Death is on the path between Lazarus and where he's going; but that path passes through death to another destination, *the glory of God*. The human race is also on a path that will eventually face death. Whether death is the end of the path or only a bump in the road to the glory of God depends on our response to the Helper when he comes.

## *Jesus Delays his Coming*

*"Now Jesus loved.... So when he heard that he was ill, he stayed two days longer in the place where he was"* (Jn. 11:5). If he loved Lazarus and his sisters, why did he stay two days longer in *his place* before beginning his journey to *their place*? This question started me on the search for the real meaning of this story. If his love and the glory of God are driving this story, why the two day delay? It's not enough to say God will get more glory if Lazarus is in the grave four days instead of two. There may be truth to that, but it doesn't seem sufficient, especially in John.

*"Let us go into Judea again"* (Jn. 11:7). Jesus charts his course but doesn't tell the disciples why he desires to return. He isn't yet ready to call them friends and tell them everything he's doing (see Jn. 15:15). He can't draw them into his confidence; their preconceived notions still influence their understanding of the way he's leading them. Anxiety rises in them because they're aware of the danger of returning to Jerusalem, the center of the misuse of religious power.

*"Rabbi, the Jews were but now seeking to stone you, and are you going there again"* (Jn. 11:8). Jesus knows his hour of departure is approaching rapidly. The disciples also sense the danger; they'd seen the hostility of the Jewish leaders the last time they were in Jerusalem. John draws attention to this awareness of danger so we can connect the developments in this story with Jesus' journey from Galilee to the cross. He's on his way to lay down his life for all who are in need of his help.

### Light of This World

*"Are there not twelve hours in the day"* (Jn. 11:9). Here we have the light and darkness theme again. There is day, when light rules; there is night, when darkness rules. In the light, one can see what's there. In the night one isn't able to see without lanterns, torches, or some form of light. John intro-

duces the light theme because the destination—Jerusalem, where Jesus will face the power of darkness head on.

*"If anyone walks in the day, he does not stumble, because he sees the light of this world"* (Jn. 11:9). When John emphasized the light of *this* world he was indicating natural light apart from revelation. The light of this world is useful for those who walk in this world. When everything's going well, in times of prosperity and health, it's difficult to know who's following this world's light and who's following Jesus, the *true* light of the world. In physical and economic struggles, in the 'dark night of the soul,' it's difficult to know what's ahead or to see where you're going. When a person lights a lantern in the night, he's clearly depending on the light of this world.

## The Stone of Stumbling

*"But if anyone walks in the night, he stumbles, because the light is not in him"* (Jn. 11:10). Those who light a torch can see dimly what's in front of them in the natural. Like Balaam, they can't see the angel posted to resist them in the way they've chosen (see Num. 22). The Jewish resistance Jesus will face in Jerusalem will come from those who see by the light of this world. Those leaders will stumble over the chief cornerstone because they think the see clearly.

The problem with this stumbling is that you don't know you're stumbling. You probably think you're coping well. The soldiers who arrested Jesus stumbled backwards. But they could cope with that. They got up, dusted themselves off, and continued their agenda. Balaam also continued on his way after encountering the angel and the talking donkey. They weren't aware of the seriousness of their stumbling because it was night and the only light they had was the torches of their natural discernment.

## The Inner Light

"*...Because the light is not in him.*" In Jesus' arrest, we noticed that the reverse is also true. If a person has light in him, he won't stumble even when it's night. Jesus is the only Son of Adam who's ever been able to walk without stumbling. He has the light in him. He is the light of the world because his Father, who is light (see I Jn. 1:5), is in him. That light lets him face the dark night of his trial and crucifixion without stumbling over the obstacles the enemy placed in his path. The disciples stumbled that night because the light hadn't yet broken into their bubbles.

## Death and Sleep

"*Our friend Lazarus has fallen asleep, but I go to awake him out of sleep*" (Jn. 11:11). Here we see the heavenly perspective of death. The one who can create everything out of nothing and give life to his creatures has no illusion that death is a problem. Raising the dead is as simple as waking the sleeper. The early Church took this perspective and referred to death as sleep. The question here is: "What will it take for Jesus to wake Lazarus from his sleep?"

"*Lazarus is dead; and for your sake I am glad that I was not there*" (Jn. 11:14). The disciples didn't understand that Jesus referred to death as sleep so Jesus had to tell them. Another wake up call came to me when I noticed that Jesus said, "I am glad." On the surface that seems to be an inappropriate response. Jesus understands something about what's about to happen that makes him glad. What causes Jesus to rejoice? The answer may be hard to find because he becomes greatly distressed when he comes to the place where Lazarus is buried. Let's keep our eyes open for an answer to this question.

## Following without Understanding

*"Let us go, that we may die with him"* (Jn. 11:16).
Thomas says this because he knows Jesus is walking into
danger. He's not aware of the full implications of what he's
saying. John includes his statement to remind us that disciples must take up their cross and follow Jesus. In light of all
the disciples' responses during the Passion Week, it's clear
that Thomas didn't really understand what he was saying.

We must die with him to be resurrected with him and
enter into the newness of life that will be available after
his resurrection (see Rom. 6:3-4). There is no resurrection
without a death experience. You must die to your self-life in
order to come alive to God.

At the same time, experiencing the resurrected Lord
does not bring us to the maturity we're after. Even after the
resurrection Thomas doesn't believe until he is personally
invited to put his hands in Jesus' side. He does follow Jesus
to Jerusalem knowing the danger (but not the implications)
that is waiting for them there.

## The House of Sorrow

*"Now when Jesus came, he found that Lazarus had
already been in the tomb for four days"* (Jn. 11:17). If we
take biblical chronology seriously (as some early Church
Fathers did), we have another possible parallel between
Lazarus and Adam. What follows stretches things a bit, but
this stretch helps us follow the point of the story. "With the
Lord one day is a thousand years, and a thousand years is one
day." (II Peter 3:8) There were roughly four days (four thousand years in biblical chronology) from Adam to Christ.

God gave the son of promise to Abraham about two days
(two thousand years) before Christ. The journey of the Son
began then, two days after the separation of Adam from God,
when Adam became ill and died. When Christ arrived, Adam
had been 'in the tomb' four days (four thousand years). All

mankind was dead in trespasses and sins—dead to God and alive to sin. From the fall of Adam to the coming of Christ Adam's entire race was dead in sin.

## Human Consolation

*"Many of the Jews had come to Martha and Mary to console them concerning their brother"* (Jn. 11:19). In that day, professional mourners came to be with people who had lost a friend or family member. They came to aid in the grieving process. The professionals were good at weeping in such a way that everyone would be able to release their grief through crying. These Jews may or may not have been professionals, but they were there to help Martha and Mary grieve. It's easier to cry when others are also crying. But that's the extent of help available through human sources. They can help you grieve.

## Martha Responds Quickly

*"When Martha heard that Jesus was coming, she went and met him, while Mary sat in the house"* (Jn. 11:20). It's important to notice the different responses here. Some, like Martha, actively seek Jesus and go to him as soon as there is a report of his movements. She takes the lead in this story because she's a woman of action. Others, like Mary, remain where they are and wait. She's more of the retiring personality who lets life come to her. Mary is also the one who poured ointment on Jesus' feet. Our point here is that the Father has a place for all different personalities in his household. We don't all have to be the same or act in the same way to have a place in the Father's bosom.

*"Lord, if you had been here, my brother would not have died. And even now I know that whatever you ask from God, God will give you"* (Jn. 11:21-22). Many get caught in the 'if only' syndrome. Focusing on the past makes it difficult to hope, because hope has its eyes on the presence of God

and future possibilities with him as our Helper. However, Martha isn't stuck in the past. She expresses her faith that Jesus can ask anything of the Father and it will be granted. On the other hand, even though she has hope in the presence of Jesus, she's not yet fully focused on the future he has in store for her.

## The Promise of Resurrection

"*Your brother will rise again*" (Jn. 11:23). Even today we use phrases like this to console those who've lost a loved one. "He's happier over there now. Besides, you'll see him in heaven some day." This can be a valid way of comforting those who've experienced loss. Of course, Jesus has more in mind than that; but we shouldn't be surprised at Martha's response. What Jesus has in mind is always more than we expect, and it's better than we can imagine with our mind's eye.

"**I** *know that he will rise again in the resurrection at the last day*" (Jn. 11:24). This confidence doesn't nullify her earlier expression of faith that Jesus could ask anything of God and it would be done. Raising Lazarus from the dead isn't in her mind when she expresses her faith. Four days is a long time for a body to be in a tomb. On the first or second day she might have hoped that Jesus could still raise him up. But by now she's resigned herself to her brother's death.

She's not expecting anything today. She's jumped from her *if only* focus on the past and what could've happened. She's now in the *some day* of the distant future. Someone once called this, "Pie in the sky when I die by and by." Again, the future she has in mind isn't the same future Jesus has in mind for her brother.

## Clarifying the Promise

"*I am the resurrection and the life; He who believes in me, though he die, yet shall he live*" (Jn. 11:25). Lazarus is dead. He'd certainly believed before he died, so this promise is for him. He shall live; but Martha takes that to mean he'll live after general resurrection. Jesus is drawing her much like he drew the woman at the well. She's on the path to a deeper revelation. Jesus wants her to see resurrection as something available today, here and now.

Jesus had said earlier, "...*the hour is coming, and now is, when the dead will hear the voice of the Son of God, and those who hear will live*" (Jn. 5:25). Those who hear the voice and live are those who were dead in sin (see Eph. 2:5). As they hear and believe the gospel, they receive life that is eternal — life in the bosom of Father God. One with this eternal life will experience natural death as a bump in the road on the way to the final and ultimate resting place in the Father's house.

"*Whoever lives and believes in me shall never die*" (Jn. 11:26). This is as radical as what Jesus said in chapter 6, "*I am the living bread that came down from heaven; if any one eats of this bread, he will live for ever*" (Jn. 6:51). The prospect of never dying is difficult to grasp with our natural mind. Even those who were raised from the dead in Jesus' day were still on their way to natural death. This statement may not have given Martha much hope.

She could've been thinking, "If the one who believes will never die, Lazarus must not have believed or he wouldn't have died." She's probably confused. Confusion is normal in the process of being drawn into revelation. Nicodemus was confused. The Samaritan woman was confused at first. Peter was confused at the arrest and trial. Confusion shouldn't trouble us; it should alert us to the dawning of revelation.

This insight couldn't have come to anyone before Jesus' resurrection, even though Jesus spoke clearly. Here we have another indication of the way John uses the stories as signs pointing to what can only be seen as we follow the arrows and come to meet the resurrected Lord. As it was for those who lived it, so it is for those of us who read. We must stay on the path until we see more deeply.

## Call to Faith

*"Do you believe this"* (Jn. 11:26). What Jesus spoke to Martha is truth. He doesn't ask if she understands. She probably doesn't. In our culture we relate believing to doctrines and propositions. We think we can't believe unless we understand the doctrines. We tend to withhold believing until we've seen the logic of the proposition. He asks if she believes, even though he knows she doesn't yet understand.

Jesus challenges Martha to commit herself before she understands. She must believe before she comes to see what he's talking about. *Believing precedes seeing.* If you believe, you will see (see Jn. 11:40). This is another mark of believing in John's gospel: believing is a *commitment to trust* even in the absence of clear vision or full understanding.

*"Yes, Lord, I believe that you are the Christ, the Son of God, he who is coming into the world"* (Jn. 11:27). Her answer doesn't seem to fit the question. He's asking about his statement concerning resurrection; she responds by affirming her faith in him. Earlier we noticed that biblical faith is tied to a person, not to doctrines and propositions. She's saying, "Lord, I'm confused by what you just said, but I believe in you. I'm committed to you." Here we have the good confession—"Thou art the Christ"—in the mouth of a woman, a *'Martha'* at that. (All you 'Marthas' out there be encouraged!)

## Martha Calls Mary Out

*"The Teacher is here and is calling for you"* (Jn. 11:28). The leader's responsibility is to point to the Teacher who is calling. The Baptist had recognized Jesus first; the two disciples followed after his testimony. One of them, Andrew, became a leader when he went to bring his brother to Jesus.

This is the way true leadership among disciples always works. Any person who tries to get other people to accomplish his or her personal dream is not a leader in the biblical sense of the word. Leaders must experience the presence of God before they approach the people and call them to involvement.

This is also true in the Old Testament. Moses saw the Lord on Mount Sinai before he went to tell the people that God was calling them. Someone aptly said, "You must experience God at the burning bush before you talk to people about the burning bush." The prophets also spoke from a place of seeing and hearing long before the Messiah came to join us in the flesh. Isaiah, for example, was in a place where he was able to see the Lord in his holy temple (see Isa. 6:1). The words Isaiah spoke to Israel were from the Teacher who was calling them. Only a few responded to the call.

## Mary Responds Quickly

*"And when she heard it, she rose quickly and went to him"* (Jn. 11:29). Mary stands for all who respond quickly to the call of the Teacher even when the call comes through a human agency. She goes to him quickly. In answering the call, we often have to leave the presence of those who surround us to comfort us in our sorrow. They can only console us in our grieving; they can never be the Helper we really need. We need one who can bring us out of the House of Sorrow. We need a Teacher, a Rabbi, a Helper, who can take us to the next level of believing and receiving; one who can take us out of our helplessness and loneliness into the next level of intimacy with the Father.

*"Jesus had not yet come to the village, but was still in the place where Martha had met him"* (Jn. 11:30). Mary has to leave to meet Jesus because he hasn't come to the village yet. She leaves Bethany, the House of Sorrow, to find the one who's coming to be her Helper. He is in a place outside the

Bethany where the wake is in process, but he's on his way there—to the House of Sorrow. Mary is willing to leave *her place* at the wake to come to *his place*. As Jesus makes his move toward the village, Martha and Mary make their move toward him.

## Inadequate Human Understanding

*"When the Jews...saw Mary rise quickly and go out, they followed her, supposing that she was going to the tomb to weep there"* (Jn. 11:31). When a person responds to the call of the Teacher, the people of Bethany will often follow and try to make sure they continue to weep and be sorrowful. They only want to help, but they're not the Helper.

The reference to weeping and the tomb connect this story with Jesus' burial and to the garden tomb where Mary will meet the resurrected Lord. In this way John prepares us to hear the true message of this story.

*"Lord, if you had been here, my brother would not have died"* (Jn. 11:32). This is the same thing Martha said when she first came to Jesus. It's human nature to question the Lord's timing. Neither of these women expects that Jesus will do anything about the situation. It seems they only expect Jesus to join them in their mourning. In their minds' eye there's only the continuation of mourning over the death of their brother and the knowledge that Jesus could've helped if he'd been there earlier. He's late according to their timing, but he's never late by his personal 'day timer.'

## Jesus is Moved and Troubled

*"When Jesus saw her weeping, and the Jews who came with her also weeping, he was deeply moved in spirit and troubled"* (Jn. 11:33). Jesus is touched on the deepest level when he sees this example of human suffering. He really did join them in the House of Sorrow. Our God isn't like the god of the Greeks who's never moved, who doesn't feel what we

feel. He feels what we feel because he cares deeply. He loves us even while we are in the throes of the House of Sorrow. He doesn't wait for us to pull ourselves together. He comes to us where we're at.

*We serve an emotional God.* "For we have not a high priest who is unable to sympathize with our weakness, but one who in every respect has been tempted [tested] as we are, yet without sin" (Heb. 4:15). Anyone who thinks the Father doesn't feel pain hasn't seen the Father who dwells in the Son. The Father's emotions are manifested in the emotions of the Son who only does what he sees the Father doing. When we see Jesus deeply moved and troubled, we see the emotions of the Father displayed. Our Father cares deeply.

## His Place and Our Place

*"Where have you laid him"* (Jn. 11:34). Jesus asks the same question Mary will later ask at the open tomb after the resurrection. John includes this question to help us connect this story to the resurrection scene. There are several points of contrast and comparison that help us connect the stories.

In this story Lazarus is still in the tomb. When Mary asked the question at the garden tomb, Jesus was already raised and was standing in front of her beside the tomb even though she didn't recognize him. In this story the stone is still covering the opening to the tomb while the stone had already been removed in the story of the resurrection of Jesus. After the resurrection of Jesus, Mary will look for the dead body of Jesus. In the story of Lazarus, Jesus is looking for one who is asleep. John wants us to connect the raising of Lazarus with the resurrection of Jesus. This we will do.

## Mary's Invitation

*"Lord, come and see"* (Jn. 11:35). Mary responds to Jesus' question with the same invitation he had offered to the first two disciples who were seeking the abiding place.

What an invitation Jesus had given. "Come over to my place; join me in the Father's bosom." It's quite an honor to be invited over to the house of a person who occupies a high position in society. It's a much greater honor to be invited into the bosom of Father God. Imagine the eternal Father of all creation saying, "Come over to my place and hang out with me."

In Mary's invitation, however, the situation is radically different. Mary is inviting Jesus to join her in the House of Sorrow. She's inviting him to the place of death and corruption. Jesus has been waiting for this invitation. He has been ready to accept that invitation from the beginning of time. That's why he came—to be our Helper, to *take our place in the tomb* and *give us his place in the Father's bosom.*

"*Jesus wept*" (Jn. 11:35). John doesn't give any personal commentary on this weeping of Jesus. Perhaps he weeps because of the emotion in the atmosphere coming through the mourners. He really does care about the suffering of others. He weeps with those who weep. Or this weeping may reflect the prayer in the garden of Gethsemane. That garden is the 'place' where Jesus met secretly with his disciples and with his Father. He's weeping because he knows what it'll cost him to come over to our place of death in the tomb. He also knows many will refuse to receive what he will accomplish for them here. That may also be one reason he's weeping.

He never forces his way on anyone. He does all he can to prepare hearts to receive. But having done that, he asks where the problem is—where we've laid it—and waits for an invitation. We must invite him to come see our place of death and impotence. He's always waiting for our invitation. Those who aren't willing to admit their impotence will never invite him over to their place.

"*See how he loved him*" (Jn. 11:36). The Jews who had come to console Martha and Mary read the weeping as an expression of his love for Lazarus. Whatever else the weeping indicates, it's certainly an expression of his love for the one who has God as his Helper but who has not yet received that help. He always weeps for those who are still in the grave, those who are dead in their trespasses and sins.

### Jesus Comes to the Tomb

*"Then Jesus, deeply moved again, came to the tomb; it was a cave, and a stone lay upon it"* (Jn. 11:38). When he approaches this tomb he's aware that this will soon be his place. He's deeply moved again. The first time is when he identified with the sorrow of those who were mourning over the death and corruption that was in their midst. This time he's agonizing in his approach to the *abiding place of the dead*, that place where men are dead in their trespasses and sins.

He knows there's no exit from that place apart from the work he was sent to accomplish on the cross. *No one will ever be able to come over to his place until he comes to our place of death—to our tomb—to make a way to the other side.*

### Delegated Responsibility

*"Take away the stone"* (Jn. 11:39). The stone has a purpose. It's designed to keep death out of sight and to keep the odor of death from bothering others. The stone is much like the fig leaves Adam used to avoid being exposed in his shame. Of course we all know God can see through fig leaves. We're really hiding from one another. In the beginning, fig leaves were enough to cover the shame. When death began to reign (see Rom. 5:17), something more than fig leaves was needed: something that could keep the smell of corruption from coming across to others.

Those who are spiritually dead still protect their shame with 'stones.' For fear of being exposed to others, they protect their stones from being rolled away. Jesus is saying, "Remove the stone that hides the corruption." *Darkness reigns behind the stone because the light doesn't shine there.* This is like the call to walk in the light, to allow ourselves to be seen as we really are. It's a challenge to acknowledge deadness and the need of a Helper who can bring life where death reigns. *But dead men can't remove the stone from their own grave.*

## Desire for Cover-up

*"Lord, by this time there will be an odor"* (Jn. 11:39). Mary is covering the condition of her brother. Love covers a multitude of sins. She doesn't want him exposed. Everyone knows there's death and corruption behind the stone. As Brennan Manning reminded us, we are all ragamuffins. Some 'let it all hang out,' but most people prefer to keep a lid on it. It's right to avoid exposing another, unless it's the Lord who's asking us to remove the stone. He wants the death to be exposed to him so he can deal with it as no one else can.

We don't mind removing other people's stones and airing their dirty grave clothes. That's what Adam and Eve were doing when they played the blame game. They were exposing the other to avoid personal exposure. They weren't trying to let the light of God's love shine into their corruption. That manipulative maneuver keeps everyone's attention focused on someone else. Whether we 'let it all hang out' in public or expose other people's filth, this kind of exposure only increases the lack of intimacy and maintains the breach in our relationships. It helps no one.

All we can accomplish by exposing others by our own human light is just that. They're exposed with no possibility of dealing with the corruption. We are not the Helper they need. Even if we expose them "for their own good", it seldom turns out for the good of either of us. Exposure only increases the lack of intimacy and promotes more death. The help we try to offer apart from Father's love is like the blind leading the blind into the pit.

The only real solution is to expose corruption to the Son who came to take our place in death and to offer us his place in the bosom of the Father. When we cover our blushing face in shame, or when we cause others to hide their face, we're not reflecting the Father's face that welcomes the presence of another unconditionally. Intimacy is only possible in a face-to-face encounter, with each face open to the other without conditions.

But a dead man can't remove the stone from his own grave. A dead man can't expose himself to the welcoming face of the Helper. It's like the paralytic who is incapable of coming to the pool when the water is troubled. We need a Helper. By suffering as a victim of those who were dead in sin, Jesus exposes the sin of mankind for what it is. In this way he becomes our Helper and calls us to roll away the stone.

The work of evangelism includes exposing corruption. Peter did that after the day of Pentecost. "[You] killed the Author of life, whom God raised from the dead," was his way of exposing the corruption (see Acts 3:15). Peter joined the Helper by removing that stone, but only to allow the light of the gospel to enter the grave and offer forgiveness—"that your sins may be blotted out, that times of refreshing may come from the presence of the Lord" (Acts 3:19). We have a responsibility to expose sin, but only for the purpose of reconciliation and redemption.

*"Did I not tell you that if you would believe you would see the glory of God"* (Jn. 11:40). There's no record of Jesus speaking these words to Martha. They're implied when he told her he was the resurrection and the life. When he asked if she believed, he was challenging her to lay aside the blinders of her preconceived notions and allow her bubble to remain empty until he filled it with reality. He can't fill her bubble with reality until she's willing to remove the stone that covers what she thinks is real.

The grave is not the end; *death does not have the last word*. Lazarus is only sleeping. But she doesn't know that yet. She must remove the stone to discover the truth about death. We will never discover the truth about our sin and corruption until we allow the light of the Father's love to shine into our darkness. *Sin does not have the last word.* Jesus is himself the true Word of God concerning our sin. Sin is covered by his love. It's forgiven by his blood. It has been taken outside the camp and deposited in the abyss.

## Coming out of Hiding

"*So they took away the stone*" (Jn. 11:41). Notice Jesus doesn't take away the stone. He'll never force the world out of its hiding place, at least not until the final day when every knee will bow and every tongue confess that Jesus Christ is Lord (see Phil. 2:10-11). Until that time it's the Christian community's responsibility to allow death and corruption to be exposed to the light of his presence. Forced freedom is an oxymoron.

*The light of his presence is the light that exposes sin and forgives in the same movement.*

Only in this way can he can give life to that which is dead and call into existence things that do not yet exist in us (see Rom. 4:17). He can't do this for us or for the world as long as we're trying to expose others by criticizing and judging them for what they're hiding behind their stone. When we do that, we're behaving like ordinary men (see I Cor. 3:3). Exposure must be in loving obedience to the prompting of the Holy Spirit. We must be conformed to the image of the Son who brings the love of the Father into the world of sin and corruption with forgiveness and cleansing.

As long as we spend our time and energy whitewashing gravesites so people will think everything is okay, his life—which is the light of man—isn't coming through us into the world. He won't remove the stone for us. That would be controlling and manipulating. Love never insists on its own way. He's still waiting for the Church to love as he has loved. He's already made his move. The resurrection scene tells us that the stone is already removed from his side. He makes his next move as we move the stone on our side of the abyss and welcome others to life in Father's bosom.

## Jesus' Prayer

*"Father, I thank thee that thou hast heard me"* (Jn. 11:41). Where is the prayer? He's thanking the Father for hearing him; but the prayer isn't recorded, at least not in this text. Where is the prayer the Father has heard? We've noticed that John often introduces an issue in one place and elaborates on it in another. Has the prayer mentioned here been recorded somewhere else in the Gospel?

A short side trip will be necessary before we can answer this question. All the stories in John are related to one another. Sometimes John places stories or statements in the reverse order from what we would expect, especially if we're familiar with the other Gospels. I'll give some examples.

The story of the cleansing of the temple is placed in the final week in the other Gospels. It's at the beginning of the ministry of Jesus in this Gospel. The story of the disciples' fishing all night with no catch is at the beginning of the other Gospels, but it's found as the last story in John's Gospel. There are other less obvious examples, but these are enough to make our point. The stories are presented in an order different from our expectation.

We'll not enter the debate about whether these events happened twice. We are not concerned with whether there were actually one or two incidents of cleansing the temple. Even if we were able to offer incontrovertible evidence that there were two almost identical incidents that occurred at different times, it would only be counting the hairs between the knuckles of the pointing finger. The real question is; "What is John trying to help us see?"

## *Lazarus is the Key to the Mystery*

John opens this story by saying that Lazarus' sister Mary was the one who anointed the Lord with ointment and wiped his feet with her hair. That story isn't recorded until chapter 12. John introduces Mary in this story as though she's already anointed Jesus' feet. That may be just an editorial style, but it's more likely that John is trying to get us to connect some of the elements in the two stories. We had no trouble seeing that he wants us to connect Mary to the resurrection scene by Jesus' question, "Where have you laid him." Let's look at some of the elements in the story of the anointing to see if we can find the connection.

## *Anointing for Burial*

The story of the anointing in chapter 12 begins, *"Six days before Passover, Jesus came to Bethany, where Lazarus was, whom Jesus had raised from the dead"* (Jn. 12:1). It's clear from the beginning that John wants us to connect the anointing of Jesus' feet with the raising of Lazarus. The mention of the Passover draws our attention to the Passover Lamb on its way to the slaughter. This Lamb of God will take our place in the grave behind the stone.

Judas Iscariot spoke in opposition to this extravagance of Mary. *"Why was this ointment not sold for three hundred denarii and given to the poor"* **(Jn. 12:5).** Our present concern is not with Judas and his motives. We'll focus on Jesus' response.

*"Let her keep it* [some texts have, "she has kept it,"] *for the day of my burial"* (Jn. 12:7). Whether you accept the texts that say, "Let her keep it" or those that say, "She has kept it," it's clear that John wants us to connect the anointing of Jesus' feet to the *burial* of Jesus. The fact that it was his feet that she anointed is an anticipation of the washing of the disciples' feet, which is recorded in chapter 13. So we actually have three chapters connected by the mention of feet.

The washing of the disciples' feet is a sign of the death and shed blood of Jesus. The focus in chapters 11 and 12 is the feet of Jesus (not the disciples' feet) being anointed for burial. *Our feet are washed on our way to life in Father's house; his feet are anointed on his way to burial in our tomb.*

John connects these three stories to point to something beyond the stories themselves. All three chapters point to the death, burial, and resurrection of Jesus. The question of the prayer Jesus prayed still remains to be answered, but we learn from this introduction to chapter 12 that the prayer must have something to do with his impending death. We'll look at the events subsequent to the anointing story for an answer.

## *Lazarus in Chapter 12*

Lazarus is side by side with Jesus throughout chapter 12. First, the crowd that gathered to see Jesus came, "*not only on account of Jesus, but also to see Lazarus, whom he had raised from the dead*" (Jn. 12:9). Then, the chief priests wanted to put Lazarus to death along with Jesus because "*on account of him many of the Jews were going away and believing in Jesus*" (Jn. 12:11). The crowd that gathered for the 'Triumphal Entry' had heard the witness of those who had been present when Jesus called Lazarus out of the tomb. The reason this excited crowd came to meet him is "*they heard he had done this sign*" (Jn. 12:18).

This many references to Lazarus makes it clear that John is connecting these stories to point to something other than merely entering the city. Let's consider the events that followed Jesus' entry into the city.

When some Greeks began to seek Jesus, he said, "**The hour has come for the Son of man to be glorified**" (Jn. 12:23). The hour of the Son's glory is the hour of his death. This is reflected in his next statement. He spoke of the grain of wheat that must die. Jesus recognizes that he must die in order to become the 'first fruits' of those who would be raised from the dead (see I Cor. 15:20). The mention of first fruits implies much more fruit to come. All those who, like Lazarus, have lived outside that place where the Helper is available, those who are dead in their trespasses and sins, now have a Helper who can call them forth from their tomb. *We can become the fruit that sprouts from the death of this grain of wheat.*

## Jesus' Prayer for the Father's Glory

Immediately after that we hear an echo of Jesus' response when he came to the tomb of Lazarus. *"Now is my soul troubled"* (Jn. 12:27). He is troubled also in the story of Lazarus. This is the same word used to speak of the troubling of the water in the healing of the paralytic (see Jn. 5:7). In the story of Lazarus we suggest that Jesus is himself the bearer of the troubled water—his spirit is troubled.

He considers two possible prayers. The first is, *"Father, save me from this hour"* (Jn. 12:27). He does consider that prayer; but he doesn't pray it. We find the same idea in the other Gospels: "If it be possible, let this cup pass" (see Matthew 26:39). He does consider that option, but that's not the essence of his prayer.

*"No, for this purpose I have come to this hour. Father, glorify thy name"* (Jn. 12:27). That's the prayer he chose to pray. His Father responds to this second prayer in a voice of thunder that comes from heaven. *"I have glorified it, and I will glorify it again"* (Jn. 12:28).

Personally, I believe this prayer, "Father, glorify thy name," is what John wants us to hear in the situation before Lazarus' tomb. He began the story with the proclamation that Lazarus' illness is unto the glory of God. This story is pointing to that work of Jesus which glorifies the Father's name. When Jesus calls Lazarus out of the tomb, he isn't seeking glory for himself; he's glorifying his Father. But the ultimate glory to the Father is when Jesus took our place in the tomb and offered us his resurrected life. The Father glorifies the Son in the resurrection because the Son glorifies the Father in his death.

## The Crowd and Thunder

The crowd around Jesus heard the sound and thought it was thunder. The thunder is reminiscent of the Mount Sinai account where Moses heard God speak but the people heard thunder (see Ex. 19). The multitude never heard the voice of God; they only heard thunder. John is connecting the crowd at Mount Sinai with the crowd of the Triumphal Entry and the mourners in front of Lazarus' tomb. The same condition is reflected in chapter 5 where the multitude under the five porticoes was under the law but never heard the voice (see Jn. 5:37). Moses heard the voice on the mountain. Jesus heard the voice in the valley of the shadow of death.

## The Resurrection of Lazarus

Now we can return to the prayer in front of the tomb where Lazarus had been laid.

*"I knew that thou hearest me always, but I have said this on account of the people standing by, that they may believe that thou didst send me"* (Jn. 11:42). He's actually addressing the people in this part of his prayer. I am reminded of a time when a visiting preacher had been invited to pray. He was in disagreement with a doctrinal position held by the local pastor. His prayer was a sermon addressed to the people rather than a prayer to God.

Jesus was doing something similar to that, but with a different spirit. There's a genuine intimate communication between the Father and the Son at this grave site. Jesus responds with thanksgiving for the sake of the people who only heard thunder. This thanksgiving is probably tied to the gladness mentioned earlier when Jesus said he was glad he was not present when Lazarus died.

The Son's prayer of determination to do what's necessary to glorify his Father evoked a thunderous voice of approval from above. With that affirmation, Jesus can move on to the next step toward our place—the grave with all the hidden corruption of Adam's race. *The blessing of the Father sustains the Son in his journey to the cross.*

*"When he had said this, he cried with a loud voice"* (Jn.11:43). The loud voice immediately brings to mind his cry from the cross recorded in Luke 23:46, "Into thy hands I commit my spirit." In John's Gospel this is the voice of the Son of God who calls to the dead and gives life to those who hear (see Jn. 5:25). The loud voice is the voice of the agony from the one who lays down his life for the one he loves. How else could he set Lazarus free? He must take his place. The blessing of the Father sustains the Son.

*This is the great exchange—he takes our death and gives us his life.*

## The Word of Command

*"Lazarus, come out"* (Jn. 11:43). The deed is done. The invitation is issued. "Come forth from your place, all you who have been away from my Father, separated from your source of help. Come over to my place all you who are dead in your trespasses and sins. All you who are weary and heavy laden join me in my Father's bosom. I've prepared a place for you here where I AM (is). I AM (is) taking your place so you can come over to my place. The Spirit and the Bride say come!" Who can refuse an invitation like that? Only those who prefer their bubble.

*"The dead man came out, his hands and feet bound with bandages, and his face wrapped with a cloth"* (Jn. 11:44). How does a *dead man* come out? For that matter, how would a man *bound from head to foot* come out even if he were alive? How does a dead man get out of the grave with his eyes covered? How does Lazarus get out of the tomb?

It's a work of the Father's love from start to finish. Lazarus doesn't do anything to get out. The omnipotent Word of God spoken to him brought him out with no help from Lazarus. Apart from the work of Jesus on the cross, all of us are still paralyzed (bound head to foot) and blind (the face wrapped with a cloth). We all need a Helper.

When we hear the voice of the Son of God we are empowered to turn within our spirit and see who he really is. We will notice in the next chapter that Mary first "turned" and saw Jesus, but did not recognize him. This is the condition of the disciples before the resurrection. They saw him as a fellowman, and he was that; but they had not seen the Father. They had not seen the reality of his person as the Son in the bosom of the Father.

The two disciples had "turned" to follow him, but they didn't yet see until they followed for some time. We'll notice that Mary "turned" again when Jesus spoke her name. When Jesus called your name the first time, he was calling one who was dead. Each time he sees you resting in yesterday's blessing or sinking in yesterday's tragedy, he will call your name again. He is calling you out of the place where you have been comfortable in your misery back into the place he prepared for you in the bosom of the Father.

## Lazarus is Still Bound

"...*His hands and feet bound with bandages, and his face wrapped with a cloth*" (Jn. 44). Later when Peter and John enter the tomb, they will find the bandages and the cloth with no body wrapped in them. Here the dead man comes out still wearing his grave clothes. When we are first brought into this new life in Christ, we're often still carrying some baggage from our former corruption. This baggage makes it difficult to see and walk on the path we have entered. We experience release and joy from being out of the grave, but life is difficult. We need some help to get rid of the baggage we brought with us from our former death.

## *Our Responsibility*

*"Unbind him and let him go"* (Jn. 11:44). Jesus speaks these words to the Church, the ones standing by to receive the one who was dead and who is now alive. When he washed the disciples' feet he instructed them to wash one another's feet. Here he is instructing them to take responsibility for the freedom of those who come out of death into life. Removing grave clothes is similar to washing one another's feet. We are called to walk the same way Jesus walked. That means we must become a helper of those who have not yet experienced complete freedom in this new life in the Spirit.

Have you received the promise of eternal life here and now? Have you been willing to remove the stone that covers corruption? Are you helping others to experience freedom from their bondages?

In the next chapter we'll turn our attention to the death, burial, and resurrection of Jesus. This is the point to which the whole Gospel has been pointing from the beginning. Every sign recorded in this Gospel has an arrow pointing to this event. Rise, let us go hence.

# CHAPTER 11

# The Christ Event

—∿∿—

In the previous chapters we've seen that unconditional love is available for Adam's entire race. Jesus prepared a place in the Father's bosom for all who will follow. True disciples follow without full understanding. We saw two sinful women, the woman at the well and the Samaritan woman, who were signs of those who receive unconditional love as Jesus draws them into a revelation of Father's love.

We wrestled with the difference between Judas and Peter to find the meaning of true discipleship. We clarified the issue of discipleship by observing Jesus' act of washing the disciples' feet. We then saw the story of Lazarus as a sign of Jesus taking our place in the grave and releasing us to life with one another and with God. We now turn to the reality which all the signs in John point to.

## The Center of History

The death, burial, and resurrection of Jesus mark the very center of human history, but not the mathematical center where there's an equal amount of time on each side. Before his death, life was a one way street with a *dead-end*, literally. Everything moved from life to death. Every human being was born facing death as his or her future. Death was the end of life. When Jesus died, death itself was "swallowed up in victory" (see I Cor. 15:54). *Jesus blew a hole in the dead-end street.*

After his resurrection all things are made new. There is a New Creation. His death is the end of death. His new life is the beginning of eternal life for all who will receive. Those who believe in the Father who sent Jesus enter *a one-way street out of death into life* (see Jn. 5:24). This road doesn't have an end. It goes on forever.

## Promise and Invitation

The presence of the Incarnate Son of God is a promising presence. He didn't come to be the 'cause' of an inevitable 'effect'. In other words, we can resist and refuse what he did. He came with a promise from his faithful Father and with an invitation to enter the way that leads from promise to fulfillment. His presence in every generation is the presence of Love, and love "does not insist on its own way" (see I Cor. 13:5).

Love isn't a first cause; it's a welcome mat on the threshold of the door to Father's house. Love can be spurned and rejected. The welcome mat is the cross, and we must take up our own cross to enter this new way. For those who choose to accept this invitation, it becomes clear that death is not a dead-end after all. It's the door to a new, resurrected life in the Spirit.

## Three Events as One

Death, burial, and resurrection: we must consider these three as one event. Without the resurrection his death would be meaningless, because the new life would not be available. Without his death there would be no atonement or reconciliation between God and man. Even if one were raised from the dead like Lazarus, he would only return to the one-way street on his way to eternal death in the pit. Anything resembling new life without the reality of atonement and reconciliation through the shed blood is nothing more than the old life in a different form, like turning over a new leaf. Turning the pages in a book called *"Alienated from God"* is pointless.

At the same time, his death and the resurrection are two totally different events. They are as different as life and death. And more so: his death and his life are radically different from our life and our death. Our human intellect can't even begin to calculate this difference. His death precedes his life; our life precedes our death. His life is eternal; ours is mortal. His death is effective; our death is impotent. His life is available to others; our life is unto ourselves. Who can measure these differences?

## *The Burial Separates Two Creations*

The grave stands between the death and the resurrection like a chasm that had never yet been crossed. The grave marks the dead-end of all natural life in the old creation. Jesus' death is the end of the old. His resurrection is the beginning of the New Creation on the other side of the chasm. The first man (Adam) is dead. "In Adam all die," that's the bad news. "In Christ shall all be made alive," that's the good news (see I Cor. 15:22). The last Adam became a life-giving spirit (see I Cor. 15:45-50). This 'life-giving spirit' produced a second man who is from heaven. "As was the man of dust [the first Adam], so are those who are of the dust [any who are not born of God]; and as is the man of heaven [the second man], so are those who are of heaven [all those who are born of God, from above]" (I Cor.15:45-50).

## *The Christ Event as a Vortex*

All history is sucked into the vortex of this Christ Event. Human history is the history of man alienating himself from God and from other men because of his failure to believe God really loves him. Adam and Eve thought God was holding out on them. This is the original sin. We tend to think God is holding out on us today when things don't go our way.

All failure to believe in God's love before the cross and all failure to respond to God's love after the resurrection is sucked into the vortex of the love demonstrated in the death, burial, and resurrection of Jesus Christ. That's what we mean by the center of history. All history is pulled into this one event. Death reigned before the event; life reigns after the event. This radical change is accomplished by this Christ Event.

## *The Old Way: From Life to Death*

Israel's history—indeed all world history before Jesus' death—was going toward this event. The Exodus prefigured it. The Israelites passed through the sea on dry land leaving the old life of bondage behind. Their enemy was drowned in the sea—the grave. They came out on the other side to meet the Lord at Mount Sinai. They had a new life with God. By keeping the feast of Passover the Israelites continually remembered the Exodus and looked forward to the coming of another deliverer. All the rites and rituals of the Levitical system were signs pointing to the Christ Event. Even the Tabernacle was a picture of the coming glory of God. All this pointed to Jesus Christ, the incarnate God, crucified and resurrected in human history.

The prophets also predicted his coming in every generation. But they "inquired what person or time was indicated by the Spirit of Christ within them when predicting the sufferings of Christ and the subsequent glory" (I Pet. 1:11). Like the disciples, they did not understand, but they followed the word that came to them. Isaiah must've wondered about his proclamation, "For to us a child is born.., his name will be called... Mighty God, Everlasting Father..." (Isa. 9:6). He was faithful to speak the word as he received it, but he was probably confused as to how a child can also be the Mighty God, Everlasting Father.

Remember, confusion is normal when new revelation is dawning. The day wouldn't dawn to shed light on Isaiah's prophecy for over seven hundred years.

The first Adam and his descendents, with all their sin and rebellion, were always on their way to *this death* — the death of the last Adam on the cross. In Jesus' death we have the complete and final result of Adam's sin. Many innocent victims died in the various sacrificial rites in all cultures, including Israel. Many cultures practiced human sacrifice. Even in Israel human sacrifice was practiced by some kings (see I Ch. 33:6). But those human victims were not innocent like the sacrificial animals. Those rites were all designed to cover (Israel) or deny (Pagan) personal or corporate guilt and shame.

## The New Way

God, the Son, with all his love and righteousness, was also on his way to this death from the beginning. In *religion*, man sacrifices to God; he gives his life over to his God. In *Christianity*, God gives his life over to his creation. In religion, man says to God, "Will you accept my sacrifice?" In Christianity, God says to man, "Will you accept *my* sacrifice?" Father God doesn't want our sacrifice; he wants *us* in his presence. He desires that so intensely that he's willing to send his Son out from his bosom as a sacrifice to bring us into the intimacy of his bosom.

## The Great Awakening

*"They shall look on him whom they have pierced"* (Jn. 19:37, a quote from Zech. 12:10). All the sin and rebellion of the sons of Adam in our day are also drawn back into the vortex of the Christ Event. Our sin and our rebellion find their full expression in the death of Jesus. He *bore the brunt* of our sin when he was on the cross. His death *exposed* our sin as well.

303

Today the world is called to look upon him as the one they have pierced. Some look and see what the Pharisees and the Romans saw: a deluded and dangerous man who deserved to die. Others look and recognize the results of their own sin and rebellion. A great awakening occurs when we really see what we humans did at the cross and when we realize that God was also doing something.

## Adam's Way: Victimizing or Forsaking

In this death we see the tragedy of Adam's way of dealing with his own sin and the sin he perceives in others. We can also see the beauty of God's way of dealing with the sin he sees in us. First we will focus on Adam's way.

Adam's way leads to personal death and murder. Adam and Eve hid themselves behind fig leaves. When they realized God could see through their cover-up, Adam blamed Eve and Eve blamed the snake. They didn't take responsibility for their action; they didn't walk in the light. Their cover-up shut down intimacy between them and brought death into the world. Cain could not effectively blame Abel because Abel was blameless, so he killed him. He killed because his own deeds were evil (see I Jn. 3:12).

That's Adam's way of dealing with sin. He's willing to victimize others either by blame or murder to avoid personal exposure. That's the only way Adam knows. The sons of Adam who become religious leaders have always ignored, persecuted, and killed the prophets who exposed their sin. The general populous, the crowd, is also guilty of failing to take responsibility. They never had enough courage or understanding to confront those who killed the prophets. Like the disciples, they ran away in the night.

### We Will even Kill God

The death of Jesus was not simply *in spite of the fact* that he was righteous. He died *because he was righteous* and his righteousness exposed the sin in the hearts of the sons of Adam. Like Cain, they killed the one who was able to walk upright before God. They projected their own guilt onto him. The deceivers accused him of deceiving the people. The demon-possessed accused him of having a demon. The blasphemers who said, *"We have no king but Caesar"* (Jn. 19:15), accused him of blasphemy. Jesus said to those who were sons of Beelzebub, *"You are of your father the devil"* (Jn. 8:44). These are the ones who accused him of casting out demons by Beelzebub. To accomplish their agenda they had to make him look like the guilty one. But the guilt they put on him was their own guilt.

By looking on this innocent victim we see what our selfishness and fear of exposure are capable of doing. *We will even kill God* to have our own way. Or, if we do not actually perform the deed, either we join the crowd in demanding his life or we run away in the night in fear and allow him to die alone. *We will forsake God* to avoid confrontation.

He was speaking to us when he said, "...as you did it not to one of the least of these, you did in unto me" (Matt. 25:45). The way we treat our fellowman is the way we would have treated him if we had lived in the days of his flesh. Whether we attack our fellowman or withdraw when he is in trouble, we are exposed in our likeness to those who victimized Jesus to protect themselves.

## Legalized Murder

The crucifixion was the *legalized murder* of an innocent victim from the perspective of what man did (see Marcus Barth and Vern Fletcher, *Acquittal by Resurrection*). By looking on him whom we pierced, we see the effect of our weakness. We see what happens when we fail to allow him to be our Helper. We see the results of our refusal to take responsibility for our own sins. Jesus on the cross is a dying example of what happens when we blame others for our problems or refuse to stand with those who are being perse-cuted for righteousness sake.

Jesus gave his life in our stead, but he did not give it to a blood-thirsty god. The Father sent him into the world system with the full knowledge that Adam's race would kill him. Jesus gave himself over to a blood-thirsty crowd and to power-hungry religious and political leaders of the world system of 'order-through-violence' (see *The Girard Reader* for further insights). The Father so loved the world that he gave his Son over—sacrificed him to this violence—to expose Adam's sin for what it is. Only when we *look on him whom we pierced* and see ourselves clearly in this light, only then can we repent and receive his gift of love.

## The Father's Way: Self-Giving

However, when we look at what the Father and the Son were doing, we see the unconditional love of God the Father and God the Son. The Father loved the world and sent his Son. The Son submitted himself to the Father's mission to the world. The Son died because he was *unable to stop loving* the ones who were victimizing him. The Father allowed his Son to die because he was *unable to stop loving* the world. If the Father had ceased loving he would've ceased being God, for God is love. God can't cease being God; therefore he can't withhold his love from sinners. Sinners may reject his love, but he can't withhold it.

This is God's way of dealing with sin: he gives himself and his life *for* sinners and *to* sinners even as they crucify him. He can't and won't close himself off to us because of our sin and corruption. Our Father will never reject us when we stumble in our attempt to find our way to him. Nor will he reject those who seek to kill him. God is love.

When we forsake him he weeps, but he doesn't with-draw his love. When we do not respond to his invitation, he doesn't withdraw his welcome. He won't force us to accept his invitation. Like the prodigal son, we may walk away; but the Father is always waiting for our return. In the story of the prodigal, it was his memory of his father's welcoming presence that drew the son back to the father's house. God's love comes into our 'far country' to draw us back to himself. The Father doesn't drag us to Jesus; he draws us (see Jn. 6:44).

## He Takes our Sin upon Himself

A number of years ago I had a vision of sorts. I saw myself as a little boy in the presence of Jesus. He was sitting with an open lap and was inviting me to come. He was dressed in dazzling white, bright as light. I was dressed in the smut and dirt of darkness. I was afraid to approach him because he was so clean and I was so dirty. I thought if I climbed up in his lap I would get his clothes dirty. He continued to beckon me to come. His eyes were pure love, his countenance was welcoming, and his voice was total acceptance. When I finally had enough courage to allow him to pick me up and put me in his lap a very surprising thing happened. All my smut and dirt was absorbed into his light and disappeared without a trace. I was suddenly dressed in dazzling white.

His love for sinners sets us free when we accept his invitation to come. That's his way of dealing with sin.

## The Man-Forsaken Man

Jesus is fully man and fully God. In his humanity he was *a man rejected by men*. (I am grateful to Jurgen Moltmann, *The Crucified God*, for the following insights.) He was a man indicted by the religious leaders as a *blasphemer* because he claimed to be the Son of God. The Roman government convicted the Prince of Peace as a *threat to the peace* of the community. The crowd condemned the true Messiah as a *false messiah*. He was abandoned by his followers as a failure because they thought he was unable to do what he came to do. He was a man victimized by both leaders and followers. It was the "will of the Lord to bruise him" (Isa. 53:10), but it was the will of man that condemned him to death and forsook him to die alone. He was a victim of those he came to save.

We humans tend to condemn and violate those who threaten our self-righteous reputation in the community. The scapegoat (the innocent victim) must be driven out because he's a reminder of our weakness and corruption. Or, if we aren't leaders in the system, we deny and forsake those who give themselves over as victims. Fear of the violent mob keeps us from standing with the victim.

Like Simon Peter, we don't understand and don't know what to do, so we deny our relationship to the victim. We withdraw our support. Or, like the crowd, we get caught up in the spirit of the mob and join the leaders in driving out the innocent scapegoat. We project our sin on him and expel him. Jesus (and martyrs) willingly embrace this expulsion and thereby expose our sin for what it is: fighting violence with violence or failing to support those who are being violated.

## The God-Forsaken Man

He was also a *God forsaken man*; "Why have you forsaken me" was his cry from the cross (see Matt. 27:46). No human being has ever experienced this depth of abandonment. We have never been forsaken by this God. We may forsake him, but he does not forsake us. Even in this forsakenness he *did not stop loving*. On the cross he received the vinegar (sour wine) so that the New Wine would be available to us (see Jn. 19:30). He drank the cup his Father gave him.

## The Man-Forsaken God

But he was also *God forsaken by man*. In his divinity he was a forsaken God. He was God, forsaken by his own people. He was God, forsaken by the ones he had come to save. He was God, forsaken by his own creation. Mankind forsook him; he was a *man forsaken God*. Mankind, Adam, has forsaken this God from the beginning. We often think of ourselves as God forsaken men; but we have never been forsaken by this God.

We forsake him and alienate ourselves from him then blame him for the alienation. "When a man's folly brings his way to ruin, his heart rages against God" (Prov. 19:3). But God is ever ready to receive us back into fellowship if we'll only return to his bosom from whence we came. In all this he remains "The Waiting Father," to borrow a sermon title from Helmut Thielicke.

## The God-Forsaken God

He was also a *God forsaken God*. His Father, God, could have saved him from this hour; but not without ceasing to love the world. The Father was experiencing as much pain as the Son because the Son is the one in whom he delights for all eternity. The Father has to watch his beloved Son die this cruel death at the hands of the ones he loves in the world. Jesus on the cross is the *Son forsaken by the Father for the sake of those who are killing him*. Neither the Father nor the Son can stop loving without ceasing to be God. "Why hast thou forsaken me?" is the cry of the Son of God as well as the Son of Man. The Father is allowing his Son to be separated from him. Here we have God separated from God. How could that be?

## His Torn Flesh: A Place Prepared

*At the cross there is a tear in the fabric of the unity of the Father and the Son.* That may not be a proper way of expressing it, but something deep was happening in God himself. In the natural, his tunic was not torn by the soldiers because it **"was without seam, woven from top to bottom"** (Jn.19:23). But the soldier's spear did tear the 'fabric' of his flesh and make an opening. **"And at once there came out** *blood and water*" (Jn. 19:34). The flow came from the tear in the body of Jesus. John uses this contrast between fabric and flesh to help us see where the real tear was inflicted. The tear was in the fabric of the Suffering Servant's towel—his flesh.

This is how Jesus prepared a place for us. We have access to the Father through this torn curtain which is his flesh (see Heb.10:20). When we come to the Father through Jesus, we are inserted into the Body of Christ—into this tear. We have access to his life in the river (blood and water) that flows from the throne of God—from the torn side of the Lamb of God seated on the throne. This is the river of God's love for humanity. It will never stop flowing because God will never stop loving.

## Two Kinds of Pain

We are called to abide in his love. When we're being offended or unjustly punished, we tend to *stop loving* the offenders. We think we can avoid more pain by ceasing to love. But when we withhold love, we experience another kind of pain, the pain of broken relationships. Torment, which is more than mere pain, comes because of our un-forgiveness.

The second kind of pain is destructive. It destroys the one who refuses to forgive and blocks his ability to have intimacy with anyone, including God. The first kind of pain, the pain of being rejected, can become a redemptive pain if we embrace it with Jesus' words, "Father, forgive them; for they know not what they do" (Luke 23:34). We abide in his love as we allow ourselves to be torn for the sake of another. Only in this way can we live the new life of the Spirit.

## A Breach in the Dead-End

So when we look on the crucified, the one we have pierced, we see our sin in bold relief. But in light of the resurrection we also see God's love fully manifested. Without the resurrection one might as well join Judas in his suicide. We would be forgiven but would have no ability to receive that forgiveness and no power to overcome sin. New life would not be available.

Those disciples who chose to join Peter in his willingness to stick around were rewarded with a post resurrection manifestation of Jesus. Those who came to the place where they could look on the *resurrected* Lord were radically changed. Conversion doesn't come by seeing the crucified in isolation from the risen Lord. It comes through a life-giving encounter with the crucified one who is risen and exalted to the right hand of the Father. He's not only alive forever more, he has become a life-giving spirit (see I Cor. 15:45).

## *Jesus Enters the Chasm*

The burial of Jesus stands between his death and resurrection. We often miss the significance of the burial because we concentrate on the death and resurrection. As we said above, the grave is like a deep chasm that drops off into the abyss when we die. From the perspective of the natural world there isn't another side to this chasm. The grave is evidence of the dead-end of this road called life. There is nothingness and void on the other side. The grave is a place where there's no hope and no future.

When someone is in the grave we morn their absence and celebrate the memory of their life if they lived a good life. If their life made us miserable in some way, we may even rejoice in their absence and try to erase the memories connected to their life. In either case we have no expectation to see them when we get up the next morning. There is finality in the grave.

Nicodemus and Joseph of Arimathea "*took the body of Jesus, and bound it in linen cloths with the spices as is the burial custom of the Jews*" (Jn. 19:40). They bind the spices into the grave cloth because of their expectation that this body will decay. That's what bodies do in the grave. The spices are placed there to minimize the odor. As far as the disciples are concerned, it's all over. Nothing more can be expected from one who's already been placed in the grave.

They'd seen Jesus raise the dead. Those whom he raised were back on the one-way street; now he had come to that dead-end himself. The one who had this extraordinary power over death is under the power of death. There's no longer anyone around with power over death. *Death appears to have the last word.*

## The Good News

The ugliness of the crucifixion becomes a sign of hope when we receive the atonement and reconciliation available through the death of the resurrected one. The glory of the resurrection becomes a daily possibility for us when we meet the risen Lord and begin our journey with him into the bosom of the Father. *But the grave still retains the aura of finality.* However, that finality becomes *good news* rather than bad news. Our old nature, with its sin and rebellion, has been drawn into the vortex of the burial of Jesus.

*All our rebellion and selfishness have been left behind in the abyss.* Our sins have been cast into the sea. "We were buried therefore with him by baptism into death, so that as Christ was raised from the dead by the glory of the Father, we too might walk in newness of life" (Rom. 6:4). Our old nature—the one that would even kill God—has been left behind in the tomb. The finality of the grave becomes great freedom for those who join the risen Lord. But the disciples didn't see that yet. The light of the New Creation had not yet dawned.

*"Now in the place where he was crucified there was a garden, and in the garden a new tomb where no one had ever been laid"* (Jn. 19:41). There were public burial places where the common people were buried, and there were the tombs of the kings where royalty were buried. But men of wealth loved to have a burial place cut out of stone on a

mountain side and to beautify it with a garden. These men hired gardeners to care for the site and see to it that no one was buried there. They wanted to have a new tomb for themselves when they died.

Jesus was buried in a place where no one had ever been laid. No one ever died the death he died, and no one was ever buried where he was buried. Others may have been laid in that geographical location later. But his burial was in a new tomb, a new place, because his death was a unique death. No one could and no one can follow him there. In his burial he went to a depth in death that had never been experienced by the sons of Adam.

## *On the Other Side*

From *this depth* he was able to bring with him all the prisoners when he took death captive and returned from the grave (see Eph. 4:8). It was from *this depth* that he was raised. Because of his willingness to descend to the lowest level in creation, his new life is a power that overcomes death and decay as well as sin (see Rom. 8:21).

In his resurrection we can see there's another side to the chasm. Others had been raised from the dead, like Lazarus, but they returned to the one-way street and died again. They had only returned to *this side*. They'd not been raised to *that life* which is on the *other side of the chasm*. This chasm, the grave, separates death from life and life from death. On this side of the chasm there is only the old life on its way to the grave. On the other side is newness of life; death is left behind. Life becomes an eternal abiding place in the bosom of the Father, not merely some day, but even today. But again, the disciples didn't know that yet.

We're unable to cross this chasm; we can only be swallowed up by it. We need a Helper. Jesus was able to cross to the other side because of the life he lived in the bosom of the Father. He glorified the Father by walking as he walked, right into the clutches of death, trusting his Father to be his Helper. The Father glorified the Son by raising him from the dead. Jesus didn't raise himself from the dead. He was really dead; dead people can't raise themselves. His Father raised him up and gave him a place at his right hand. Jesus resumed his place in the bosom of the Father having prepared a place in his side for us to join him there.

## Meeting the Resurrected Lord

We'll now focus on the series of events surrounding the resurrection. As we unpack the story, remember we're looking at the crucified in his resurrected form. We mustn't ever forget that connection. Focusing on the death without resurrection is morbid, as though there's no hope. Focusing on the resurrection without the death is idealistic, as though there's no price to pay, no place for suffering. We must hold the two together. We must also hold before us the question, "How can I, a son or daughter of Adam, get to the other side of this chasm and join him in the Father's bosom?

## Mary Magdalene Approaches the Tomb

*"Now on the first day of the week Mary Magdalene came to the tomb early, while it was still dark"* (Jn. 20:1). It's significant that the first person to approach the empty tomb is a woman, a sinful woman. It isn't Mary, the mother of Jesus, whom the church sees in terms of purity. John is drawing our attention again to one who represents the bottom rung of society. Jesus is a friend of prostitutes and sinners; and they all feel very comfortable in his presence. As Jack Frost often says, the righteous were uncomfortable when he was around; sinners loved to hang out with him.

This woman is coming to the tomb early because she's eager to mourn the death of her friend. She had anointed Jesus' feet for burial, now she's the first to come to the grave site. She comes while it's still dark. The light of revelation hasn't yet begun to shine. The sunrise of the new creation is not yet visible.

## Too Dark to See

She *"saw that the stone had been taken away"* (Jn. 20:1). That's all anyone can see before the light of revelation dawns. The stone is already rolled away; the grave is opened. The body isn't there. The open grave is not revelation. It only shows where Jesus is not. Mary comes to the conclusion that someone has taken the body away. The tomb belongs to someone else and the body should not have been put there. Not knowing what else to do, Mary runs to Simon Peter and the other disciple (that would be John). She'll need their help to find the body.

*"They have taken the Lord out of the tomb, and we do not know where they have laid him"* (Jn. 20:2). There are confusing elements in this report. First she refers to him as Lord, and then she expresses her concern over where they laid him. How is he Lord if someone (whoever "they" are) can take him away? How can she expect him to be laid in a prone position if she really believes he is Lord? For that matter, how could he be dead if he is Lord?" The nature of the Lordship of Jesus, the Suffering Servant, is not yet clear because it's still dark. Confusion is inevitable when the light of revelation hasn't dawned.

## Peter and John Arrive

*"They both ran, but the other disciple outran Peter and reached the tomb first; and stooping to look in, he saw the linen cloths lying there, but he did not go in"* (Jn. 20:4). The only thing they're able to see in the dim light of the dawning revelation is the linen cloths. Peter arrives and goes into the tomb. His vision is also limited. All he sees is the grave cloths. The natural eye can see grave cloths under the light of this world. What they must see to have new life is not

yet evident. The question rises, why would those who took the body leave the grave cloths behind? That question may have occurred to the disciples.

This brings up the question of the Shroud of Turin. Is it genuine? Some say yes; some say no. But it doesn't matter for our purposes. It's only cloth, and of itself can give no revelation. All we can know is the body is no longer wrapped in that cloth, if it ever was. The question, "Where have they laid him?" will always be a valid question for those whose eyes have not yet been exposed to the light of revelation.

## Believing without Believing

*"The other disciple...also went in, and he saw and believed; for as yet they did not know the scripture, that he must rise from the dead"* (Jn. 20:8). Here we have another set of confusing statements. First he "saw and believed," then we discover they "did not know the scripture, that he must rise from the dead." If they don't know of the resurrection, then exactly what do they believe? The text doesn't tell us. Perhaps John's point is that the dawning of revelation has come but the full light is not yet shining. The tacit question, "Why were the grave cloths left behind?" prompts the same level of belief we found in the official in John 5, whose son was ill. He believed the word but later believed on a deeper level.

*"Then the disciples went back to their homes"* (Jn. 20:10). Here's another indication of the weakness of their believing. If they're aware that Jesus has been raised from the dead it seems they would begin to seek him. If they believe, they should tell Mary not to look for a dead body. Unlike Mary, they don't linger around the tomb. They don't expect to find him there and it's doubtful they expect to find him in their homes. Again we have evidence that full revelation has not yet dawned on them.

## Light Begins to Dawn

"*But Mary stood weeping outside the tomb, and as she wept she stooped to look into the tomb; and she saw two angels in white sitting where the body of Jesus had lain*" (Jn. 20:11). I wonder if those two angels were in the tomb when Peter and John went in. Angels are often present without being seen or recognized. The fact that she sees the angels is an indication that the light of revelation is increasing. The presence of the supernatural is being exposed. But the light is not yet bright enough to see what's really there. She doesn't realize at this time that they're angles. The question of the whereabouts of the body is still puzzling her.

"*Why are you weeping?*" the angels ask (Jn. 20:13).

"*Because they have taken away my Lord and I do not know where they have laid him*" (Jn. 20:13). She's looking for a dead Lord. She expects to find him in a prone position. The Jewish funereal practice was to mourn the death of a loved one at the site where the body was laid. Mary wants to mourn the death of her friend and is frustrated by her inability to find the body. Grieving is our way of slowly separating ourselves from one who has left us behind, while at the same time remaining attached. The presence of angels doesn't alert her to the Lord's living presence.

## Seeing without Seeing

"*She turned round and saw Jesus standing, but did not know it was Jesus*" (Jn. 20:14). This is the first of two turns Mary makes on this first Easter morning. When she turns this time, she sees Jesus *standing* but she doesn't recognize him. Perhaps she doesn't recognize him because she's looking for a body in a prone position. Dead people don't stand up. He's there as one whom she doesn't know because she still perceives from her bubble.

"*Jesus said to her, 'Woman, why are you weeping?*'" (Jn. 20:15). She's thinking, "That's a dumb question. Why would anyone weep at a grave site? Isn't it obvious I'm grieving over the death of someone I love?" She's so absorbed in her grieving process that she doesn't really hear the implication of the question that now comes to her for the second time. If she had ears to hear the question the way Jesus and the angels intended it, she would've heard, "Why weep over one who is alive?" The sun continues to rise during the course of the events of this early morning. It's about to burst through the clouds and shine into Mary's consciousness.

"*Whom do you seek*" (Jn. 20:15)? The first question Jesus asked in chapter one was, "What do you seek?" Now that the discipleship journey has come to this crossroad, the question has changed from 'what?' to 'whom?' *Seeking the abiding place has brought the disciples to this garden in front of this tomb*. This is the same question Jesus asked the band of soldiers who arrested him. However, the question now has a new significance since he has been crucified. Jesus knew the soldiers were seeking him to arrest him. Mary's desire is to find her friend. She's seeking the one she loves.

### Mistaken for a Gardner

"*Supposing him to be the gardener…*" (Jn. 20:15). This is amazing. The resurrected Lord can be mistaken for a common gardener! How could that be? During his life the disciples see him as the promised hero who will bring victory to Israel. They don't understand his mission but they were certain he would be able to miraculously win justice for the Jewish nation. That's the content of their preconceived notions.

They see him as a "mighty man of God" before his death. His death seriously challenges the content of their imagination. After his resurrection Mary thinks he's a gardener. The sunlight has not yet burst through the cloud. But her unbelief is on its way to believing because the cloudy veil is about to be lifted from her mind.

*"Sir, if you have carried him away, tell me where you have laid him, and I will take him away"* (Jn. 20:15). The gardener's job would've been to carry away any cadaver placed in this tomb. Mary still expects the body to be in the prone position. "If my dead Jesus is a bother to you, I'll take him away so you don't have to deal with his presence." How many modern Christians are ashamed of their dead Jesus? They may not be aware they think of him as dead, but they don't expect him show up and do anything. Dead people don't do anything. Is that why most of us limit our witness to a secure place behind the four walls of a church building? No one knows what we do behind those walls, that is, no one accept the others among us who are also ashamed of their dead Jesus.

Then again, Jesus may be the original Gardener—the one who planted the garden in the Genesis creation story. Perhaps he has been guarding that place to keep dead bodies out (dead in sin that is). If so, he has now come to bring new life so that we can all join him for a walk in the garden with his Father. I wonder if John also wants us to connect the garden where Jesus was arrested with this garden by the tomb. I can imagine that Adam's eating of the forbidden fruit arrested God's ability to be the Helper.

*"Jesus said to her, 'Mary'"* (Jn. 20:16). It's Jesus who is speaking her name; but she hasn't yet recognized him. This is the same man she mistook for the gardener. She hadn't recognized his voice when he asked why she was weeping. But now, suddenly she realizes this man knows her name, he knows who she is. "This must be someone I know, someone who knows me," she thinks. So she looks more closely, and as she turns, the veil is removed. The Light shines in.

## The Light Shines In

*"She turned and said to him in Hebrew, 'Rabboni!' (which means teacher)"* (Jn. 20:16). This is the second time

she *turns*. She had turned to see the gardener. Now she turns to see Jesus. This second turning is possible only in the light of full revelation. "When a man turns to the Lord, the veil is removed" (I Cor. 3:16). She could not have made this turn if Jesus had not been there calling her name. This is an inner turning of her spirit made possible by the presence of the Lord. She turns away from her bubble and away from her preoccupation with grieving. She turns to the presence of the Lord who has been there all along. She's able to make this turn because he opened her eyes to see.

Her response is one word: "Rabboni." This is an echo of the response of the first two disciples when Jesus asked the question, "What do you seek?" They had said, "Rabbi." She says, "Rabboni." As we noticed earlier, the first is the address expected by any teacher with disciples following him, and the second was used only to address the most honorable teachers of teachers. The disciples had begun to follow a great teacher among other teachers only to discover they were following the Teacher of all true teachers.

## My Father and Your Father

"*Go to my brethren and say to them, I am ascending to my Father and your Father, to my God and your God*" (Jn. 20:17). This reminds me of what Jesus said to the Samaritan woman, "...*you* will worship the Father." For her it was a coming hour; it was not yet a reality. In this statement Jesus indicates the hour has come: "My brethren, my Father and your Father, my God and your God." Martha is now *more than a friend* of Jesus. She's a *sister* to him because they have the same Father. She's a sister to the resurrected Lord. She's a *daughter* of the Father of all creation. For the Samaritan woman it was a sign looking forward to a coming hour, for Mary the hour has arrived. She is now on her way to the bosom of her Father.

Jesus commissions her to tell the others who are also his brothers and sisters, sons and daughters of his Father. The Samaritan woman had understood this mission intuitively. But her testimony was related to a man who had told her about herself. Her invitation, "Come and see," was all about *this man*. The death and resurrection of Jesus was all future for her, a coming hour. Now the announcement is: "The crucified Lord has returned as the risen one. We are now his brothers and sisters. We are sons and daughters of his Father."

The form the invitation took for those who were truly his disciples during the days of his flesh was different from the form it must take for us today. "Come see a man…," was the testimony then. Today it must be an announcement followed by an invitation: "He is risen! Come, meet the resurrected Lord. Become sons and daughters of his Father. He has prepared a place for you in his Father's house, even in his Father's heart."

## Peace be With You

*"On the evening of that day, the first day of the week, the doors being shut…Jesus came and stood among them…"* (Jn. 20:19). It's still the first day of the week, the same day Jesus revealed himself to Mary and sent her to the other disciples. That was morning; now it's evening. It's dark outside again.

The first two disciples had come to abide with him the tenth hour. That would be shortly before sundown: after the time of crucifixion when the earth was darkened because the sun refused to shine. Now it's evening and they're in need of light again. They've heard the report of his resurrection, but they haven't met the resurrected Lord themselves.

The closed doors indicate more than the fear of the Jews. The fear that prompted them to shut the doors is the barrier Jesus will have to overcome to reveal himself to them. Fear and unbelief are related. In this case we're looking at an incomplete belief rather than crass unbelief. But incomplete belief also breeds fear. He had overcome Mary's barrier, her insufficient faith, by calling her name. The process of overcoming this barrier in the disciples begins when Jesus shows up in the room.

*"Peace be with you.... When he had said this he showed them his hands and his side. Then the disciples were glad when they saw the Lord"* (Jn. 20:19-20). The word *then* is revealing. The disciples apparently don't recognize the Lord until he shows them his hands and his side. Like Mary, they may not have recognized him at first. He brings these men to revelation by showing up and showing his hands and his side.

Jesus can still walk through closed doors. He only does that for those whose hearts he knows are searching and open, to those responding to his Father's drawing. We are surprised by some of the people he encounters because we judge outer appearance. He did it for Saul of Tarsus, a murderer. He did it for St. Francis of Assisi, the selfish son of a rich man. Many reports have come in from Islamic, Buddhist, and animistic cultures. People all over the world have been having dreams and seeing visions of Jesus. Whole villages are often converted as a result of a dream or vision. He commissioned us to go, but he is going before us. These are days for missionaries to be bold. He is coming.

## As the Father Sent Me

*"Jesus said to them again, 'Peace be with you. As the Father has sent me, even so I send you"* (Jn. 20:21). The Father sent the Son to represent him to the world. 'Represent' here must be understood in the sense of re-present or make present again. Jesus' presence is the presence of the Father because he does only what he sees the Father doing. Jesus said to the disciples, *"...apart from me you can do nothing"* (Jn. 15:5).

The Father lives his life in the Son. The disciples are sent to allow the Son to live his life in them. Paul lived his life in this way. "It is no longer I who live; but Christ who lives in me" (Gal. 2:20). But how are the disciples to fulfill their mission? How are we to fulfill our mission? How can we *represent* Jesus to our generation?

## The New Creation

"*He breathed on them, and said to them, 'Receive the Holy Spirit*" (Jn. 20:22). The language here is significant. There is a Greek verb for 'breathe' that is related to the word 'spirit' (*pneuma*). But that's not the word used here. The word used here means something like 'puff into'. This is significant because the same situation is found in the Genesis account of the creation of the first Adam where God breathed into Adam's nostrils the breath of life.

There is also a Hebrew word for 'breath' that is related to the word 'spirit' (*ruach*). The word used in Genesis is a different Hebrew word that means 'to puff'. God puffed into Adam the breath of soul-life. That was the old creation. Jesus puffed into these disciples the breath of spirit-life, the Holy Spirit. That's the New Creation. He's giving them new life for the new garden.

In the old creation, God gathered particles of red earth and formed the body of the first Adam. In the New Creation, Jesus gathers particles of humanity and forms a new body, the Body of Christ.

It's impossible to do the work of God with soul-life. His work can only be done with spirit-life. The soul-life is related to the idea of the flesh. "*The Spirit gives life, the flesh is of no avail*" (Jn. 6:63). The word for soul-life (*psyche*) was used by Jesus when he said, "*He who loves his life [psyche] loses it, and he who hates his life [psyche] will keep it for eternal life*" (Jn. 12:25). The only way anyone can do the will of God is through the Holy Spirit. The risen Lord brings the Holy Spirit so that no one need be left without the ability to do the will of the Father. Only by the guidance and power of the Holy Spirit can we participate in the New Creation.

## Grace for Doubters

*"Unless I see in his hands the print of the nails, and place my finger in the mark of the nails, and place my hand in his side, I will not believe"* (Jn. 20:25). Thomas was not with the other disciples when Jesus appeared to them. We must not judge Thomas too quickly. Peter and John had walked away from the tomb with no expectation of finding the risen Lord. When they gave their testimony, "We have seen the Lord," Thomas spoke the words quoted above. These are words of doubt and unbelief. How does the risen Lord respond to doubt and unbelief?

*"Put your finger here, and see my hands; and put out your hand, and place it in my side; do not be faithless, but believing"* (Jn. 20:27). Jesus comes again eight days after his first appearance to the disciples. Thomas is with them this time. Jesus overcomes the barrier, the closed door of his heart, by inviting him (not forcing him) to put his hands in his side. This invitation brought Thomas to the place Jesus had prepared for him, to the tear in his side.

When Jesus invited him to place his hand in his side he reveals that the wound is still an open wound. It may be that Jesus has chosen to wear these wounds in eternity. When we meet him 'over there' we may see those open wounds as a reminder of his love for us. This is the wound where we are inserted. We live in the river that flows from this tear. This will be our place eternally. He is in the Father's bosom with these wounds, and we are in him, inserted into the tear.

## My Lord and my God

Several years ago I was meditating on these open wounds and suddenly realized that we human beings have made a mark in eternity by our rebellion and sin. There is something 'up there' that is man-made—the wounds in the hands and side of Jesus. I felt the Lord was saying to me, "Don't become proud. You would never have made those marks if I hadn't taken to myself a human body. Even then you wouldn't have been able to pierce these hands or tear this side unless I had willingly offered them to the soldiers. These wounds are a result of my work, not yours."

It's the gracious love of God from the beginning and will continue to be his loving grace in all eternity. Our Father and our big Brother love us enough to give themselves to us and for us in this way.

Even his death was not our work. We did murder him when he made himself available; but God raised him from the dead. We did bury him in the hope that he would no longer be a bother to us; but he conquered the grave. He returned to give eternal life to those who rejected him and murdered him. We can't even have this insight apart from the Holy Spirit who comes to us and reveals the risen Lord to us. Only then can we recognize our Lord. Only then can we serve him effectively in the New Creation.

*"Thomas answered him, 'my Lord and my God'"* (Jn. 20:28)! When full revelation breaks through the barrier of our self-centeredness and unbelief we can only worship his majesty. We can never know him in this way apart from revelation. But when the revelation comes we can know him intimately. We are gathered into the Body of the New Creation. He is the risen Lord, and we are raised with him and made to sit with him in heavenly places (in the Father's bosom), in Christ Jesus (see Ephesians 2:6). We are with him *there* because he is with us *here*.

## No Witnesses to the Resurrection

Notice an important point here. No human being witnessed the resurrection. That event occurred in the darkness with no one watching. The crucifixion was accomplished in the sight of the multitude. There were many witnesses to his death. To be a witness one must be present on the scene when the deed is done. The whole world was asleep (figuratively) when the stone was rolled away and Jesus was raised.

We can't be witnesses to the resurrection as such today because that happened almost two thousand years ago. But it's possible to meet the resurrected Lord today. If we've met him, we know the resurrection occurred because we have been encountered by the resurrected Lord. *If we doubt the resurrection it can only be because we have not yet had, or we have forgotten, this encounter.*

Our testimony shouldn't focus on the resurrection as an event occurring two thousand years ago. That was the most important event in history up to that point; but it's not to be the focus of our testimony. In a court of law a testimony is allowed only if the witness was on the scene and heard with his own ears and saw with his own eyes. Our only testimony, if we have one, will be, "I have met the resurrected Lord! And because I've met him I know that the old has passed away and the new has come." The testimony should be followed by an invitation: "Come and see. Become a part of the New Creation."

## *Personal Encounter is Necessary*

The crucial question isn't whether you believe the doctrine of the resurrection. That's obviously a very important doctrine. The real question is, "Have you met him personally?" Closely connected to that question is another set of questions, "Are you following him into the bosom of the Father? Are you in the abiding place? Does your daily life issue out of this place in Father's bosom?" That's our inheritance as those who participate in the New Creation.

Several years ago I had the privilege of spending extended time with a Jewish Rabbi who was known internationally as a teacher of Jewish history and philosophy. The question of Jesus' resurrection came up in our conversation. He looked out the window, closed the curtains (he'd been influenced by Auschwitz) and said, "I know Jesus was our Messiah. I know he was raised from the dead; but I can't change."

I was confused by this. "If he knows, why is he reluctant to change?" I thought to myself. "My experience has been that we are automatically changed when the risen Lord shows up." Later I realized the great distinction between believing the facts of history and knowing the person to whom those facts point as a sign. Knowing that Jesus was raised is not the same as knowing him. Knowledge of facts never brings anyone into the bosom of the Father. We get there only by following the risen Lord to that place and becoming a part of the Body of this New Creation.

One question remains to be answered in our last chapter: "Where do we go from here? We have met the risen Lord; now what?"

# CHAPTER 12

# Do You Love Me?

—m—

Abiding in him is abiding in his love. It's an active participation in the inner life of the Trinitarian God. As the Father and the Son reach out by the Spirit to the lost and hurting world to bring life and liberation, we are invited to join the journey. When a believer is connected to the Vine, allowing the *rhema* word to flow through his life, he becomes a disciple and begins to know the truth by experiencing a transformation in his life and in his relationships.

Jesus allowed his flesh to be torn and his blood to flow so that we may receive *this* Love-life. He could not stop loving, and he calls us to live a life of loving even when we are being rejected.

## *What's Next?*

Readers of the Gospel often respond with surprise when they come to chapter 21 for the first time. We find seven disciples together wondering what they should do next. They've encountered the risen Lord twice, and they've received the Holy Spirit, but they still don't know what to do or where to go. Their confusion over their purpose and destiny didn't evaporate when they met the risen Lord.

Our surprise comes because we believe the early disciples were fundamentally different from us. Most Christians today are just as unsure about the purpose of life after their conversion experience. Something more or something else seems to be needed to have clear direction.

## A Puzzling List

There's something about the list of disciples that puzzles me. I'll mention it briefly before we turn to the development of the story and dialogue of this chapter. Simon Peter, Thomas, and Nathaniel are named. Then there are the sons of Zebedee (that would be James and John) and *"two others of his disciples"* (Jn. 21:2). Why were the two others not named? Throughout the book the 'other disciple' is the one whom Jesus loved and we've identified him as John, the author of the Gospel.

Perhaps John wants us to read his book of signs again and identify with the 'other disciple' whom Jesus loved. Our next time through, some of us may be like Simon, some like Philip, some like Nathaniel, and some in the background like John. But the next time through we'll have an idea of where we are going and what we can expect at the end of this journey.

We'll also begin to discover our own tendency to follow the script of the movie that plays on the screen of our imagination rather than allowing Jesus to take the lead. Like Simon Peter, we'll experience our journey as a process of transition from what we were (Simon) to what we're becoming (Peter). Each time we read the Gospel we'll leave more of the "Simon" behind and embrace more of the "Peter" we're becoming. And we'll experience that as the 'other disciple whom Jesus loves.'

## The 'Other' Disciples

The number of disciples who fall into the 'other' category increases after the resurrection and continues to increase as others enter the path. These two, along with the other five, have become sons and daughters of the Father and they have received the Holy Spirit. They still don't know what to do next. Most of us are in that spiritual condition periodically. In this final chapter we'll join these disciples as they try to discover their identity, purpose, and destiny after their encounter with the risen Lord.

## The Need to Do Something

*"Simon Peter said to them, 'I am going fishing.' They said to him, 'We will go with you'"* (Jn. 21:3). Simon, on his way to becoming Peter, isn't one to just stand around wondering what to do. He's a man of action. The absence of the risen Lord means he must decide for himself what to do. Simon isn't willing to wait. He'll go fishing even if no one goes with him. But men of action become leaders of others who also don't know what to do. The others simply agree to *follow Simon Peter.* Since fishing became a code word for evangelism, we suggest that the activity of these men is a sign pointing to an attempt to do the work of God without the presence and direction of the risen Lord.

*"But that night they caught nothing"* (Jn. 21:3). It's night again. Light had dawned with his resurrection, and Mary had seen the risen Lord. The disciples received the Holy Spirit on the evening of that same day. He had appeared to them again eight days later to draw Thomas to his side, but his presence wasn't an *abiding, manifest presence*—not yet. They were facing another experience of what St. John of the Cross called a "dark night of the soul." We often experience this dark night when we just do what we think is right, simply because we don't know what else to do.

Night doesn't necessarily indicate the absence of the Lord. It can also refer to times when we aren't *aware* of his presence. Night and day in the creation story indicates the separation of light from darkness and the division of time. Time is divided into darkness which hides what's there, and light which reveals it. Light doesn't cause the thing to be present; it reveals its presence. Our attempt to fill dark times with activity may be the very thing that keeps us from experiencing his presence in those times. When we're busy filling our time with undirected activity, we're too distracted to notice him on the beach cooking breakfast for us.

## *More Revelation*

"*Just as day was breaking…*" (Jn. 21:4). Here's another example of dawning revelation. One isn't able to see when it's night. Any activity in the darkness of night is the work of the natural man unless you're following Jesus in the darkness. We usually relate works of the flesh with sin and degradation. But religious activity is also a work of the flesh if we do it without him.

We so much want to please the Lord that we just go fishing for lack of any clear direction from him. We fail to empty our time so he can fill it with his presence and Spirit-directed activity. We're afraid of empty time. We want activity and involvement. We feel guilty or worthless if we're not doing something, as though our value is in *doing things* rather than *being sons and daughters* of God.

## *A New Revelation?*

This question rises to the surface, "If this is a story of revelation, what is about to be revealed? They already know he is risen. They've received the Holy Spirit. What additional revelation is needed? I'm sensing a direction for the answer, but it's difficult to find language—that's a common experience when talking about spiritual matters.

I'll try this. When a baby is in the womb, he is tied to the mother and doesn't know anything other than what he's feeling. When he's born, it takes time for him to separate himself from his mother in a way that will allow him to recognize he's not still a part of his mother. He can't experience a person-to-person relationship until he recognizes who he is as distinct from his mother. During that time of development he'll try to use crying and whining to force his mother to conform to the image of what he feels a mother ought to be.

That picture is not exactly what I see, but it will help. Simon had been attached to his *image* of the Messiah and had identified himself with the Jesus of his bubble. That attachment (which is distinct from connection) was so tight he tried to force Jesus to be conformed to his image of the Christ. Peter actually thought he and Jesus were together in this venture. Jesus had to go away so Simon would detach himself from the 'Jesus' of his imagination. It was a necessary separation which also allowed Simon to forsake his image of himself as a 'holy hot-shot' and to acknowledge he was a fisherman.

## Breaking Our Commitment to the Bubble

Peter's detachment began when Jesus rebuked him for striking the High Priest's servant. The detachment reached another level when he denied the Lord around the charcoal fire in the courtyard of the High Priest. When Simon Peter goes fishing, he's simply being who he is apart from Jesus. Now that he has embraced his heritage, this fisherman can connect to Jesus without trying to prove he's a mighty man of God. Now that Simon has embraced his own identity, Jesus can come to him and draw him into a meaningful relationship that will radically change his destiny and his identity.

In this story Jesus reveals to the disciples who they really are in relation to who he really is. Disciples who have been filled with the Spirit are dangerous until they learn they aren't God's 'man of power for the hour.'

The image of the Vine and the branches comes to mind. Peter was *attached* to Jesus before the resurrection, but the life flow was from his own flesh. He's about to become *connected* so the life of God can flow through him. When we embrace our identity as men and women, as weak humans that need a Helper, then we can connect to man's 'God of power for the hour' and simply watch as God does his work through us.

## Jesus Standing Again

"*Jesus stood on the beach*" (Jn. 21:4). I get the impression Jesus had been there all night watching these disciples' fruitless activity. They were outside the abiding place. There's no possibility of bearing fruit apart from abiding in the Vine and allowing the life of the Vine to flow. Jesus isn't judging them; he didn't come to judge. He hadn't condemned the woman caught in the act of adultery; and he didn't condemn these men for trying to do something apart from him. He comes to them in their fruitlessness to bring them to himself. When this vital connection of the Vine and the branches is completed, they'll bear much fruit.

He's standing on the beach waiting for the right time to reveal himself to them in a new way. *He's standing.* In the first story of the Gospel, Jesus was standing in the crowd when the representatives of the Jewish authorities were questioning John. He was standing as one whom they didn't know. We interpreted the standing position as an indication that he'd not yet begun his ministry. There he was in transition from his ministry in the Old Testament to his ministry as the Word become flesh.

When the first disciples began to follow they thought they were following a holy hero, one who would effectively inflict violence on those who were violating the Jewish nation. At the end of the Gospel he is fully clothed in his humanity—mistaken for a gardener at the tomb and unrecognized on the beach. Here he's in transition from his ministry in the flesh to his ministry in his Body, the Church.

## Unrecognized Again

*"Yet the disciples did not know that it was Jesus"* (Jn. 21:4). He was standing on the beach as one they didn't know. Here we have an echo of the situation with Mary at the resurrection. Jesus was standing there as well. He was standing in front of one who was a devoted friend and disciple. Mary didn't recognize him in the garden tomb.

When Jesus said to her, *"Do not hold me, for I have not yet ascended to the Father"* (Jn. 20:17), he indicated it wasn't yet time for his post-resurrection ministry to begin. He came to the disciples and breathed upon them the evening of that day. They became the Body of the New Creation at that time. But time for ministry had not yet arrived.

This makes one wonder how often Jesus is present to the Body of Christ today without our recognizing him. They didn't know because the light had not yet exposed his presence to them. Only a few days or a few weeks earlier they'd seen him clearly. Now they do not see. We experience time in two ways: as times of obscurity (night) and times of clarity (day).

We shouldn't condemn ourselves when we fail to see nor should we condemn others when they fail to see. Seeing comes with the dawning of the light of the presence of the resurrected Lord. *Man can't control the dawn nor can he control the dusk.* Jesus is coming out of hiding in this text. He's coming to bring the disciples to a new level of trust in him even when they're not consciously aware of his presence.

## The Question of Productivity

*"Children, have you any fish"* (Jn. 21:5). He addresses them as children. They'd only been 'born again' for a few days, or a few weeks at the most. What a tender, loving way of addressing those who don't recognize him. There's no condemnation, no critical or sarcastic remarks. There's only a simple question, "Children, how are you doing on your own? How's your program working for you?" The question isn't designed to bring shame but to begin the process of recognizing who they are apart from him and to draw them into the intimate connection that will bear fruit.

They'd not yet understood what he meant when he said they would not be able to do anything apart from him (see Jn. 15:5). He's not upset that they don't understand. He's confident of his ability to bring them to the place he's prepared for them. If we become anxious when others do not understand, it may be because we are not confident in our Big Brother's ability to bring them to the place he's prepared for them.

## A Personal Experience

I fully understand this from personal experience. Over thirty-six years ago the Lord came to me when I doubted his willingness to do miracles today. I'd been trained to believe all the gifts of the Spirit were limited to the first century. He'd been trying to get my attention as a teacher by healing some of my students. I tried to explain it away, but I really wanted it to be true. My commitment to my bubble-images was too strong to simply accept the facts in front of me. I did begin to read some testimonials with the hope of coming to believe. My doubt was still standing strong.

One evening as I was reading, the Lord appeared to me. I could've counted the locks of his hair. He spoke these words deep into my spirit, "Fount, you haven't been believing me, have you?" That's all he said. There was no condemnation in his voice, only love and tender concern. I began to weep and sob uncontrollably, repenting for my unbelief. I was suddenly aware that I had been fishing all night and caught nothing. From that time to this I've never doubted his love and willingness to be my Helper day and night. But I'm always pleasantly surprised when he works a miracle through my act of reaching out to hurting people.

*"They answered him, 'No'"* (Jn. 21:5). It's difficult for us humans to admit our program isn't working when we're only comparing ourselves with ourselves. If another leader or someone from another church asks, we tend to cover up our fruitlessness with statistics that have nothing to do with abiding in the Father's bosom or bearing fruit. We talk about what we're doing as though that amounts to something.

It's refreshing to meet someone who's honest with themselves and willing to confess their fruitlessness to others. These disciples don't know they are speaking to the Lord. They're willing to confess their fruitlessness to one they think is a total stranger.

## Obedience without Knowing

*"Cast the net on the right side of the boat, and you will find some"* (Jn. 21:6). Peter and the sons of Zebedee are professional fishermen. They know how to catch fish if there are fish to be caught. These men are on a path leading to revelation. Like the woman at the well, they don't know they are on the path, but they are on it none the less. When this 'total stranger' suggests they cast to the right, they could laugh at him. They could insist on their superior abilities as fishermen, or just ignore him. They could leave the path, but they don't.

*"So they cast it, and now they were not able to haul it in, for the quantity of fish"* (Jn. 21:6). We see amazing results when we respond obediently to the voice of the one who is in the bosom of the Father. But these men didn't know it was the Lord. Peter had responded on an impulse when the

'stranger' spoke. All of us have had experiences where we acted on an impulse only to discover later it was the Lord. Sometimes the impulse isn't from the Lord when we think it is. Later we discover the Lord was doing something else. Those of us who don't move until we're certain usually don't move. We discover later that the Lord left us behind. How can we know for sure? Do we *need* to know for certain?

### Recognizing the Lord

*"The disciple whom Jesus loved said to Peter, 'It is the Lord'"* (Jn. 21:7). Why does the beloved disciple tell Peter? Why doesn't he jump in the water and go to the Lord? John isn't a man of impulsive action like Peter. John likes to analyze the situation before he does anything. In the book of Acts, Peter and John are often together. Peter is always the one speaking and the one acting. John is just there observing. He is very much involved but he doesn't initiate anything. He doesn't avoid situations that might bring him into conflict with the authorities, but he never causes the conflict.

John is the last of the apostles to put his insights into written form because he needs time to process what he sees. The depth of John's writings may be a result of his willingness to wait until he's seen more clearly.

### Peter and John Respond

*"When Simon Peter heard that it was the Lord, he... sprang into the sea"* (Jn. 21:7). It may be that he was eager to be reconciled after he had denied the Lord three times. The issue of his denial had not come up in the previous encounters with the risen Lord. Knowing his nature, however, it's more likely he didn't even think; he just acted. That's the way he was. "Make your move and think later," seems to have been his motto. But he's making his move toward the Lord. That's a good thing.

*"But the other disciple came in the boat, dragging the net full of fish"* (Jn. 21:8). John knew it was the Lord, yet his concern was for the fish. Why wasn't he eager to have fellowship with the Lord? If those fish represent the fruit of evangelism, his concern is justified. Taking care of the fresh catch of fish would be the love issuing from the bosom of the Father toward the new children in the family. We have *fellowship* with the Father and with the Son *as we take care of one another*, washing feet, removing grave clothes, and bringing in the net lest the fish return to the sea.

## Invitation to Breakfast

*"When they got out on land, they saw a charcoal fire there, with fish lying on it, and bread"* (Jn. 21:9). Jesus had already prepared breakfast for these fishermen. In the story of the Samaritan woman the disciples had gone away to the city to buy bread. When they returned, Jesus had already eaten. We learned in that context that the real food is to do the will of the Father.

In this fishing story Jesus had prepared them a meal since they had worked all night to earn bread and had nothing to show for it. The great catch of fish was a result of hearing the voice and responding in obedience, but it wasn't necessary for their sustenance. Breakfast was already provided.

The early church saw the fish as a symbol of Jesus Christ and the bread was the Body of Christ. He is offering himself to them as their source and sustenance to do the Father's work as the Body of Christ. Only by partaking of him will they be able to accomplish the Father's will. Apart from him we can do nothing.

*"The net was not torn"* (Jn. 21:11). Seasoned fishermen know what happens to nets when the catch is too heavy for the test of the net. The mention of the net indicates John saw it as a miracle that the net wasn't torn. When our Father does a work with us or through us, he doesn't ruin our equipment.

The equipment he gives us to do the work of ministry will not be damaged in use when we hearken to the voice, even if we don't know it's him speaking.

*"Jesus said to them, 'Come and have breakfast'"* (Jn. 21:12). The invitation to come and eat reminds us of the invitation to come and see. This is a sign of the fellowship meal prepared in the abiding place. Jesus prepared a place for them and he prepared a meal (a feast?) in that place. He invites them to bring some of their miraculous catch to the charcoal fire.

The only fish allowed on this charcoal fire are those the Lord himself provides. John wants us to connect the fish Jesus prepared with the fish the disciples caught in obedient response to his voice. We participate in the work of the Father as we hearken to the voice of the Son. Hearing and responding to the voice provides nourishment for doing the Father's will.

## Knowing with Uncertainty

*"Now none of the disciples dared ask him, 'Who are you?'"* (Jn. 21:12). When John informs us that they didn't *dare* ask, he implies they really did want to ask. For some reason they didn't have enough courage. They wanted to ask because they were not absolutely certain. John had already recognized him and announced his presence; but apparently they were still uncertain on some level.

*"They knew it was the Lord"* (Jn. 21:12). If they knew, why did they want to ask? If they wanted to ask, why did they not *dare* ask? This is another one of those strange 'contradictions' John is so fond of using to tempt the reader to go deeper.

Above we noticed the disciples didn't recognize the Lord when he was standing on the beach. They didn't even recognize him when he spoke. They obeyed him without knowing it was him they obeyed. The first level of revelation in this story of the breaking of day is the *hearing* of his voice *without recognizing* it as his voice. That was also Mary's experience at the tomb. In this experience they are exposed as fishermen who do not recognize the voice. The second level is *recognizing* him as Lord *with less certainty* than we as humans are comfortable with.

## Learning to Hear His Voice

In the coffee house days of the early seventies a group of young zealots (I loved those kids) had asked me to come teach them how to hear the voice of the Lord. I was much like the disciples in this story. I wasn't certain of my own ability to hear him. I went to John chapter 10 and read about the Good Shepherd who, *"goes before them, and the sheep follow him, for they know his voice"* (Jn. 10:4).

My insecurities rose up. I wondered if I were even a sheep since I didn't hear his voice regularly. I had even followed the other shepherd's voice a few times. Then I noticed, *"A stranger they will not follow"* (Jn. 10:5). Fortunately for me and for the young zealots, the Lord drew my attention to the difference between sheep and lambs.

Sheep are the mature of the flock that have become confident in their Shepherd, they have learned to recognize and respond to his voice consistently. The lambs are the immature that have not yet learned. The Shepherd uses his goad to pull lambs back when they start following another shepherd. If they kick against this goad it hurts. Lambs mature and become sheep that know the voice of the Shepherd as they experience the goad.

How much pain we have to experience on our way to learning to recognize the voice is related to how quickly we submit to the goad. *The real issue, then, isn't certainty; it's submission to discipline as a disciple.* This fits the pattern we've noticed. We enter into a deeper relationship as we follow the path even without understanding.

## Breakfast is Served

*"Jesus came and took the bread and gave it to them, and so with the fish"* (Jn. 21:13). This act of taking and giving bread reminds us of the feeding of the multitude. In John 6 there's a clear sign pointing to the Lord's Supper. The question of the Jews in that context is, *"What must we do, to be doing the works of God?"* (Jn. 6:28). The text connects food with doing the will of the Father there. At this breakfast by the sea we also have a pointer to the doing of the will of the Father. They caught no fish except in response to the Son's voice.

The fish already on the charcoal fire may be a reference to the *"other sheep, that are not of this fold; I must bring them also, and they will heed my voice. So there shall be one flock, one shepherd"* (Jn. 10:16). All the fish are together on the grill. These fish are not from the same school, but they're together in unity on the fire. Are you willing to take your place on the grill beside fish from the other school?

Notice the disciples don't help themselves to the bread; Jesus selects the specific portion each will receive. We're not at liberty to choose our place in the Body as it accomplishes the will of God. The Head of the Body places each of us in the Body; we receive the place he went to prepare for us. We'll always be frustrated if we try to choose a place for ourselves because of the prestige or prosperity available there. But when we willingly receive the portion Jesus gives us we experience fulfillment even if there's pain or suffering in that place.

## The Third Time

*"This was now the third time that Jesus was revealed to the disciples after he was raised from the dead"* (Jn. 21:14). The *third time* reminds us of the third day when the disciples entered into the abiding place (see Jn. 1:39). The wedding feast was also on the third day. At that third day wedding

feast, Jesus did his first sign and "*manifested his glory; and his disciples believed in him*" (Jn. 2:11). At the end of the Gospel His glory is cloaked in a humanity that we can fail to recognize on the beach.

This 'third time' breakfast is about overcoming our insecurity over his identity as Lord and accepting our identity as those who need a Helper. Notice that the same issue appears here as in Peter's denial. That event was also around a charcoal fire. He denied his discipleship (his identity) around a charcoal fire in the courtyard of the High Priest. And by that denial, he also denied the Lord.

*Here our recognition of his identity is tied to our recognition of our own identity.* The question of who He is has been settled by the resurrection. The question before us in this final chapter is how our identity is affected when we believe in him. This time the question is settled around a charcoal fire in the 'courtyard' of the new High Priest.

## *Tying the End to the Beginning*

It's clear from these connections between the beginning and the end of the Gospel that John is folding the Gospel together as a unified whole around two major themes: Jesus as the way to abiding in the Father and the revelation of himself as the Son in the Father's bosom. All other themes, including discipleship, are integrated into these.

But, as there was a prologue (see Jn. 1:1-18), there is also a postscript (see Jn. 21:15-25). The prologue answered the question of the identity of Jesus and his relationship his Father and to the world he created. He is the Word of God become flesh, the Son who makes the Father known. The postscript is answering the question of the identity of the disciples: who we are in Christ and our relationship to other disciples.

By implication this postscript also shows the relationship all disciples have with Christ and with one another. Our identity is always in relation to others, never as isolated individuals. We were created with a longing for intimacy, for knowing and being known, for holding and being held by one who is faithful. There is no fullness of life apart from finding our identity in an intimate relationship with our Father and his other children.

## *Simon, Do You Love Me?*

*"When they had finished breakfast, Jesus said to Simon Peter, 'Simon, son of John, do you love me more than these?'"* (Jn. 21:15). In the beginning of this Gospel Jesus gave Simon a new name, "You will be called Cephas (which means Peter)." Throughout the Gospel John refers to him as Peter or Simon Peter; but Jesus never calls him Peter—not even once. Here at the close of the Gospel we are back to Simon, son of John. Simon had tried to become Peter, to find his own identity by his own strength and wisdom.

All his attempts to become the Peter he was called to be had failed. Why had he failed? We know what he had done wrong, but why had he denied the Lord? What had he failed to see? What had he failed to understand?

*"Do you love [agapao] me more than these?"* The transition from what we are in the natural to what we are becoming in the bosom of the Father has something to do with love. That should not be surprising since God is love. But Peter is not alone in failing to see this. The Church through history has failed to become everything it's called to be for this very reason. We've not yet understood or practiced love properly.

## *Two Kinds of Love*

In his excellent book, *Agape and Eros*, Anders Nygren traced the development of the love motif from the early church all the way through to Martin Luther. He demonstrated that the key to the apostasy of the church in the Middle Ages was a direct result of a failure to remain faithful to the

New Testament use of the word *Agape*. The Church adopted the concept of *eros* (a love that only appreciates and desires things of value) even though that word never appears in the New Testament. What did the Church miss? What have we missed? What had Peter missed?

When Jesus asked, "Do you love me?" he used the word *agape*. *Agape* is not a popular word for love among the Greeks. It refers to a love that's not concerned with the quality or value of the one loved or what value the beloved might bring to the relationship. *Agape* is a love *unmotivated by anything external to itself.*

The Greeks prefer a love that reflects their good taste. Jesus and his Father love sinners and outcasts of society. That doesn't indicate good taste on God's part, at least not from our human perspective. It doesn't make him look good to the religious 'lovers of God' who only loved 'good' people and only love God because he makes them look good.

Bob Mumford in his book, *The Agape Road*, describes *eros* as "love with a hook in it." It's a love that relates to the beloved because of some good that comes back to me. This raises the question of our motive in seeking God. Do we seek him, or love him, only because of the good he has for us? In Luke 15 the prodigal son only wanted the inheritance. He was not looking for a relationship with the Father. The elder brother was only interested in the Father's house as a place to entertain his friends. Both brothers loved with *eros* love—"*What's in it for me?*" The father loved with *agape* love—"*All I have is yours.*" The difference between these two kinds of love is obvious.

Jesus is asking Simon if he loves him "more than these," that is, with a love that's willing to look bad in the eyes of others. "Do you love me more than you love the approval of these others?" is the essence of the question. "Will you be willing to follow me even if you lose the respect of others?"

The Father certainly has special blessings for those who seek him. He rewards those who seek him (see Heb. 11:6). But, if we are seeking him because of the rewards, it is the rewards we are really seeking. To love God means to love him with no hidden agenda. Loving him simply means "I want to be with him no matter what that costs me personally." This love is tied to the Father, not to the things available to us in his house or from his storehouse.

## Simon Prefers Friendship

*"Yes, Lord; you know that I love [phileo] you"* (Jn. 21:15). Simon, on his way to becoming Peter, didn't answer with the word *agape*. He used the word *philia*, which refers to a friendship love. Jesus had said, *"No longer do I call you servants...; but I have called you friends"* (Jn. 15:15). Simon has reason to think Jesus will be pleased with his affirmation of friendship. But Simon still hasn't become Peter. He thinks he can do better than Jesus is asking. "Jesus, you are asking for *agape*. I can do better than that; I love you like a friend."

The Greeks considered friendship one of the highest forms of love. If I am a friend, that means I have a friend. Having that friend really makes me feel good. If that friend is a person of high position, his friendship makes me look good in the community. Simon is offering the best he knows; but it's not what Jesus is asking for. Even this offer of friendship still has a tinge of *eros* in it. He's still interested in what's in it for him.

C. S. Lewis wrote of the danger lurking beneath the various kinds of human love. In his book, *The Four Loves*, he warned that each of the loves can become a demon if it tries to become a god. Jesus certainly offers us friendship, and he desires our friendship. But when we set our idea of friendship love above him or above the will of the Father, our 'love' takes on a demonic form that has a life of its own and draws us away from the love the Father is offering us.

This demonic love also serves to keep true intimacy out of all our relationships. There can be no intimacy if either party is out for himself at the expense of the other. *Eros* in itself is not the problem, just as *philia* in itself is not the problem. The problem is *eros* or *philia* isolated from the *agape* love of God.

## John's Use of the word Friend

Jesus does call us friends. We can't afford to leave that behind us as we follow this text. Let's consider the concept of friendship found in John before we proceed. We don't want to make the same mistake that led the Church astray in the Dark Ages. They read the *eros* concept into *agape* which should imply a love for the beloved that is willing to lay down its personal agenda. We are in danger of thinking of friendship in terms of *eros* if we're looking for personal gain, even good feelings, from the friendship.

There is personal gain in knowing him, but our driving desire must be to know him, to be with him, not just to have the advantages of his friendship. So we want to understand friendship from John's perspective rather than reading into this context the Greek or our own American concept of what it means to be a friend. In our culture we think of friends as peers who enjoy one other's company, who have a fond affection for one another. Is that what John meant?

## Jesus as Father's Friend

The first mention of friendship in the Gospel is in chapter 5. *"The Son can do nothing of his own accord, but only what he sees the Father doing"* (Jn. 5:19). We have already related this to the concept of abiding. Here we will focus on the relationship between the Father and the Son. The Father initiates; the Son responds. This isn't a peer relationship as we think of it. There's a clear leader and a clear follower. Jesus, in his humanity, was *under* the Father and the Father was *over* him.

In our culture we dislike over/under relationships, unless we're the one who's over. That's the nature of *eros*. Even in our 'friendships' we compete for the over/under position. To be a friend of God, however, is to willingly embrace the under position.

Jesus continued, *"For the Father loves [phileo] the Son and shows him all that he himself is doing"* (Jn. 5:16). The friendship between the Father and the Son consists of the Father letting the Son in on the plan and the Son implementing that plan. In a wealthy household, servants only do what they are told. They don't need to know the full plan. Children of the household are like servants until they arrive at that level of maturity called 'sons' (see Gal. 4:1).

When a father brings his son into his counsel, he begins to show him things about the operation of the family business that neither the servants nor the children know anything about. But, until the business is handed over to him, he's still *under* his father. During that time of mentoring, the friendship is a matter of the son doing what he sees the father doing. He is able to see because the father shows him.

### *Jesus Calls us Friends*

This theme of friendship is taken a step farther in chapter fifteen. *"No longer do I call you servants, for the servant does not know what the master is doing...."* There are many 'servants of God' who do not have the foggiest idea what God is doing. Jesus continued, *"...but I have called you friends [philia], for all that I have heard from my Father I have made known to you"* (Jn. 15:15-16). When we become friends of Jesus *we do not become peers*. He is our Big Brother and we remain in an *under* position. He will show us what his Father is doing with the intent that we will embrace the *under* position of doing what he shows us.

## The Nature of Biblical Friendship

Submission is more basic than simply a relation between man and God. It's a reality in God himself. The Son submits to what the Father shows him. The Holy Spirit is also submitted. *"When the Spirit of truth comes, he will guide you into all truth; for he will not speak on his own authority, but whatever he hears he will speak"* (Jn. 16:13). Notice the Holy Spirit does not say whatever he wants to say. The Holy Spirit submits himself to the authority of the Father and the Son.

The text continues, *"He will glorify me, for he will take what is mine and declare it to you"* (Jn. 16:14). It's through this submission of the Holy Spirit that we can receive direction in doing the will of the Father. This submission is an integral part of the friendship within the Holy Trinity and it's the model of our friendship with the Son.

## The Father is Our Friend

The next step of the development of the friendship theme is later in chapter 16. The context is about our relationship with the Father based on our relationship with Jesus. *"In that day you will ask in my name; and I do not say to you that I shall pray the Father for you; for the Father himself loves |phileo| you, because you have loved |phileo| me and have believed that I came from the Father"* (Jn. 16:26-27). Because we are Jesus' friends, willingly embracing the under position, we're also friends of the Father. He will show us what he's doing by the ministry of the Holy Spirit because we are abiding in Christ.

Friends in the natural enjoy doing things together. That is also the case with our friendship with God. He wants to show us what he's doing, but he doesn't want us to walk away and do it alone. In fact, apart from him we can do nothing. He wants us to join him in his doing and allow him to join us to make our doing effective.

## *Returning to the Question*

Now we can return to the context of Jesus questioning Simon's love.

*"Feed my lambs"* (Jn. 21:15). This is Jesus' response to Simon's claim to be a friend. "Simon, if you're my friend as you say, you'll be interested in doing what I'm showing you. My concern is for the lambs of my flock." This is an echo of what happened earlier when Peter jumped out of the boat and waded to meet Jesus on the shore. He left John to take care of the catch of fish. We raised the question there why John had not raced to Jesus. John's concern had been for the fish; Peter left the fish for someone else to care for because he was in a hurry to get to Jesus. Changing the metaphor from fish to lambs, Simon had left the new converts, the lambs, so he could run to Jesus.

*"Simon, son of John, do you love [agapao] me"* (Jn. 21:16)? Jesus returns to the original question concerning Simon's willingness to love in a way that would not necessarily make him feel good about himself or look good in the eyes of others. Friendship is a good thing; Jesus does call us friends and he does show us what he's doing. But we'll remain weak in our ability to do what he shows us if we don't willingly embrace the love that has no concern for its own life or reputation. Jesus may show us to do something that will make us look bad in the eyes of the community. He may even lead us to do something that will cause the religious people to reject us. They may even crucify us. Do you love (*agapao*) Jesus?

## *Simon Still Prefers Friendship*

*"Yes, Lord, you know that I love [phileo] you"* (Jn. 21:16). Simon, becoming Peter, still doesn't get the point. He's holding on to the concept of love he has in his bubble. He's not yet ready to commit himself to the kind of love Jesus is calling for. He's not yet willing to submit his friendship to the higher form of *agape* love.

We must be careful not to set ourselves up as Simon's judge. Few of us have come to fully embrace the call to a love that always chooses the will of God over our own way. If we harbor resentment, for example, we have not yet chosen to forgive as we have been forgiven. We think we have a right to hold on to our bitterness. That makes us feel superior to those who have offended us. Or, to give another example, we become jealous of another who seems to have a more prestigious ministry. We begin to compete for the attention of the flock. Bob Sorge calls this "flirting with the Bride." Think about that.

*"Tend my sheep"* (Jn. 21:16). Again we find Jesus more interested in the care of his flock than in having our attention turned to him. As a matter of fact, attention given to the lambs and the sheep is attention given to him. Lambs are immature and need to be fed so they can grow and become sheep. Sheep are the mature of the flock but they have not yet come to the place of tending themselves.

I'm not sure sheep ever come to a place they can tend themselves. We'll always need the ministry of those who are called to tend the sheep. Even those who are already tending other sheep must be willing to receive the care of others. Leaders who fail to receive care from someone are in danger of coming to a place where they actually destroy themselves and the flock that is under their care.

## The Radical Question

*"Simon, son of John, do you love [phileo] me"* (Jn. 21:17)? This third time Jesus questions whether Simon is his friend. Simon hasn't grasped the fact that Jesus is calling him to a higher form of love. He thinks he's offering Jesus a more intimate form of love than he's requesting. When Jesus questions Simon's friendship, he gets his attention. Peter is grieved.

*"Lord, you know everything, you know that I love [phileo] you"* (Jn. 21:17). Simon is very confident that he's a friend of Jesus. He may not fully understand what it means, but he is a friend and he knows it. He also knows that Jesus knows he's a friend. His confidence is not shaken by the question even though it grieves him. But he hasn't understood or embraced the *agape* Jesus is asking him to embrace. He's resisting, but he's still on the path in the presence of Jesus.

*"Feed my sheep."* Mature sheep still need to be fed. The call is for Simon to concern himself with what concerns the chief Shepherd. Take care of the flock. Intimacy doesn't come to those who simply desire to come into the Father's bosom to feel good. Goose bumps are pleasurable; but they don't do anything for the flock. Jesus had told the disciples how to have the intimacy with himself and with his Father. *"He who has my commandments and keeps them, he it is who loves [agape] me; and he who loves [agape] me will be loved [agape] by my Father, and I will love [agape] him and manifest myself to him"* (Jn. 14:21).

It's as we lay down our own self-serving agenda and receive the commission of the moment from the Father's bosom that we inter into true intimacy with the Father and the Son. *True friendship can only come through the exercise of agape love.* Otherwise even friendship can take on a demonic form that excludes those outside the circle. Everything apart from *agape* is pretense at best and is on its way to becoming demonic if we aren't willing to submit to

Jesus' attempt to adjust our thinking. Simon is still on the path but he has not yet arrived.

## *Insight from the Song of Songs*

We can learn something from the Bride in the *Song of Solomon*. She begins her journey with the Bridegroom with a desire for "the kisses of your mouth" (see 1:2). Her desire is to have him in the bedchamber (see 2:6). The Bridegroom calls her away to the vineyard (see 2:10-13), but she wants to stay where she is and let him go out and do his thing without her (see 2:17). He calls her again, this time "from Lebanon," from her desire for mountain top experiences (see 4:8).

Because of her slow response to his call she loses contact with him again and goes through hard times (see 5:7). He finally comes to her when she responds to his call by going down to the orchard; she takes an interest in his agenda rather than her own desire for intimacy on her terms. Then he offers his love to her as she follows him into the fields and the vineyards: "...there I will give you my love" (see 6:11-12). Her focus moved from "My beloved is mine," to "I am my beloved's, and his desire is for me" (2:16 and 7:10).

In the *Song of Solomon* we see that *eros* is a good thing if it submits to *agape* by laying down its own agenda and taking up the Bridegroom's agenda. It's in this *philia* friendship of doing things together that the *eros* intimacy is available without taking on its demonic form of self-centeredness. It's only by being in Christ, doing the will of the Father through the Spirit, that we can find true intimacy.

There's no intimacy with the Lord that's not related to what he's doing in the earth. Throughout the *Song of Solomon* there are moments of intimacy, but that intimacy is not a self-enclosed intimacy. The call is always to the fields and the vineyards, to the flock and the fishing net. We want to be close to him because it feels good. That's *eros*. He wants to be close to us so we can do what he's doing—that's *philia* friendship. Abiding in the bosom of the Father isn't just a 'goose bump' experience. It's a dynamic relationship where the will of the Father is done on earth as in heaven through our involvement in his fishing trip.

## Dealing with Envy and Jealousy

*"When you are old, you will stretch out your hands, and another will gird you and carry you where you do not wish to go"* (Jn. 21:18). This is referring to the manner of death by which Peter would glorify God. Peter will be crucified. Simon becomes Peter when he takes up his cross and follows Jesus. When he walks away from his own agenda (takes up his personal cross), he becomes a true friend (*philia*) who loves (*agape*) God.

At the Last Supper, Jesus told Simon he would be allowed to follow later (see Jn. 13:36). The cross was not in the path Simon had in mind when he wanted to follow, but it is in the path Jesus was calling him to travel. That cross would be his ultimate demonstration of friendship (*philia*) and love (*agape*). A demonic love will never embrace a cross. It always insists on its own way and its own comfort.

*"Follow me"* (Jn. 21:19). Simon becomes Peter simply by following Jesus the way Jesus is leading him. But he turns and sees John, the beloved disciple, following them. When he makes this turn, when he turns his attention to the other disciple, he turns his attention away from Jesus. The thing Jesus has been after in Simon is exposed. Now he can become Peter if he will listen to Jesus' answer to his question.

*"Lord, what about this man"* (Jn. 21:21)? Simon's jealousy is exposed. He is in competition with the other disciple. John had lain close to the breast of Jesus at the Supper. He had gained the confidence of Jesus enough that he would identify the betrayer without being concerned that John would mess it up by confronting Judas. Simon knew that Jesus did not trust him on that level. His attempt to take matters into his

own hands at the arrest may have been, in part, an attempt to gain the upper hand over John.

Simon is still measuring himself, trying to find his identity, *over against John*. Jesus is calling him to simply embrace his rightful position as Peter under the Son in the presence of the Father by the Spirit.

## Simon, Follow Me

*"What is that to you? Follow me"* (Jn. 21:22). If Simon is to become Peter, he must lay down his desire to be number one. His competitive nature must die. His jealousy over what Jesus is doing in and through others must die. His only desire must be to be with Jesus in the presence of the Father, doing what he shows him to do. Like Jesus, he will have to glorify God by doing what he sees the Father doing. He must concern himself with being the one he was created to be and doing the thing that pleases the Father. This won't necessarily put him outside the fellowship of others nor will he become superior to others. He will be among others as their servant, feeding and tending the sheep.

*"What about this man?"* The point of this question comes clear when we change the perspective a little. I have often wondered if John may have been a bit jealous of Peter. Peter got the lead part in the first part of the book of Acts. John is there with Peter, but Peter is always the leader. We hear what Peter said but we never hear anything from John. I can almost hear John asking, "Why does Peter always get the lead part? Why do I have to be in the background all the time?"

Of course we have no evidence that John felt that way; and he probably didn't. But most of us have these kinds of thoughts when we see some other disciple in the limelight. I've certainly struggled with being placed in a support role while the leader has what seem to be all the advantages. The 'other disciple' always seems to have the advantage over us. We tend to think that their gifts are more important than ours. Their place in the Body appears to be more prominent. That's our old natural way of thinking.

Peter is probably saying something like, "Why do I always have to be the one who goes first and meet the opposition? Why can't I be in the background and let someone else take the fall? Why don't you let John get in trouble next time?" The point is that there are different functions within the Body. We don't get to choose which portion of bread we receive. Each of us is called to function in that place Jesus went to prepare for us.

Until we come to willingly embrace the place he prepared for us we will continue to be jealous of the 'other' disciple. *Agape* willingly receives the place offered by the Lord and joyfully allows others to be in their prepared place. *Agape* sets us free to become friends, *philioi*, doing the will of the Father with the Son and with the Spirit. In this relational structure we are able to experience intimacy, *eros*, with God and with those whom he loves in the world.

## *Make it Personal*

Each must hear the Lord say, ***"What is that to you; Follow me,"*** just as we must each hear the first question, ***"What do you seek?"*** Each must learn to follow him in the way he is leading. We must come to rest in the fact that he calls others to be different from us.

This brings us to another point. Many try to insist that others be like them. We often set ourselves up as the standard by which the 'other' disciple is judged. "How could you be a genuine Christian if you are not like me?" Conformity to a standard is not the way of the Body of Christ. We are called to be conformed to the image of the Son who does only what he sees the Father doing. There's no other standard. Hearing his present word and responding in obedience is the only call that is standard for us all.

There are those like Peter and Martha who are persons of action. Their action needs to be a response to the presence and direction of Jesus in their lives. There are those like John and Mary who are quiet, retiring persons. Their quietness needs to be in response to the presence and direction of Jesus in their lives. If either allows the other to determine their activity or their stillness, they are not following Jesus.

Many years ago I wrote in the margin of my Bible at the end of John: "*Lord, give me the grace to be everything you called me to be without comparing myself to others, and give me the grace to allow others to be everything you called them to be without comparing them to me.*"

## *A Challenge and an Invitation*

I conclude this devotional commentary with a challenge and an invitation.

Seek the abiding place. Go forward toward that place in the bosom of the Father where true intimacy is available. Seek that place with all your heart, soul, mind and strength. I cannot tell you how to get there. I can only challenge you to seek it. Seek it above the desire to be number one in the community. Seek that place above the desire to have a good reputation or a big ministry. And don't seek it just for yourself. Invite others to join you in the loving embrace of Daddy God.

Don't worry about the 'other' disciple. Let him be who he is. Focus on being who you are. Life is much simpler when we resign from general overseer of the Church of Jesus Christ. It is much easier to have good relationships within the Body of Christ when we resign from a judge's bench. Give up your gavel. You will be happier and people around you will not be so miserable.

That's the challenge. Now here's the invitation. "Come and see the abiding place." Don't be satisfied with seeking. Get on the path and follow it until you come to see the place and actually begin to abide with him there, and bring as many with you as you can. Again, I cannot tell you how to stay on that path. I can only tell you that you will see as you follow Jesus in the way he leads you each day. You can't get there by following the way Jesus is leading the 'other' disciple.

I can't take you there; I can only invite you to come. I have been there. It's an awesome place of rest, peace, joy and productivity. I desire to go even deeper into that experience today. Join me on the way. Follow your Leader the way he leads you.

## The Beginning

# About the Author

—⁓—

FOUNT SHULTS was born in Lovington, New Mexico in 1936. He was born again in 1945 and overwhelmed by the Father's love in 1957 in an Air Force barrack while he was in Japan. He received a call to teach God's Word at that time and began to pursue that goal as soon as he returned to the States.

He received a BA and MA in Religion from Eastern New Mexico University, Portales, New Mexico and a PhD in Hebrew Studies from The University of Texas at Austin. He taught Bible and Theology on college campuses for 40 years, the biggest part of that time being at Elim Bible Institute in Lima, New York. He retired from the campus in 2004 to spend his "Golden Years" doing seminars and retreats for churches and training leaders in third world countries.

Fount is the founder of On Word Ministries and part of an apostolic team making resources available to churches and leaders worldwide. He has held leadership conferences and seminars in Mexico, Colombia, Ukraine, Korea, Indonesia, India, Canada and the United States. He posts an "almost daily" reflection on Bible topics on the reflections blog of his website http://www.onword.org. His itinerary is also posted on the website, on the ministry blog.

Fount has been married to his wife, best friend, and partner in ministry, Lynda, since 1964. They have six children and ten grandchildren. Their home and ministry base is in Myrtle Beach, South Carolina.

Fount is available for speaking engagements. For further information regarding his itinerary and scheduling details visit http://www.onword.org.

Printed in the United States
78475LV00001B/85-1599